D0119840

The Sunday Times
Wordpower Guide

The Sunday Times
Wordpower
Guide

GRAHAM KING

Selected from *The Sunday Times*
One Hour Wordpower Series

LONDON NEW YORK SYDNEY TORONTO

This edition published 1993
by BCA
by arrangement with
William Heinemann Ltd

First published 1993
Copyright © Graham King 1993

CN 8014

Printed and bound in Great Britain
by Clays Ltd, St Ives plc

Contents

The Sunday Times
Wordpower Guide

You've seen the headlines: *Literacy Skills Lacked by Six Million Adults*; *1 in 4 Students Poor at Punctuation*; *One in Ten is a Dunce at Spelling*; *The Language is Languishing* . . . and dozens more.

What they all spell out is that many of us are losing our skill with the English language. It may be that we don't care much about it any more, content with sloppy speech and writing; or that we have been seduced by fashions that include near-Neanderthal speech and an incomprehensible grammarless code that passes as writing.

At the same time the world has become more ruthlessly competitive. The demand for real skills and knowledge is insatiable. But for anyone who has difficulty communicating their skills and knowledge, the future is bleak. The need to speak and write clear, unambiguous, interesting English has never been greater.

Obviously this background has had much to do with the success of *The Sunday Times* One Hour Wordpower series of self-help books on the English language. The books, with their invitation to learn about a variety of aspects of English usage in an hour or so appealed instantly to tens of thousands of busy people.

Once read, however – often on a train journey, a business flight, during a lunch hour – the Wordpower books proved to be concise but valuable works of reference, which is why a selection of them has been gathered together to make this book.

The key to good English is an understanding of its grammar. This is not as difficult as it sounds, and the *Good Grammar* section proves it. You know more about grammar than you think, and *Good Grammar* builds on this basic knowledge to help you renew your acquaintance with the language and its workings.

Word Bank draws your attention to the importance of possessing a good working vocabulary, so essential to effective communicating. Almost effortlessly, it will help you add hundreds of useful, apposite and elegant words to your everyday vocabulary.

Owning a good supply of words is one thing, but it is also worthwhile knowing how to spell them. Words like *sacrilegious, fuchsia, inoculate* and *obbligato* are well-known stumpers; Spell Check lists not only these but 996 other deceptive, puzzling and troublesome words that often hold us spellbound.

The *Word Check* section is about using words correctly. It lists the correct meanings of some 500 look-alikes, grammatical mischief-makers and chronically misused words and explains the differences between such confusing couples as *obligate* and *oblige, among* and *amongst, flammable* and *inflammable, lay* and *lie,* and *who* and *whom.*

Finally, *Crisp Clear Writing* will show you how to put it all together to create prose that is unambiguous, interesting and a delight to read. Be warned, however: it contains explicitly brutal language in its condemnation of jargon, circumlocution, verbiage, euphemism and clichés.

Enjoy *The Sunday Times Wordpower Guide* for browsing, and keep it by your side as a handy reference book to help you polish your usage of the English language.

Acknowledgements

Consultant on Grammar and Linguistics in Chapter 1: Paul Coggle, Senior Lecturer in German, University of Kent at Canterbury.

The following works provided the definitive sources for meanings and usage in Chapter 2:

> *The Oxford English Dictionary, Cassell's English Dictionary, Webster's New Twentieth Century Dictionary, Collins English Dictionary, Funk & Wagnalls Standard College Dictionary, The Encyclopaedia Britannica, Fontana Dictionary of Modern Thought.* Also *Fowler's Modern English Usage*, Eric Partridge's *Usage and Abusage, The Facts on File Encyclopedia of Word and Phrase Origins, Chambers Science and Technology Dictionary*, Robert Claiborne's *The Life and Times of the English Language* and *The Cambridge Encyclopedia of Language* by David Crystal.

The publishers would like to thank Collins English Dictionaries for permission to reproduce the extract on page 117

The ultimate authority for Chapter 3 has been the *Oxford English Dictionary and Supplement*. Other works consulted include *Cassell's English Dictionary, Webster's New 20th Century Dictionary, Webster's Dictionary of Proper Names.*

The publishers are grateful to *The Times* and *The Sunday Times* for permission to reproduce extracts.

The following works provided the definitive sources for meanings and usage in Chapter 4:

The Oxford English Dictionary, Webster's New Twentieth Century Dictionary, Cassell's English Dictionary, Collins English Dictionary, Longman New Generation Dictionary, The Encyclopaedia Britannica, Fontana Dictionary of Modern Thought. Also Fowler's A Dictionary of Modern English Usage, Eric Partridge's Usage and Abusage, Harry Shaw's Dictionary of Problem Words and Expressions, John Bremner's Words on Words, Alexander Witherspoon's Common Errors in English and William Safire's On Language and What's The Good Word?

The author and publishers would like to thank the following for their kind permission to reproduce extracts in Chapter 5:

Cassell plc: The Second World War (VI): Triumph and Tragedy, by Sir Winston Churchill; Thames and Hudson Ltd: A Good Enough Parent, by Bruno Bettelheim; copyright © 1987 Bruno Bettelheim; Macmillan London Ltd: The Way Through the Woods, by Colin Dexter; London 1992; Oxford University Press: Fowler's Modern English Usage (Second Edition), ed. Sir Ernest Gowers; Oxford 1965; The Plain English Campaign: Gobbledegook – an anthology of bureaucratic writing, by Martin Cutts and Chrissie Maher*; The Daily Telegraph: extracts pages 386–387, 392 copyright © The Telegraph plc 1992; The Sunday Telegraph: extract pages 431–32 copyright © The Telegraph plc 1992; The Independent: extracts pages 386, 394, 432 copyright © The Independent 1992; The Sun: extract page 431 copyright © The Sun 1992

The publishers have made every endeavour to trace the owners of copyright and apologise for any inadvertent omissions.

*The Plain English Campaign was founded by Mrs Chrissie Maher, who had been illiterate until she was sixteen. It wages non-stop war on obscure and confusing language in official and other public writings. Address: Outram House, Canal Street, Whaley Bridge, Stockport SK12 7LS.

Grammar

Introduction

Learning and obeying all the rules of grammar will not automatically bestow excellence on your speech and writing; but completely ignoring them will almost certainly consign you to inarticulate semi-illiteracy.

Users of the English language tend to fall into three groups. The smallest consists of those who really care about the language even to the extent of believing they are its guardians. To them a mispronounced word, a split infinitive, a double negative, are anathema.

Slightly larger, probably, is the group that neither knows nor gives a damn about correct usage; yet, paradoxically, it is the one that contributes more colour and consternation and more new words and novel expressions to the language than the others, even though, initially at any rate, its offerings may be as welcome as a coachload of shellsuit yobbos.

By far the largest group are those who retain an awareness of the language, some respect for correct spelling and pronunciation and who on occasions will consciously do, or think of doing, something about improving their mastery of English and its grammar. Members of this group probably own dictionaries.

This chapter has been written with all three groups in mind. Many of the 'don't cares' would love to kick some words around if they could only find a book or course that made grammar accessible, interesting and understandable.

Even among our top group there are many people who are enviably articulate and fluent yet often find themselves at a loss over some grammatical point. For these people, as with those in the large middle group, this chapter will provide the missing or forgotten knowledge without the need for a long and laborious re-education.

Not even the highest grammatical authorities can ever claim they know it all. H. W. Fowler, the doyen of correct usage, and Robert Burchfield, compiler of the great *Oxford English Dictionary*, have both suffered the embarrassment of making the most rudimentary mistakes. A Mensa advertisement asked: *'Can you solve this problem faster than me?'* (Grammatically punctilious, *Me* was boggled!) Even *The Times*, that paragon of grammatical certitude, trips up with comforting regularity. It recently wrote, 'According to the Adult Literacy and Basic Skills Unit, one in four 16- to 20-year-olds have reading problems and more than one third have trouble with spelling.' (*have* should read *has*). To make matters worse it appeared in an editorial on the need for the rigorous teaching of grammar.

None of us can ever assume we're on top of a pernickety language that chops trees down and then chops them up; that has parents telling their children to sit down at the meal table and to then sit up; that has marriages breaking down and then breaking up; that has court cases open and shut at the same time; and has some unfortunate with a toothache pondering over the dentist's remark that the extraction will be 'fairly painless'. Either it's going to hurt or it isn't.

This is what usage is all about, and it's what makes our language so frustrating but at the same time so fascinating. Every day it changes, perhaps imperceptibly, and we all contribute to the changes. If enough of us, a majority, insist that black means white, then, the linguists say, it *does* mean white, and the old meaning goes out of the window. This is why, today, most books on grammar avoid insisting that this usage is 'correct' and that usage is 'wrong'. *The Wordpower Guide* doesn't completely go along with this, believing that most readers will have bought this book for some positive straightforward guidance. However, every reader is also free to disagree with it.

This chaper on grammar has been designed as a refresher course, a fast update or a kickstart, depending upon your needs and your present relationship with the language. It does not set out to teach, but to convey, step by step, a lively awareness of the workings of grammar and the possibilities of using it to improve your speaking, writing and reading.

The text has been subjected to some extensive road testing, and care has been taken to keep grammatical terms to a minimum. In the interests of simplicity the term grammar (and grammarian) is used in the widest sense, encompassing, at times, syntax, morphology, phonology, semantics and orthography. You should be so lucky.

What is Grammar?
Why Use It?

This won't take long.

A language requires two elements to fulfil virtually all the needs of communication – a vocabulary and a grammar.

The vocabulary is the language's stock of words: combinations of symbols, signs or letters that have meanings that identify things and ideas. But words by themselves can never constitute a language. Imagine somebody having all the words required to express the message in the first sentence, but no method of putting them together. An attempt might look like this:

> Grammar about what what time take long no little yes

It would be like trying to build a wall with tennis balls. What is needed is some cement or glue to stick them together. In the case of a language this glue is a mixture of rules called grammar.

Languages aren't created in a day; some evolve over hundreds, even thousands of years. The users of a language must invent all the time, and when they don't invent they borrow. English has borrowed from just about every language on earth. Not only words were purloined, but rules, too. English grammar contains rules that can be traced back to the Greeks and Romans: rules that helped the early users of our language to string their words together to create more complex and clearer messages. They enabled that meaningless jumble of words above to take shape as a recognisable sentence:

> I tell you what grammar is will need not little time not long time but some time

An improvement, but still the language required some more words and rules. The speaker wanted something more precise than *tell*, like *explain*. Also needed was a system for building phrases with their own meanings, and another system for adding inflections to basic words: *explain, explaining, explained*. With such improvements, the sentence becomes shorter but also more accurate:

> Explaining what grammar is will not take a long time.

Then users began to get really clever by inventing idioms like *not too long* to say in three words what it took nine words to say in an earlier version. They also learned to relate sentences to each other. Having asked the question in the chapter headline, why should the opening sentence repeat the same information? So we arrive at:

> What is Grammar? Why use it? This will not take long.

And, then, finally, in the quest for even greater economy, the newly invented apostrophe was brought into play, saving yet one more word:

> This won't take long.

None of this will surprise you, because if you are a native user of English you are also an intuitive user of its grammar, and probably a very skilful user, too. Nevertheless, this quick dip into the origins of grammar will provide a foundation for all that follows in this book.

The Thirteen Gremlins of Grammar

1. Correct speling is essential.
2. Don't use no double negatives.
3. Verbs has got to agree with their subjects.
4. Don't write run-on sentences they are hard to read.
5. About them sentence fragments
6. Don't use commas, that aren't necessary.
7. A preposition is not a good word to end a sentence with.
8. Remember to not ever split infinitives.
9. Writing carefully, dangling participles must be avoided.
10. Use apostrophe's correctly.
11. Make each singular pronoun agree with their antecedents.
12. Join clauses good, like a conjunction should.
13. Proofread your writing to make sure if you words out.

And, above all, avoid clichés like the plague.

You Know More About Grammar Than You Think

Although you may not know what a prepositional complement is or what it does, and may never have heard of subordinator conjunctions or modal auxiliaries, it is nevertheless very likely that you know a lot more about grammar than you think you do.

Whether your memories of what you were taught about English grammar are fresh or distantly hazy, pleasant or mordantly painful, a good deal of it has undoubtedly stuck. And on this foundation, through daily conversation, reading newspapers and watching television, you have, if you are an ordinary person, built up a handy working knowledge of grammar.

To demonstrate this to yourself, try the following test, consisting of twenty examples of right and wrong grammatical use of the language. A tip before you begin: rather than try to analyse the examples, try to 'listen' to what is being said.

(Answers and Score Sheet, page 16–19)

1. One of these isn't a sentence. Which one is?

   A. *Any failure of the buyers to comply with any of the conditions, the damages are recoverable by the seller or the Auctioneers.*

   B. *Any failure of the buyers to comply with any of the conditions may result in damages recoverable by the seller or the Auctioneers.*

2. Here's another pair of sentences. One contains a fairly common mistake. Which is correct?

   A. *On Sunday we heard the first chaffinch sing, we have several that come into the garden for crumbs.*

   B. *On Sunday we heard the first chaffinch sing; we have several that come into the garden for crumbs.*

3. This one demands closer inspection. Which one do you think is considered correct?

   A. *A thousand visitors are not unusual on an average weekday.*

   B. *A thousand visitors is not unusual on an average weekday.*

4. You can add to your score by spotting the inconsistency in one of these sentences. Which is consistent?

   A. *The team, which is playing in Manchester next week, were badly out of form on their last performance.*

   B. *The team, which is playing in Manchester next week, was badly out of form on its last performance.*

5. If you read these sentences carefully, you will see that one doesn't make sense. Which one is clear and correct?

   A. *She remained unimpressed by both evidence and argument.*

   B. *She remained both unimpressed by evidence and argument.*

6. Because it asks you to decide between who and whom, this question is one of the toughest in the test. But try, anyway, to pick the correct usage:

   A. *The Foreign Secretary, whom we are pleased to see is now fully recovered, will speak at tonight's meeting.*

   B. *The Foreign Secretary, who we are pleased to see is now fully recovered, will speak at tonight's meeting.*

7. Here's one you should answer without even blinking. Which is correct?

   A. *The shop supplied all his shirt's and suit's and most of his ties.*

B. *The shop supplied all his shirts and suits and most of his ties.*

8. If you think about the meanings of either and neither, you should have no trouble choosing the correct sentence:

   A. *In my view either of the hotels is fine, but neither has what I would call a decent bottle of wine.*

   B. *In my view either of the hotels are fine, but neither have what I would call a decent bottle of wine.*

9. A minor error, perhaps, but it would have irked the late Graham Greene. Pick the correct statement:

   A. *Do you remember when his novel the* Third Man *came out as a movie?*

   B. *Do you remember when his novel* The Third Man *came out as a movie?*

10. One of these sentences contains two errors, so you can score 4 points by spotting them and identifying the correctly written sentence:

    A. *She would agree to go neither to the match nor to the cocktail party afterwards.*

    B. *She neither would agree to go to the match, or to the cocktail party afterwards.*

11. Back to single points for picking the correct usage of among and between.

    A. *The pudding was shared among the three of them.*

    B. *The pudding was shared between the three of them.*

12. Don't get carried away by the racy prose; there's a fundamental error in one of these sentences. Which is the sentence without the error?

    A. *Then, as he lay silently beside her, she cried: A broken, hoarse cry that sprang from a lost memory of adolescence.*

B. *Then, as he lay silently beside her, she cried: a broken, hoarse cry that sprang from a lost memory of adolescence.*

13. Try to/try and choose the correct sentence:

    A. *The teacher asked her to try to do better.*

    B. *The teacher asked her to try and do better.*

14. Question marks can be troublesome. Which sentence uses the question mark correctly?

    A. *Her mother was always asking? 'When are you going to get married.'*

    B. *Her mother was always asking, 'When are you going to get married?'*

15. There are some discordant notes in one of these sentences. Which one is consistent and harmonious?

    A. *If one is to live happily among one's neighbours, you must learn to mind your own business.*

    B. *If you are to live happily among your neighbours, you must learn to mind your own business.*

16. If you listen carefully to what is being said here, one sentence will be clear and one will confuse you. Which is the unambiguous sentence?

    A. *After the game he talked at length to the captain and the manager.*

    B. *After the game he talked at length to the captain and manager.*

17. Something weird is happening in one of these sentences. Which one avoids a rather bizarre atmospheric condition?

    A. *Tearing down the motorway at 80 mph, the fog suddenly enveloped the car, forcing me to pull over.*

B. *As I was tearing down the motorway at 80 mph, the fog suddenly enveloped the car, forcing me to pull over.*

18. Your ear should guide you here; which sentence sounds right and is right?

    A. *Penny and Tony each realised what each other was trying to do.*

    B. *Penny and Tony each realised what the other was trying to do.*

19. A somewhat strange rule is in play here, but, again, your ear should tell you which is correct:

    A. *Every man, woman and child is requested to assemble in the departure lounge.*

    B. *Every man, woman and child are requested to assemble in the departure lounge.*

20. Finally, let's find out how well you know your plurals! Which of these three sentences is correct?

    A. *One year's training is satisfactory, but three year's apprenticeship ensures greater rewards.*

    B. *One years' training is satisfactory, but three years' apprenticeship ensure greater rewards.*

    C. *One year's training is satisfactory, but three years' apprenticeship ensure greater rewards.*

If you wish to know where you stand on your knowledge and use of English grammar, you should have attempted to answer all twenty questions. If you have made a guess at some of them, don't feel too guilty: some guesses will be right and others will be wrong.

Now turn to page 17 for the answers and explanations. The correct answers to questions considered to be more difficult receive higher scores than those to easier questions.

The total score for all correct is 50. If you score 20–25 you are certainly in the 'above average' category – which means that, grammatically speaking, you are halfway there. If you score in the 25–50 range, you are among those who take considerable care over their speech and writing.

But whatever your score (even if it's 50!) you will never regret taking an hour or two to polish your native know-how of English and its workings, and to renew acquaintance with its sheer utility, its complexity, its beauty and its genius for contrariness.

Answers to the Grammar Test

Check your answers to the Grammar Test on pages
10–14 with the correct versions and explanations and
enter the results on the scorecard below

Grammar Test Scorecard

Question	Score for Correct Answer	Your Score
1	3	
2	2	
3	3	
4	3	
5	2	
6	4	
7	1	
8	3	
9	2	
10	4	
11	1	
12	2	
13	2	
14	1	
15	3	
16	3	
17	2	
18	1	
19	2	
20	6	
TOTAL	50	

Answers

1. B. is a sentence. A is not because it is incomplete and makes no sense. See *Let's Look at a Sentence*.

2. A is what is called a 'run-on' sentence: the kind that someone in a state of excitement might breathlessly blurt out! It should have stopped and started again after *sing*, but as the two thoughts are closely related, the better idea is to keep them in the same sentence and separated with a longer pause – a semi-colon. So B is the sentence that is preferred.

3. B is correct. *Visitors* is plural, but *A thousand visitors* is short for 'to have a thousand visitors'. In other words the number of visitors has become a single unit, and therefore requires a singular verb, *is* and not *are*.

4. Sentence B is consistent. The problem with sentence A is that, quite correctly, it treats the team as a collective noun at the beginning (which *is* playing) but then switches to treating it as a lot of individual players (*were* badly out of form) towards the end of the sentence. See *Collective Nouns*, page 45.

5. A is quite clear and correct. If you study B closely enough you will see that it makes no sense. The only way that *both* would work in that position would be in a sentence like: *She remained both unimpressed and amused by the evidence and the argument.*

6. B is correct. In this case, apply the *he = who*/*him = whom* rule. As the Foreign Secretary (*he*, the subject) is fully recovered, and will speak (the object), *who* is called for. There's further discussion on the *who*/*whom* conundrum under *Twenty Sore Points*.

7. B is correct. The plurals of *shirt* and *suit* and *tie* are *shirts*, *suits* and *ties*. No apostrophes are needed.

8. *Either* and *neither* require singular verbs, so Sentence A, using *is* and *has* rather than *are* and *have*, is correct.

9. B is correct. The full title of Graham Greene's novel and subsequent film is *The Third Man*, not the *Third Man*.

10. A is correct on both counts. B contains what is known as a misplaced correlative (*neither would agree*), and also breaks the accepted *either/or, neither/nor* rule.

11. You share *between* two, or *among* three, so A is correct.

12. You capitalise at the beginning of a sentence, but not after a colon, so version B is correct.

13. Both are acceptable. The form *try to* is considered to be grammatically correct but the idiomatic *try and* is now very widely used.

14. B is correct; the question mark always follows the question.

15. B is correct. The problem with A is that the pronouns lack concord: it begins with the personal pronoun *one* but then moves on to *you* and *your*. A correct sentence using *one* would read, '*If one is to live happily among one's neighbours, one must learn to mind one's business*'. The neighbours, on the other hand, might take a dim view of anyone talking like that.

16. A is unambiguous because it makes clear that he talked to the captain *and* the manager – two people. B is unclear, because he could have talked to the captain/manager – one person.

17. The 'something weird' in one of the sentences is

the 80 mph fog tearing down the motorway!
Version B is correct. See *Danglers and Manglers*,
page 77.

18. Grammatically, A has *each other* as the subject of
the verb *realised*, which is plainly wrong and also
sounds wrong. B is right, and also sounds right.

19. A is correct, because *every* refers to each individual.
So regardless of how many men, women and
children there are, a singular verb is called for.

20. C is the sentence correct on all points. *One year's
training* requires a possessive apostrophe. So does
three years' apprenticeship, but because we now have
the plural of *year* = *years*, the apostrophe comes
after the *-s*. And because *three years' apprenticeship*
is plural, *ensure* (and not *ensures*) is needed. Getting
all this right is certainly worth a score of six!

Let's Look at Sentences

Every time we speak we use sentences. They are the easiest of all grammatical units to recognise, so it seems sensible to begin with them.

Easy to recognise, yes; but hard to define. In his *Dictionary of Modern English Usage*, H. W. Fowler gives ten definitions by various grammarians, including:

- A group of words which makes sense
- A word or set of words followed by a pause and revealing an intelligible purpose
- A combination of words that contains at least one subject and one predicate
- A combination of words which is complete as expressing a thought

None of these, however, exactly fills the bill, although it is difficult not to agree with the *Oxford English Dictionary's* definition: 'Such portion of a composition or utterance as extends from one full stop to another.'

More important is what sentences are for:

- To make statements
- To ask questions
- To request action
- To express emotion

From a practical standpoint, a sentence should express a single idea, or thoughts related to that idea. A popular rule of thumb is that a sentence should be complete in thought and complete in construction. And again, from a practical point of view, you will soon find that certain rules must be observed if your sentences are to be clear, unambiguous, logical and interesting to the listener or reader. That said, you still have plenty of scope to fashion sentences of almost any size and shape.

Here is a sentence: the opening sentence to Daniel Defoe's *The Life and strange surprising Adventures of Robinson Crusoe*.

'I was born in the year 1632, in the city of York, of a good family, though not of that country, my father being a foreigner of Bremen, who settled first at Hull: he got a good estate by merchandise, and leaving off his trade, lived afterward at York, from whence he had married my mother, whose relations were named Robinson, a very good family in that country, and from whom I was called Robinson Kreutznoer; but, by the usual corruption of words in England, we are now called, nay, we call ourselves, and write our name Crusoe, and so my companions always called me.'

Very few novelists today would have the nerve or the skill to begin a novel with a long sentence like that; for apart from its length it is also a skilfully wrought passage: clear, unambiguous, supple, flowing and ultimately riveting. If it were written today it would most likely appear as a paragraph of several sentences:

'I was born in York in 1632, of a good family. My father came from Bremen and first settled at Hull, acquired his estate by trading merchandise, and then moved to York. There he met and married my mother, from a well established family in that county named Robinson. I was therefore named Robinson Kreutznoer, but in time my own name and that of our family was modified to Crusoe. That's what we are now called, that's how we write our name, and that's what my friends have always called me.'

Defoe's original is a fairly long sentence by any standards. Now try this sentence for size:

'But —— !'

This one appears to defy everything we think we know about sentences, but it is a valid sentence just the same, as you will see when it is placed in its correct context:

'Jane turned abruptly from the window and faced

him with blazing eyes. "Well, you've finally done
it! You realise we're all but ruined, don't you?
Don't you!"

"But —— !" Harry was squirming. Speechless.
He stepped back in an attempt to evade the next
onslaught.

It never came. Instead, weeping uncontrollably,
Jane collapsed on to the settee.'

You can see that 'But —— !', short though it is, quite
adequately expresses a response and an action in the
context of the second paragraph (a paragraph is a string
of linked sentences with a common theme). Despite its
seeming incompleteness, it is nevertheless a complete
sentence in thought and construction, although some
grammarians might label it a sentence fragment. Here
are some more:

Her expression conveyed everything. Disaster.
Ruin. Utter ruin.

Three of the four sentences above are sentence
fragments. They're perfectly legitimate, but use them
for emphasis only, and with care.

Another kind of sentence, and one to avoid, is seen
rather too often. Typically, it is rambling and unclear,
usually the result of having too many ideas and
unrelated ideas jammed into it, like this one:

He said that the agreement would galvanise a new
sense of opportunity and partnership between the
countries and enable them to articulate the targets
with regard to inflation which was always of
concern to every family in the land.

Would you really bother to try to unravel that sentence?
No, life is too short, and the sentence is destined to
remain unread, its author's voice unheard. That's
the price you pay for writing bad sentences. To
demonstrate how the inclusion of irrelevant matter can

22

cloud the intent and meaning of a sentence, consider this:

> Jonathan Yeats, whose family moved to the US from Ireland in the late 1940s, and who later married a Mormon girl from Wisconsin, wrote the novel in less than three months.

We have to ask, what has the novelist's family to do with his writing a book in record time? Did the Mormon girl help him? If not, why mention her? By the time we've reached the important part of the sentence – the fact that he wrote the book in three months – our attention has been ambushed by two extraneous thoughts.

American presidents are notorious for irrelevant rambling. The tradition began, apparently, with President Harding, of whom, when he died in 1923, a wit observed, 'The only man, woman or child who wrote a simple declarative sentence with seven grammatical errors is dead.' For example:

> 'I have had the good intention to write you a letter ever since you left, but the pressure of things has prevented, speeches to prepare and deliver, and seeing people, make a very exacting penalty of trying to be in politics.'

But we must not grieve over Harding when we have President Bush gamely carrying the national flag of Gobbledegook:

> 'I mean a child that doesn't have a parent to read to that child or that doesn't see that when the child is hurting to have a parent and help out or neither parent there enough to pick the kid up and dust him off and send him back into the game at school or whatever, that kid has a disadvantage.'

Well, enough of warnings. The point to remember is that although a sentence may be as long as a piece of string, long sentences may land you in trouble. A good sentence will be no longer than necessary, but this doesn't mean that you should chop all your sentences to a few words. That would be boring. To keep the reader alert and interested you need variety. If you examine this paragraph, for example, you will find a sentence sequence that goes *short/long/long/short/medium/long/short*. That's aiming in the right direction.

When a 'Sentence' isn't a Sentence

Here are some exceptions to all the sentences you've read so far:

> Are unable to fill any order within 21 days
> Date for the closing of
> Thinking it a good opportunity

Clearly, there's something wrong here. What is wrong is that these examples do not make sense because they are incomplete. They are incomplete because they are ungrammatical and do not adequately express a thought or carry any recognisable information. It has nothing to do with length, either; the following examples are extremely short but are grammatical and convey the intended information in such a way as to be unambiguous:

> *'Waiter!'*   THIS WAY   *Stop!*   Amount Due

Types of Sentences

Single-word expressions like 'Hey!', signs, catchphrases, greetings and so on, are called irregular, fragmentary or minor sentences. Sentences which appear to have been constructed to express one or more thoughts are called regular or major sentences and these are our work horses for talking and writing. There is also a third type, called a compound sentence, that expresses two or more thoughts or which, grammatically, has two or more clauses. Let us take two simple, regular sentences:

> The money was spent on urban regeneration. The money provided hundreds of people with excellent houses.

Most of us, seeing these two sentences, would find it difficult to resist the urge to combine them:

> The money was spent on urban regeneration and provided hundreds of people with excellent houses.

That is a complex or compound sentence, and you will see that it links the two connected thoughts in an economical way. Indeed, a third thought could safely be added:

> The money was spent on urban regeneration and provided hundreds of people with excellent houses; but it did not take funds away from existing housing schemes.

Beyond this, you have to be careful, or risk confusing the reader. By the way, did you notice the two words that link the three sentences into one? They are *and* and *but*, and they are commonly used for building compound sentences.

Types of Regular or Major Sentences

Earlier, we defined four uses for sentences. Each of these uses calls for a type of sentence, and it's worth knowing what they are:

- A DECLARATIVE sentence makes a statement:

  A rose-bush grew in the garden.

- An INTERROGATIVE sentence asks a question:

Is that a rose-bush in the garden?

- An IMPERATIVE sentence requests or commands:

  James, dig that rose-bush out of the garden.

- An EXCLAMATIVE sentence expresses emotion:

  I wouldn't dream of touching the rose-bush!

It's also worth knowing about some other kinds of sentences:

- *I like eating at restaurants* is a positive sentence.
- *I don't like eating at restaurants* is a negative sentence.

The difference may seem obvious, but it's worth noting because a diet of too much negativism in your speech and writing can have an overall negative or depressing effect. Sometimes it is better to express a negative thought in a positive way:

She is not beautiful.

This is negative and also vague: she could be statuesque or handsome. A more positive and precise description might be:

She is rather homely.

Lastly, all sentences are either active or passive, and it is up to us to choose which 'voice' to use. Here are some examples:

ACTIVE   *The favourite won the 3.30 hurdle event.*
Her boyfriend bought the ring.
Very few can understand his poems.

PASSIVE *The 3.30 hurdle event was won by the favourite.*
The ring was bought by her boyfriend.
His poems can be understood by very few.

It's easy to see why one sort of sentence is called active, and the other passive; active sentences are direct and seem more interesting and exciting, while passive

26

sentences tend to be detached and impersonal. Generally, we use the active voice almost exclusively in our everyday speech and writing.

Trimming Away 'Sentence Fat'

Nobody these days wants to write more words than necessary, or to be forced to read fifty words when the information could have been conveyed in half that number. We have already seen that by combining simple sentences into compound sentences we can economise on words and even enhance clarity; but there is another grammatical convention that allows us to sensibly trim away words we don't need. It is called ellipsis, and it works like this:

WITHOUT ELLIPSIS When the children were called to the dinner table they came to the dinner table immediately.

      Mr Green had more coins in his collection than Thomas had coins in his collection.

WITH ELLIPSIS When the children were called to the dinner table they came immediately.

      Mr Green had more coins in his collection than Thomas had in his.

The reason we can get away with this trimming is that, if the listener or reader is paying attention, he or she will automatically supply the missing words from the context of what is being said. There is no loss of clarity, either; on the contrary, repetitive words can lead to boredom.

 Sometimes our economising extends to dropping what were once considered essential words:

He was kicked out the door.
She got off the bus.

If we heard these sentences spoken in an informal context, we would hardly take exception; and, nowadays, even the strictly grammatical versions look odd to our eyes:

He was kicked out *of* the door.
She got off *of* the bus.

Another common, but quite acceptable, omission, is the word *that*:

The hat (that) she bought is a disaster.
They knew (that) they would never reach the airport in time.

Such sentences are considered informal, although their meanings are perfectly clear. If a hostess greets a guest with, '*I am delighted that you could come*', isn't she being a trifle formal? More likely, the greeting would be, '*I'm delighted you could come*'; and that is becoming the accepted usage. (The other extreme is the multiple *that*: '*He claimed that that that in the sentence was superfluous.*') If you are intent on dropping *that*, be careful (that) it doesn't lead to ambiguity.

Harmony in the Sentence

Perhaps the most important principle in the construction of sentences is what is called *concord* – which means that all the units in the sentence must agree and harmonise with each other. We can spot most inharmonious constructions, because they usually jar:

February is usually a succession of *rain, hail and snowing*.

That sentence mixes two nouns and a participle, and it
28

screams out at you, doesn't it? An harmonious construction would be to group three nouns:

> February is usually a sucession of *rain, hail and snow*.

Alternatively, we could use a trio of participles:

> In February, it is usually either *raining, hailing or snowing*.

Another form of discord is the shift from active to passive voice:

> My father painted those pictures, which were left to me.

That sentence mixes active and passive voice; the following sentence is consistently active, and more direct:

> My father painted those pictures and left them to me.

Other sources of discord include shifting from personal to impersonal pronouns (or vice versa): 'If one is to keep out of trouble, you should mind your p's and q's'; shifting mid-sentence from negative to positive (or vice versa); and mixing tenses. But the most common form of discord is the sentence which fails to recognise that a singular noun takes a singular verb and a plural noun takes a plural verb. The following sentences ignore this:

> *We was* furious with the umpire's decision.
> The four *houses was* sold at auction.

They should, of course, read:

> We *were* furious about the umpire's decision.
> The four houses *were* sold at auction.

But look what happens when we 'collectivise' the subjects:

The *team was* furious about the umpire's decision.
A *number* of houses *was* sold at auction.

Because we've gathered the players together into a
team, and combined the four houses into a single group
(a number), we're back to using singular verbs. This
singular/plural business is one of the trickiest areas in
the whole of grammar, and we'll have some fun with it
in the chapter on nouns.

Starting a Sentence with 'And' and 'But'

One of the more persistent grammatical superstitions is
that you can't begin a sentence with *And*. This is
curious, because many of the best writers in the English
language – Shakespeare, Blake, Tennyson, Kipling, to
name just four – have kicked sentences off with *And*,
and so has the Bible: read the opening chapter.

The same applies to *But*:

> There is no rule to say that you can't begin a
> sentence or a paragraph with the conjunction *but*.
> When you want to express a doubt or outright
> disagreement to a statement, starting with *But* can
> emphasise and dramatise your point. *But* don't let
> it become a habit!

The *Daily Express* some years ago carried a memorable
sentence in its sporting pages that not only began with
but, but ended with *but*; and the following sentence
began with *and*:

> 'Northumberland and Humberside will each hold
> the trophy for six months after fighting out an
> exciting 1–1 draw. But if the result was indecisive,
> then the Soccer was anything but. And when all
> the medals have been engraved . . .'

The Building Blocks of Sentences: Parts of Speech

In Victorian times, when life was simpler, so, apparently, was grammar. Here is a little verse widely used to teach young children in the latter part of the nineteenth century:

> Three little words we often see,
> *Determiners* like a, an, and the.
>
> A *Noun's* the name of anything,
> A school or garden, hoop or string.
>
> An *Adjective* tells the kind of noun,
> Like great, small, pretty, white, or brown.
>
> Instead of nouns the *Pronouns* stand
> John's head, his face, my arm, your hand.
>
> *Verbs* tell of something being done,
> To read, write, count, sing, jump, or run.
>
> How things are done, the *Adverbs* tell,
> Like slowly, quickly, ill, or well.
>
> A *Preposition* stands before
> A noun, as in a room or through a door.
>
> *Conjunctions* join the nouns together,
> Like boy or girl, wind and weather.
>
> The *Interjection* shows surprise,
> Like Oh, how charming! Ah, how wise!
>
> The whole are called nine parts of speech,
> Which reading, writing, speaking teach.

This rhyme, incidentally, contains a fairly obvious grammatical error: *whole*, in the final couplet, is a 'quantity word' requiring a singular *is*, not *are*. But modernday grammarians would find far more fault with the verses than such a mere slip. 'Too simplistic', they would say, and they would be right. For example, many words defy a single classification. *Play* and *première*, for example, can be nouns and adverbs:

> They looked forward to the *première* of the *play*. (nouns)
> When the play *premièred* the critics would come out to *play*. (verbs)

Modern grammar isn't so bolted down as it was, because it has to recognise changes – in the usage of words, the coining of new words, and the migration of a word from one class to another:

> The doctor noticed the *knee jerk*. (noun/verb)
> His speech produced the expected *knee-jerk* reaction. (noun used as an adjective)
> The President's campaign strategy will rely on the art of the *knee-jerk*. (noun)

This is why we now have two broad word classes: open classes (which freely admit new words) and closed classes (which rarely do). For example:

OPEN CLASSES

Nouns	*software, gazumper, Fergie, tummytuck*
Adjectives	*neural, digital, cellular, quaffable investigative, hands-on*
Verbs	*outed, overdosed, stargaze*
Adverbs	*breezily, grandly, chaotically*
Interjections	*phew, aahhh, damn, ouch*

CLOSED CLASSES

Determiners	*the, which, my, that, your, these*
Pronouns	*I, me, we, hers, someone, whom*
Conjunctions	*and, or, but, when, since, as*
Prepositions	*at, with, in, by, to, from*
Auxiliaries	*be, may, can, will, were, must*

You can see from the examples above that the closed

classes of words are more or less static; it is difficult to invent additional determiners or substitutes for *the*, *my* and *your*. The open classes, however, are expanding all the time.

At this point a pause may be useful, because we are now using grammatical terms which may mean little or nothing to you; for many of us our grasp of such terms is at best incomplete or confused, and at worst, a hazy memory. But to make sense of grammar it is difficult to avoid familiarity with at least a few basic terms. These will, however, be kept to a workable minimum.

Let us return to the components that we use as building blocks for the way we speak and write, with a simple analysis of sentences that might look like this:

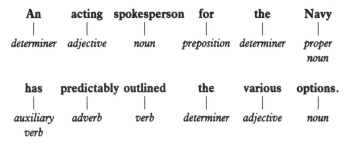

An	**acting**	**spokesperson**	**for**	**the**	**Navy**
determiner	adjective	noun	preposition	determiner	proper noun

has	**predictably**	**outlined**	**the**	**various**	**options.**
auxiliary verb	adverb	verb	determiner	adjective	noun

Nouns

A noun is a name – of a place, an object, a person, an animal, a concept, of anything:

- PLACES   street, home, Germany, Paris, heaven
- OBJECTS   plate, chair, tree, chamber pot
- PERSONS   Einstein, Michael Jackson, Caroline
- ANIMALS   pony, pig, wolfhound, chimp
- CONCEPTS   option, bad temper, ability, direction

33

We also recognise types of nouns. All nouns are either proper nouns, or names which are quite specific,

Marilyn Monroe, Saturday, The Rake's Progress, Mercedes, Brooklyn Bridge, Easter

or common nouns, which are broadly descriptive:

tea, coffee, hair, darkness, opinions, anger, ideas

You'll notice that the proper nouns begin with capital letters (not invariably, however) and that the common nouns do not.

Common nouns are further subdivided into concrete, abstract, count and non-count nouns, and these are all discussed in **Naming Things – Nouns** on page 41.

Verbs

Verbs are the engines that drive sentences and make them work. Imagine trying to get through a day without these work-horses:

eat, drink, sleeps, dream, woke, walked, go, come, talked, do, keep

You can see, even from these few examples, that verbs take various forms, some ending in *-s*, *-ed*, and so on, and in fact most verbs have four or more forms. For example:

eat, eats, eaten, ate

If you look up the words *eats, eating, eaten* or *ate* in a dictionary, in most cases you will be referred to the base verb *eat*, where the entry will include the entire *eat* family (plus derivatives like *eatable* and *eating-house*).

Apart from their multiplicity of forms, verbs are notoriously variable: they can be regular (where they follow certain rules) and irregular (where they don't);

they can be main verbs or auxiliary verbs, transitive and intransitive, finite and infinite. But don't let these grammatical gremlins frighten you; they will be exposed for what they are in **The Business of Verbs** on page 51.

Adjectives

Life without adjectives would be very difficult and extremely dull, because adjectives describe and qualify things:

> *hot, freezing, beautiful, hairy, user-friendly, brainless, distasteful, pathogenic, pliable*

Some adjectives give themselves away by their endings: *-ing*, *-y*, *-less*, *-ful*, *-ic*, and so on. They can also end with *-ly*, and can thus be confused with adverbs, which typically end with the same suffix.

Simply put, adjectives add something to nouns by qualifying,

> It was a *dreary* match.
> We made a *late* start.

or by reinforcing a noun's descriptive power:

> It was an *obvious* mistake.
> She possessed *hypnotic* charm.

You will see that all the adjectives here come before the noun, but that need not always be the case:

> Her charm was *hypnotic*.

There is a fuller discussion of adjectives and how to use them on page 60.

Adverbs

Adverbs are close relations to adjectives, as you can see:

ADJECTIVES	ADVERBS
essential	essentially
hypnotic	hypnotically
interesting	interestingly
dark	darkly

Notice that the giveaway element in adverbs is the *-ly* ending.

The difference between adjectives and adverbs is that adjectives invariably modify nouns, while adverbs modify a range of words: verbs, adjectives and even other adverbs:

MODIFYING A VERB	He *trudged wearily* along the road.
MODIFYING AN ADJECTIVE	She's an *exceedingly lucky* girl.
MODIFYING ANOTHER ADVERB	The engine turned over *relatively smoothly*.

Adverbs are often required where adjectives are used, and vice versa. A guide to their usage will be found on page 65.

Interjections

Interjections or exclamations are self-explanatory:

Wow! Hey! Shhhh! Blimey! Oh! What?

Although these examples, expressing surprise, excitement or some other emotion, are followed by exclamation marks, these are not always necessary:

Okay, let's get on with it.
Ah-ha, that's better.

Determiners

Determiners precede nouns, and the best known and most common of them are those known as articles: *a*, *an* and *the*:

> *a* party, *an* object, *the* concert

Determiners exist, however, in some variety, and help us to indicate quantity (*some* wine); ask questions (*whose* wine?); denote possession (*my* wine); and even emotion (*what* wine!).

Pronouns

Pronouns are great stand-ins for nouns and noun phrases, and are especially useful for avoiding repetition:

WITHOUT A PRONOUN	He saw James in the bar, and went over to meet James. Was I aware that Marcia is married? Yes, I was aware that Marcia is married.
WITH A PRONOUN	He saw James in the bar, and went over to meet *him*. Was I aware that *she* is married? Yes, I was aware of *it*.

You can readily see that pronouns are indispensable, and, with determiners, form a major part of our speech.

We divide pronouns (or them) into personal pronouns (*I*, *me*, *you*, *she*, *it*); reflexive pronouns (*myself*, *themselves*); possessive pronouns (*mine*, *ours*, *his*, *theirs*); demonstrative pronouns (*this*, *these*, *those*); interrogative pronouns (*who? what? which?*); relative pronouns (*who, whom, which, that*); and reciprocal pronouns (*one another, each other*).

You may experience a prickly sensation reading this, and not without good reason, for pronouns probably create more grammatical havoc than any other class of word. See the more detailed section on pronouns on page 47, and also in **Twenty Sore Points** on page 92.

Conjunctions

Think of conjunctions as link-words that join two parts of a sentence or two nouns:

> She asked him if he intended going out *and* he told her to mind her own business.
> She told him he could stay *if* he promised to be more polite.

There are two types of conjunctions – coordinating and subordinating – which are described on page 72.

Prepositions

While conjunctions link in a fairly straightforward way, prepositions link by relating verbs to nouns, pronouns and noun phrases:

> He flew to New York *in* a 747.
> She sidled *through* the open doorway.

We use prepositions constantly (try getting through a day without using *as, by, in, on, to* and *up*, to name just a few!) and misuse them occasionally. The vexing question of whether or not you can end a sentence with a preposition is answered on page 75.

Phrases and Clauses

We have now surveyed the different kinds of words we use to construct sentences. However we should also familiarise ourselves with two units or groups of words that are usually found in sentences: phrases and clauses.

PHRASES used to be defined as a number of words working together as a unit, but today's definition includes single words. The logic of this is demonstrated when we shrink a conventional phrase:

I love *that dry white wine from California.*
I love *that white wine.*
I love *wine.*

The key word *wine* is called the headword, and because it is a noun, all three phrases are called noun phrases.

There are five types of phrases, each named after the headword:

NOUN PHRASE	their first *home* (headword *home* is a noun)
VERB PHRASE	had been *burgled* (*burgled* is a verb)
ADVERB PHRASE	very *quickly* (*quickly* is an adverb)
ADJECTIVE PHRASE	too *difficult* to do (*difficult* is an adjective)
PREPOSITIONAL PHRASE	*on* the jumbo jet (*on* is the introducing preposition, *the jumbo jet* is a noun phrase)

The popular definition of a CLAUSE is a word unit larger than a phrase but smaller than a sentence. It is also more complete than a phrase. A simple sentence contains or consists of a single clause; a multiple sentence contains two or more clauses.

Because clauses can contain several elements, including verbs, conjunctions, nouns, pronouns and adverbs, the difference between clauses and sentences can be mystifying. But clauses are not constructed with the intention of being complete in themselves, but rather as a key part, or one of several parts, of a sentence. That is why clauses are described as main clauses and subordinate clauses:

MAIN CLAUSE	SUBORDINATE CLAUSE
I'll go	*to buy the tickets*
You'll never know	*what it's like*

The whole point of clauses is that they can be strung together, but always ruled by main clauses and with as many subordinate clauses as required. Fortunately, with practice, most of us seem to acquire the skills to do this intuitively. In fact, most of us could write the following sentence, or one very much like it, without ever consciously thinking of clause construction:

The Building Societies Association was almost alone in expressing relief because it meant the scrapping of the second-phase interest rise, of 3 per cent, which was announced earlier yesterday.

Here is the above sentence (from a report in a newspaper) dissected to expose its clauses:

MAIN CLAUSE	*The Building Societies Association was almost alone in expressing relief*
SUBORDINATE CLAUSE	*because it meant the scrapping of the second-phase interest rate rise (of 3 per cent,) (which was)*
SUBORDINATE CLAUSE WITHIN THE SUBORDINATE CLAUSE	*announced earlier yesterday.*

40

Naming Things – Nouns

Nouns make up by far the biggest family of words in the English language. This is because nouns name things; everything, everyone, almost every place in the world has a name. The common and scientific names of all the creatures in the natural world – from elephants to insects, molluscs to mites – add another few millions to the pile. There are about two billion people living in the world and all of them have one or more names. Not all human names are unique, of course; Korea is dominated by just four surnames, and in China, combinations of surnames and given names are often shared by several hundred thousand individuals, but it still adds up to a mind-boggling total. The names or titles of every book written, every song composed, every movie made and every brand of soap powder advertised, help expand this massive lexicon by tens of thousands of new names every day of our lives.

So while our everyday working vocabulary of verbs, adjectives, adverbs and so on remains more or less static throughout our lives, new nouns continue to pour into our memory, so that a person with a working vocabulary of several thousand words might have memory access to a hundred thousand proper and common nouns.

All names are nouns, but not all nouns are names. To make the distinction we use the terms proper noun and common noun:

PROPER NOUN	COMMON NOUN
Bentley	*car*
Boeing 747	*aeroplane*
Hoover	*vacuum cleaner*
Britain	*country*
Agaricus campestris	*mushroom*
Madonna	*singer*

That is a very basic separation. But while it is easy to identify proper nouns (by their capital letters, for a start), how do we know when a word is a common noun and not an adjective or a preposition, for example?

One way to find out is to precede the word by a determiner such as *the*, *an*, *a*, or *some*:

NOUNS	NON-NOUNS
a *racehorse*	a *racing*
the *park*	the *parked*
an *assembly*	an *assemble*
some *cash*	some *cashable*

Other tests include a noun's ability to take on singular and plural form; to be replaced by pronouns (*he*, *she*, *it*, etc); and also to accept add-ons to form new nouns:

book / booking / booklet / bookman / bookmark

Nouns can also be concrete nouns, or names of things we can see and touch, like *earth*, *sky*, *vapour*, *girl* and, yes, even *concrete*; and abstract nouns, which describe concepts, ideas and qualities, like *team*, *instinct*, *strength*, *coincidence*.

Both common and proper nouns have gender, too, which we learn at a very early age:

	MASCULINE	FEMININE	NEUTER
Common nouns	*boy, bull, cock, stallion, man*	*woman, cow, hen, mare, girl*	*letter, box, gelding*
Proper nouns	*Frank Sinatra, Peeping Tom*	*Joan of Arc, Cleopatra*	*Xerox, Aida Cold War*

Another class of noun familiar to everyone is the compound noun – again demonstrating a noun's potential to grow:

gin and tonic, scotch on the rocks, ne'er-do well, Eggs McMuffin, mother-in-law, attorney general

Such nouns throw up one of the more fascinating qualities of nouns – their capacity to be countable or uncountable, and (with some exceptions) singular and plural.

Countable and Uncountable Nouns

A countable noun is usually preceded by a determiner like *a*, *an* or *the*, and can be counted, and can also have either singular or plural form:

a *hamburger*	five *hamburgers*	several *hamburgers*
an *egg*	a dozen *eggs*	a nest of *eggs*
the *mountain*	the two *mountains*	the range of *mountains*

Uncountable nouns, as the name suggests, cannot be counted, nor do they have a plural form:

music, poetry, cement, light, luck, greed

But be careful here, because nouns, including uncountable nouns, are slippery; with a deft flick of the wrist they can become:

COUNTABLE NOUNS	The ship was lit by many bright *lights*.
ADJECTIVES	Both women had *light* complexions.
VERBS	Max did his best to *light* the fire.

Singular and Plural Nouns

Of all the chameleon qualities of the countable noun, its capacity to exist in singular and plural form is perhaps the most interesting and certainly – for most of us – the most perplexing.

Singulars and plurals have for a long time provided

gamesters and wordsmiths with a favourite playground for puzzles like these:

- Name words ending in -s which are spelt the same in singular and plural forms
  (Answer: *shambles, congeries*)
- Name a plural of a noun in which none of the letters are common with the singular
  (Answer: *cow = kine*)
- Name any plural words with no singular
  (Examples: *scissors, knickers, marginalia*)

In other words, the singular/plural phenomenon is littered with inconsistencies. For example, most nouns change from singular to plural by the simple addition of an -s:

shop, shops   *boat, boats*   *gate, gates*

This is by far the largest group. Notice, by the way, that there are no apostrophes before the -s. Then there is another group that adds an -es to become plural:

circus, circuses   *bush, bushes*   *bus, buses*

Fair enough. But now we come to other – fortunately smaller – groups, that pluralise in quaint and random ways:

mouse, mice	*loaf, loaves*	*tooth, teeth*
foot, feet	*hoof, hooves*	*child, children*
ox, oxen	*medium, media*	*index, indices*
crisis, crises	*larva, larvae*	*stimulus, stimuli*

And, finally, there are nouns like *sheep* which are both singular and plural.

We might now return to our compound nouns, which are prone to present unusual difficulties. For example:

Is it two *gins and tonic*, please, or two *gin and tonics*?

Is it *poet laureates* or *poets laureate*?

Is it *mother-in-laws* or *mothers-in-law*?

Is it *Egg McMuffins* or *Eggs McMuffin*?
Is it *scotches on the rocks*, or *scotch on the rocks's*?

These are conundrums that have tortured people for ages. There is, however, a view, which sounds reasonable, that hyphenated compounds should be pluralised by adding an -*s* at the end (with, strangely, the exception of *mothers-in-law*); and that unhyphenated compounds should have the -*s* added to the central, or most important noun. If we follow this advice, we get:

> *gins and tonic, poets laureate, Egg McMuffins* (for it is the McMuffin bit that creates the difference), and *scotches on the rocks*.

So what about *spoon full* and *mouth full*, and *spoonful* and *mouthful*? The plurals of the first pair are *spoons full* and *mouths full*; the point about the second pair is fullness, so -ful is the central part of the compound and should have the -*s* added to it: *spoonfuls* and *mouthfuls*. But remember that these recommendations are not bound by strict rules; far from it. Many respected grammarians will opt for *spoonsful* and *mother-in-laws*, and will expect to be served like anyone else when they ask the barman for two *gin and tonics*.

Collective Nouns

There are a few other categories of nouns – nouns of a kind, for example, like *species, brand, type* – but of these the most useful is the collective noun. It is also a grammatical favourite.

Collective nouns are handy because they unify things, ideas or people into groups:

> *audience*, the *Government, council, team, jury*

The effect of a collective noun is to create a singular entity, which, although many creatures (bees in *swarm*) or people (members of a *jury*) are involved, should now be treated as a singular noun:

> The *army is* outside the city gates.
> Will this *class* please behave *itself*!
> The *committee is* still deliberating.

Sometimes, however, a collective noun is more subtle, and can lead to confusion:

> A vast *number* of crimes *is* never reported at all.
> The *majority is* in favour of the wage rise.

Such nouns sometimes lead to grammatically correct but odd-sounding emissions like *none of us is going to work today*, and *a lot of things is wrong with the world today*, and this in turn has led to considerable relaxation of the old rule of always following a group or collective noun with a singular verb. While not going all the way with 'if it sounds okay it *is* okay', group or collective nouns like *team*, *government* and *committee* may now be treated as singular or plural. But, once begun, don't change in midstream:

NOT	The Tilner Committee *has* a week in which to announce *their* findings.
BUT	The Tilner Committee *have* a week in which to announce *their* findings.
OR	The Tilner Committee *has* a week in which to announce *its* findings.

Collective nouns are not all doom and gloom. Knowing the correct collectives for groups of certain birds, animals and humans can score a lot of points at Wine and Wisdom nights. Try these:

a *murder* of crows	a *convocation* of eagles
an *exaltation* of larks	a *chattering* of starlings
a *pod* of whiting	a *dray* of squirrels
a *knot* of toads	a *business* of ferrets

and these, more recent, whimsical contributions:

a *rash* of dermatologists

a *descent* of in-laws

a *fraid* of ghosts

an *innuendo* of gossips

a *piddle* of puppies

an *overcharge* of plumbers

a *failing* of students

a *slew* of dragons

How Nouns Become Possessive

We have seen that when we pluralise most nouns, we add an -*s* (*ghost*, *ghosts*). Note, no apostrophe. But when a noun changes to its possessive form, we add an -*'s*. Note the apostrophe:

a *ghost*   a *ghost's* shroud

the *team*   the *team's* triumph

Where common nouns end with -*s* (*girls*) we add an apostrophe; with proper nouns we have the option of adding -*'s* as usual, or simply adding an apostrophe after the -*s*:

The invitation went out for the *girls' party*.
Instead they went to *James's party* (or *James' party*).

As many of us often find that apostrophe spells catastrophe, there is a more detailed session on the 'upstairs comma' in **Punctuation: What's the Point?** on page 79.

You, I, Me, and Other Pronouns

As we saw in **Building Blocks of Sentences**, pronouns are versatile substitutes for nouns and noun phrases. We also noted that they spread like a rash through our speech yet at the same time have the capacity to cause us lots of problems. But before we worry about the dangers, let's find out what pronouns are.

Although perhaps academic, it's worth running through the various kinds of pronouns to see what they do:

PERSONAL PRONOUNS   We use these to identify ourselves and others, and we use them constantly. They are used in three ways:

- In the *first person*, the most intimate, which includes the person or persons doing the speaking or writing: *I*, *me*, *we*, *us*, *myself*, *ourselves*
- In the *second person*, which embraces those who are being addressed: *you*, *yourself*, *yourselves*
- In the *third person*, or 'all the others': *he*, *him*, *she*, *her*, *it*, *they*, *them*, *themselves*, *itself*

With the exception of *it*, which refers to things (and sometimes babies and animals), all personal pronouns refer to people, while *them* can refer to people or things. There are odd exceptions: a ship is not an *it*, but a *she*, or a *her*.

POSSESSIVE PRONOUNS   These indicate possession or ownership and are sometimes called possessive adjectives. Some are used as determiners, and are dependent on nouns:

my groceries, *her* hairdresser, *his* anger, *our* house, *your* car, *their* washing machine

The other possessive pronouns are used on their own:

it is *ours*, it is *mine*, *theirs* is out of date, *his* is that one there, *hers* is over there

REFLEXIVE PRONOUNS   This tribe insinuates its members into our lives in various ways: *Look after yourself*; *they keep to themselves*. Others are *itself*, *herself*, *himself*, *yourselves*, *myself*, *ourselves*.

48

DEMONSTRATIVE PRONOUNS   These help us to demonstrate something or to point to things:

> I'll take *this*. I'll have *that*.
> *These* will do. *Those* are too stale.

INTERROGATIVE PRONOUNS   These are used to ask questions: *who, what, which, whom, whose*. When you use them, make sure they are followed by a question mark:

> *Who? Who* is she? *Which* one? *Whose* are those?

RELATIVE PRONOUNS   These are *that, which, who, whom* and *whose* and we use them to introduce relative clauses, as in '*It was Claire who asked me first*'. We use them constantly and, with some exceptions, with confidence:

> The suit *that he was supposed to mend* is ruined.
> I wish I knew *whose parcels were damaged*.
> I'd like those shoes *which I saw yesterday*.
> She's the lady *to whom I gave the keys*.

You can see the traps looming, can't you? Taking the last example, many of us would avoid the formal *whom*, and say something like, '*She's the lady I gave the keys to*.' And we are increasingly dropping *that* and *which* from sentences, so that the first and third examples would customarily sound like:

> *The suit he was supposed to mend is ruined.*
> *I'd like those shoes I saw yesterday.*

INDEFINITE PRONOUNS   This is a mixed bunch, but when you see them you will immediately spot a common bond:

> *all, any, every, each, some, one, both, either, neither,*
> *few, little, less, least, many, everyone, someone,*
> *no one, something, anybody, more, most*

They all have to do with quantity: nothing at all, a little, some, or a lot. Here are a few pointers on their use:

- Note that *no one* is the only two-word pronoun
- Note that *little*, *less* and *much* should refer to uncountable nouns (a *little sugar*, but not a *little cakes*; *much trouble*, but not *much problems*; *less fat*, not *less calories*). (See **Twenty Sore Points**, page 92)
- Note that *each*, *one*, *either*, *neither*, *someone*, *no one*, *something* and *anybody* are all singular

When Using Pronouns . . .

A common piece of advice is not to use pronouns without first introducing the nouns they represent, although in practice it's done all the time:

It's very difficult, *this job*. *Here* it comes! (*the bus*)

Try to avoid using a pronoun when it results in confusion and ambiguity. It is difficult to resist bringing out the old chestnut, 'If your *baby* has trouble digesting cow's milk, boil *it*.'

While pronouns referring to people are of either gender (*he*, *she*) or unspecified (*I*, *me*, *they*) there is an historical propensity to use masculine pronouns to refer to both sexes:

Any runner who does not finish will have *his* application for next year's race reconsidered by the committee.

What does one do in this age of gender equality? One way is to use the '*his and her*' formula (Any runner who does not finish will have *his* or *her* application . . .) but this is obviously clumsy. A better way is to pluralise the sentence (Runners who do not finish will have *their* applications . . .)

The Business of Verbs

The business of verbs is to express action or to indicate a condition or a state:

ACTION He *is running* away.
STATE She *loathes* rap music.

Verbs also help us to express time:

PAST He's *been sacked*.
PRESENT He is *listening* to her sing.
FUTURE I *will come* if I *can*.

Verbs are among the most versatile of all our words. You can see how brilliant they are in these two paragraphs. The first is a fairly matter-of-fact description:

> Then the helicopter banked and almost stalled. The engines roared and the craft tilted and a body fell out of the hatch. The machine rapidly lost height and the engines died. Now only the wind could be heard. Then it began to revolve, falling out of control, throwing Kippy off and finally plunging into the sea.

That could have been a report of a helicopter accident at sea by an aviation safety officer. Here, now, is the same passage, but brought graphically to life by selective verbs:

> Suddenly the helicopter banked, shuddered, and seemed to stall, its arms rotating wildly, scrabbling and clawing the black sky for something to grip. The engines whined and screamed and the craft lurched and a body shot out of the hatch and hurtled past Kippy into the void below. The machine was now losing height, dropping at an increasing rate until the engines abruptly died, their howling replaced by the eerie

whistling of the wind. Then, slowly at first, the fuselage itself began to spin around the almost stationary rotors, gyrating faster and faster, whirling and spinning out of control, spiralling down through the tunnel of rushing air until, a few seconds after Kippy was hurled off by the force of the spin, the rotors disintegrated and the grey coffin plummeted into the wild black water.

You can easily see how certain verbs – *shuddered, rotating, scrabbling, clawing, whined, screamed, shot, hurtled, dropping, spin, gyrating, spiralling, hurled, disintegrated, plummeted* – contribute to this vivid, action-packed word picture. To heighten the effect even more, some novelists might move the verbs to the present tense, to give the reader the 'you are there now' feeling:

> . . . then, slowly at first, the fuselage itself begins to spin . . . the rotors disintegrate and the grey coffin plummets into the wild black water.

Because verbs are so versatile, it's well worth finding out what they can do, and how you can put them to work. Whole books have been written about verbs (*The English Verb* by Michael Lewis, Language Teaching Publications, 1986, is just one) so this little introduction will merely brush the high spots; nevertheless, they will be the *important* high spots.

Regular and Irregular Verbs

Verbs are divided into two groups, regular, or weak verbs, of which there are thousands, and slightly fewer than 300 irregular, or strong verbs. Regular verbs are so named because they stick to certain rules, while irregular verbs are real wild cards, as you will see.

| REGULAR VERBS | *laugh, look, advises, play, loved* |
| IRREGULAR VERBS | *begin, chosen, speak, froze, shrink* |

The difference between these two groups is in their behaviour when they change to express time: present and past time. **Regular** verbs follow a pattern; the basic form of the verb simply adds an *-s*, *-ing*, or *-ed* to express a different person, time or mood:

BASIC FORM	*laugh, look, play, advise, push*
PAST TENSE	*laughed, looked, played, advised, pushed*
PARTICIPLE FORMS (PRESENT)	*laughs, looks, plays, advises, pushes laughing, looking, playing, advising, pushing*

Irregular verbs, however, can behave quite erratically:

PRESENT	*begin, choose, speak, freeze, shrink*
PAST TENSE	*began, chose, spoke, froze, shrank*
PARTICIPLE FORMS (PAST)	*begun, chosen, spoken, frozen, shrunk*

It's the irregular verbs that can give us trouble because they change in such unexpected ways. Some verbs have more than three forms; *be* has eight. It can be most confusing:

> The verse we write we say is written,
> All rules despite, but not despitten,
> And the gas we light is never litten.
> The things we drank were doubtless drunk,
> The boy that's spanked is never spunk,
> The friend we thank is never thunk.
> Suppose we speak, then we have spoken,
> But if we sneak, we have not snoken,
> And shoes that squeak have never squoken.
> The dog that bites has certainly bitten,
> But when it fights, it has not fitten.

As a matter of fact, we conjugate verbs (for that is what this process is called) more or less instinctively and quite successfully ninety-eight per cent of the time, and tend to avoid the few oddniks among irregular verbs that trip us up. But if you would like to master these, you'll find a list of the more obstreperous of them at the end of the section.

Other Kinds of Verbs

The verbs discussed so far, whether regular or irregular, are all main verbs. Sometimes, however, they need help from auxiliary verbs to describe subtleties of action.

Auxiliary Verbs

There are two kinds of these: the three primary auxiliaries (*be*, *do*, *have*) which sometimes double as main verbs; and what are known as modal auxiliaries (*can/could*, *may/might*, *must*, *shall/should*, *will/would*) which enable us to express an amazing range of meanings: whether or not something is possible; making demands; giving permission; deducing or predicting some event, and so forth. Also, by following an auxiliary with *not*, we can express a negative. Let's track the main verb *speak* through a range of possibilities:

I speak	I do not speak
she speaks	she does not speak
she is speaking	she is not speaking
she has spoken	she has not spoken
she has been speaking	she has not been speaking
she spoke	she did not speak
she was speaking	she was not speaking
she had spoken	she had not spoken
she had been speaking	she had not been speaking
she will speak	she will not speak

she will be speaking	she will not be speaking
she will have spoken	she will not have spoken
she will have been speaking	she will not have been speaking
she would speak	she would not speak
she would be speaking	she would not be speaking
she would have spoken	she would not have spoken
she would have been speaking	she would not have been speaking
she could speak	she could not speak
she could be speaking	she could not be speaking
she could have spoken	she could not have spoken
etc, etc	

To all these variations you can add a *must speak*, *may speak*, *might speak*, *can speak* and a *shall speak* series. Further, there are several 'fringe' modals that we can trot out to contribute other possibilities: *ought to speak*, *used to speak*, *dare she speak?*, *need she speak?*; plus idiomatic modals such as *had better speak*, *would rather speak* and *has got to speak* (try working backwards from *he's got to be joking!*). It's astonishing, isn't it? It surely demonstrates how verbs, aided by their auxiliaries and a three-letter negative, can offer us so many fine shades of meaning with such economy.

Transitive and Intransitive Verbs

The distinction here is that an intransitive verb can stand alone:

> She *speaks*   He *runs*   I *smile*

while nearly all transitive verbs won't work unless they have some sort of relationship:

> He *raised* his fist.
> She *laid* the book on the bed.

Phrasal Verbs

These are multi-word verbs that incorporate prepositions or adverbs, and they are an interesting lot:

> *look up, look out, look after, look for, give up, take off, break even, called up, look forward to, listen to, fall out, turn down, run up*

You will immediately see that all these examples have an idiomatic feel about them; they are the sort of expressions that pepper our speech.

If we hear someone say 'She loves to *run down* her neighbours', we don't jump to the conclusion that she's trying to kill them with her car. The same applies to 'Will you *run up* a pair of curtains for me?' Why do we *bring up* and not *bring down* a problem? When someone *turns up*, what is that person doing, literally? Or to *go back* on a promise, *chat up* a girl, *turn down* an offer, *put up* with a situation?

Most phrasal verbs do acquire precise meanings:

> He *checked* the speedometer.
> She *checked up* on her husband.

Many phrasal verbs seem to add nothing except paradox to the original verb (*shout down, settle up, ring up*) but not even dynamite will stop us from using them.

Verbless Clauses and Sentences

Verbs are so versatile they can disappear altogether in clauses and even sentences. These are not so much aimless fragments as idiomatic expressions or deliberate constructions for effect:

> *Why all the fuss?*
> *Another glass of wine?*

> *What brilliant tennis!*
> *Nuts!*

Having begun this chapter with a paragraph loaded with verbs and concluded it with no verbs at all, one item remains, and that is the list of verbal tripwires promised earlier:

Those Disorderly, Disobedient, Deviating Irregular Verbs

Present	Past	Past Participle
arise	arose	arisen
awake	awoke	awoken
be	was	been
bear	bore	borne
bid	bad	bidden
bite	bit	bitten
burn	burned/burnt	burned/burnt
burst	burst	burst
choose	chose	chosen
dive	dived	dived
do	did	done
drive	drove	driven
forgive	forgave	forgiven
go	went	gone
hang	hung/hanged	hung/hanged
kneel	kneeled/knelt	knelt/kneeled
lay	laid	laid
lean	leaned/leant	leant/leaned
lie	lay	lain
mistake	mistook	mistaken
mow	mowed	mown
quit	quit/quitted	quit/quitted
rid	rid	rid
saw	sawed	sawn
sew	sewed	sewn

Present	Past	Past Participle
shear	sheared	shorn/sheared
shoe	shoed/shod	shod
show	showed	shown/showed
slay	slew	slain
smell	smelled/smelt	smelt/smelled
speed	speeded/sped	sped/speeded
spell	spelled/spelt	spelt/spelled
spin	span/spun	spun
spring	sprang	sprung
steal	stole	stolen
stink	stank	stunk
strew	strewed	strewn
stride	strode	stridden/strode
strike	struck	stricken/struck
strive	strove	striven
swell	swelled	swollen
teach	taught	taught
thrive	thrived/throve	thrived/thriven
tread	trod	trodden/trod
undergo	underwent	undergone
undertake	undertaken	undertook
undo	undid	undone
wake	waked/woke	woken/waked
weave	wove	woven
wet	wet/wetted	wet/wetted
wring	wrung	wrung

Describing Things –
Adjectives and Adverbs

Adjectives define and modify nouns while adverbs do the same for nouns and verbs. They are close relations in a very big family of words, and often are difficult to tell apart; so that when we use them we sometimes misuse or abuse them. It's therefore useful to know something about adjectives and adverbs and how we can use them to better effect.

Here's a sentence in which the meaning depends almost entirely on adjectives and adverbs:

You're buying the	*best,*	ADJECTIVE
	most	ADVERB
	expensive,	ADJECTIVE
	exciting	PARTICIPLE
and	*arguably*	ADVERB
highest	*performance*	ADJECTIVE/NOUN
	saloon	NOUN/ADJECTIVE
	car	NOUN

There are four kinds of modifier in this sentence: several adjectives, two adverbs, a participle (the verb *excite* turned into an adjective by adding *-ing*, discussed in the next chapter), and two nouns (*performance*, *saloon*) that are used in an adjectival way.

Writing a sentence like that is a bit like juggling four balls, but most of us manage to do it tolerably well without too many mishaps.

In **Parts of Speech** we found that we could identify many adverbs by their *-ly* endings. That's fine for adverbs with *-ly* endings, but there are many without, and there are also some adjectives with *-ly* endings. It is these that cause confusion:

ADJECTIVES	ADVERBS
He is a *slow* driver.	He drives *slowly*.
She is an *early* riser.	She rises *early*.

That's very *loud* music.	He's playing *loudly*.
It was a *straight* road.	She drove *straight* home.
He read a *daily* newspaper.	He reads a paper *daily*.

Obviously we must be wary of adjectives and adverbs that don't play by the rules. We've all seen signs that say: *GO SLOW!* and wonder, on reflection, if it ought to say, *GO SLOWLY!* Our reason is that *slow* in *SLOW LANE* is an adjective, *slowly* (by its suffix *-ly*) is an adverb, therefore it should be the latter. Correct; but in this case, modern usage allows both *slow* and *slowly*. The following examples, however, are still regarded as bad news:

She put her lips to his ear and spoke *soft*.	(*softly*)
I'm afraid I've let him down *bad*.	(*badly*)
That feels *real* great!	(*really*)

You are excused if some confusion still exists, which is all the more reason why we should subject both adjectives and adverbs to some closer study.

Adjectives

Here are some adjectives in use to show you how free-ranging they are:

DESCRIBING SIZE	It was a *huge* marquee.
DESCRIBING COLOUR	The carpet was *red*.
DESCRIBING A QUALITY	I loved the *plush* armchairs.
DEFINING QUANTITY	There were *five* windows.
DEFINING SPECIFICITY	Did you see her *Persian* rug?
. . . and so on	

Adjectives can come before a noun (*huge marquee*) and after a number of verbs: the *be* family – *is, are, was, were, am, being, been*; *look, seem, become, stay*, etc (carpet *was red*). They can 'top and tail' a sentence

(*Welsh* singing is world *famous*), follow nouns (he requested that all the journalists *present* should leave) and pronouns (did you find anything *useful?*). And of course they can be used liberally:

> What impressed her most of all were the *three big ancient green-tinged metallic Burmese religious* figures.

A bit over the top, but here we have no less than seven adjectives all adding something to the description of the figures. It's worth noting that, although no strict rules exist to tell you in which order your adjectives should be, it should follow a common-sense sequence. For example, you know immediately that something's wrong here:

> *What impressed her most of all were the Burmese religious three big green-tinged ancient metallic figures.*

An acceptable rule-of-thumb for arranging your adjectives is:

QUANTITY	*five*, a *hundred*
EMOTIVE	*lovely*, *ugly*, *rare*
SIZE	*large*, *tiny*
AGE	*brand new*, *old*
COLOUR, TEXTURE	*ochreous*, *blue*, *smooth*
SPECIFICITY	*Jewish*, *Japanese*, *Xeroxed*
PURPOSE	*dining* table, *wine* glass

which, followed to the letter, might result in something like this:

> The catalogue listed *two exquisite 23in. 18th century Peruzzi silver candle* sticks.

Recognising Adjectives

What makes an adjective? Many of them are original descriptive words like *good, dark, hot* and *rough*, many of which have their opposites: *bad, fair, cold* and *smooth*. But thousands more began life as nouns and verbs and were changed into adjectives by having endings tacked on to them. These are fairly easy to recognise as adjectives:

-able	*notable, fashionable, detestable, desirable*
-ible	*sensible, comprehensible, horrible, responsible*
-al	*natural, mortal, skeletal, oriental*
-ar	*jocular, circular, spectacular, singular*
-ed	*excited, crooked, married, cracked*
-ent	*excellent, indulgent, emergent, deficient*
-esque	*picturesque, Romanesque, statuesque*
-ful	*wonderful, hopeful, forgetful, thoughtful*
-ic	*heroic, psychic, angelic, romantic*
-ical	*periodical, magical, farcical, psychological*
-ish	*liverish, childish, quirkish, British*
-ive	*reflective, massive, defensive, offensive*
-less	*endless, cloudless, hopeless, legless*
-like	*lifelike, ladylike, childlike*
-ous	*nervous, herbaceous, piteous, officious*
-some	*meddlesome, awesome, loathsome, fearsome*
-worthy	*newsworthy, praiseworthy, seaworthy*

and two endings to watch for:

| -ly | *lonely, crinkly, sickly, prickly* |
| -y | *earthy, shaky, funny, tacky, kinky* |

These two endings provide a wildly (adverb) frothing bubbly (adjective) brew of pitfalls and booby traps. Try to separate the adjectives from the adverbs:

truly idly gravelly loyally woolly yearly holy thankfully gentlemanly brazenly properly

If you try placing each of the words before a noun (truly car, gravelly voice) you should score 100%. The adjectives are gravelly, woolly, yearly, holy and gentlemanly; the rest are adverbs.

Kinds of Adjectives

You must be aware now that adjectives cover a lot of ground. Even possessive pronouns like *many*, *this*, *my*, *his* and *her* can be used as adjectives. There are adjectives which can rove around a sentence with some freedom, and others that are locked into certain positions. The former are called central adjectives, and the latter are peripheral adjectives:

CENTRAL ADJECTIVE	This is a *new* car.
	This car is *new*.
	New the car may be, but it is far too expensive.
PERIPHERAL ADJECTIVE	The man spoke *utter* nonsense.

Here you can see that *utter* cannot be moved to any other position (*The man spoke nonsense that was utter?*); its function here as an adjective is specifically to qualify the noun *nonsense*. For different degrees of nonsense we might have used adjectives like *absolute*, *puerile* or *childish*, but in this case the old cliché does an effective job.

In an earlier example, we saw *Welsh* used as an adjective, and noted that *British* is also an adjective. These are called proper adjectives (*Chippendale* furniture, *Shrewsbury* cake) because they define a particular thing; common adjectives describe classes of things: *leafy* tree, *white* house, *angry* bull.

The Expanding Adjective

One of the most valuable services adjectives provide is a range of comparisons. Imagine trying to describe the comparative sizes of three bundles of ten-pound notes without having recourse to the words *small/smaller/ smallest* and *large/larger/largest*. Most adjectives work like that; they can express several comparative elements: the same, less, least, more, most. In some cases we add *-er* (*taller, weaker*) or *-est* (*tallest, weakest*); while in others we qualify the adjective with *more* (*more entertaining*); *most* (*most endearing*); *less* (*less enthusiastic*) or *least* (the *least likely*). All these adjectival devices enable us to describe almost anything, any action, any feeling, with extraordinary accuracy:

> It was a *big* celebration.   It was a *very big* celebration.   It was the *biggest* celebration ever. It was *bigger* than any other celebration I've seen. It was a *fairly big* celebration.   It was *quite a big* celebration.   Well, it was a *biggish* celebration . . .

etc etc. Then we can move on to *huge, vast* and *gargantuan*!

Tips on Using Adjectives

● BE AWARE OF CLICHÉ ADJECTIVES   These are what the novelist and columnist Keith Waterhouse calls 'limpet adjectives' – they always seem to stick to certain nouns:

> *widespread concern*   *drastic steps*   *utmost urgency*
> *long-felt want*   *true facts*   *full inquiry*

● AVOID REPETITIOUS ADJECTIVES   The definition of the word *history* is 'a record of past events', so why do we so often read a sentence like, '*The disagreement is now past history*'? Sloppiness or ignorance is the answer, and redundancy (or pleonasm, as grammarians have it) is the problem.

Here are some typical examples:

personal friend   *unexpected* surprise
amazing miracle *actual* fact   *mobile* van
wet puddle   a *warm* 28 degrees *tall* skyscraper

● PRACTICE ADJECTIVAL ECONOMY   To demonstrate the use of adjectives, an earlier example used a pile-up of seven of them, which is rather too many. Overloads of this sort cause confusion; by the time the reader has reached the last one the first is probably forgotten. If you find you've written a sentence with more than half a dozen adjectives, try another construction. Furthermore, make sure that every adjective you use adds something essential to the sentence: 'Her skis sliced through the *powdery white* snow on her *downward* trajectory'. Most of us know that snow is white, and believe that it is difficult to ski uphill, so the adjectives *white* and *downward* could well be returned to the dictionary.

Adverbs

As with adjectives, we use adverbs to add information and extra layers of meaning to a statement. Adverbs, however, are far more versatile; while adjectives can dress up nouns and pronouns, adverbs are regular Houdinis, modifying a verb here, boosting an adjective there, appearing in disguise to support another adverb – even bossing phrases and whole sentences about! And as we have seen, they disguise themselves so well sometimes that they can be mistaken for adjectives:

ADVERBS   The train arrived *early*. She hadn't *long* left home.

ADJECTIVES   They caught the *early* train. He drew a *long* line.

How Adverbs Work

Here is a short catalogue of how we can use adverbs to add information and meaning:

DEFINE MANNER	They played *happily* together.
DENOTE PLACE	They can play over *there*.
FIX TIME	We can all go there *afterwards*.
EXPRESS GRADATION	We never seem to see *enough*.
EXPRESS FREQUENCY	We *hardly ever* go there.
INDICATE VIEWPOINT	I would never go there, *personally*.
LINK TO A PREVIOUS THOUGHT	*Nevertheless*, I feel we should go.
INDICATE ATTITUDE	*Curiously*, she has never been there.

You will note that while many adverbs are stand-alone words like *there, enough, up, now, here, very*, etc., others have been created from existing words. The most common of these constructions is the *-ly* suffix (*personally, curiously, romantically, historically*); other suffixes include *-wise* (*clockwise, otherwise*); *-wards* (*backwards, homewards*); and *-ways* (*endways, always*).

Enough? (That's an exclamatory adverb, used as a sentence.) There is little reason to dwell on the detailed workings of adverbs like those above, because from childhood we've learned to handle them with intuitive assurance.

What is worth looking into, however, is the order in which adverbs should appear in a sentence. Because of their versatility, adverbs offer a lot of options. In his book *Rediscover Grammar*, David Crystal demonstrates this all-purpose quality with devastating effect, using a seven-way sentence:

1. *Originally*, the book must have been bought in the shop.
2. The book *originally* must have been bought in the shop.

3. The book must *originally* have been bought in the shop.
4. The book must have *originally* been bought in the shop.
5. The book must have been *originally* bought in the shop.
6. The book must have been bought *originally* in the shop.
7. The book must have been bought in the shop, *originally*.

Positioning Your Adverbs

Not all adverbs are so adaptable, however; most feel uncomfortable in certain positions while others, wrongly placed, can produce ambiguity and even hilarity. This rough guide should make you aware of such adverbial problems:

DEFINING MANNER:	adverb usually towards end of sentence
Not advised –	He rather *erratically* walked.
Much better –	He walked rather *erratically*.
DENOTING PLACE:	adverb typically towards end of sentence
Not advised –	Over *there* he threw the stone.
Much better –	He threw the stone over *there*.
FIXING TIME:	adverb best towards end of sentence
Not advised –	I *recently* saw that film.
Much better –	I saw that film *recently*.
EXPRESSING GRADATION:	adverb works best in the middle

| Not advised – | The jar is full, *almost*. |
| Much better – | The jar is *almost* full. |

INDICATING FREQUENCY:	adverb usually not at beginning
Not advised –	*Always* he is going to the pub.
Much better –	He is *always* going to the pub.

DENOTING ATTITUDE:	most effective at the front of a sentence
Not advised –	They both decided to *wisely* stay away.
Much better –	*Wisely*, they both decided to stay away.

INDICATING VIEWPOINT:	again, best placed at the front
Not advised –	I shouldn't comment, *strictly speaking*.
Much better –	*Strictly speaking*, I shouldn't comment.

Keep in mind that a guide such as this is not a rule book, for there are many exceptions. *Enough* is an adverb of gradation or degree and it is commonly placed in the middle of a sentence: *I've done enough work for today*. But look what happens when enough is placed at the end or beginning of a sentence: *Do you think they've had enough? Enough has been said on the subject of adverbs!* What has happened is that in these two examples, *enough* has turned into a noun. Look at the sentences again and you will see that this is so.

One of the most contentious adverbial placements is known as the split infinitive in which, typically, an adverb or adverbial phrase finds its way between the preposition *to* and a basic verb form:

to dearly love   to properly understand   to boldly go

This really isn't an issue any more, and many modern

grammarians will happily provide you with a nickel-plated infinitive-splitter to use to your heart's content. It is discussed in some detail in **Twenty Sore Points** on page 96.

Some Tips on Using Adverbs

• BEWARE OF MISPLACED ADVERBS   Always keep adverbs like *nearly, only, even, quite, just*, etc, as near as possible to the words they're meant to modify. *He just went to the store to buy some jeans* could mean that very recently he went to the store to buy jeans; what the writer meant was, *He went to the store* just *to buy some jeans*.

• BE WARY OF STARTING SENTENCES WITH ADVERBS   *Interestingly*, this advice is given by *The Times* to its journalists; this sentence is an example. 'Such constructions,' advises *The Times*, 'are not forbidden, but sentences starting with adverbs are normally built on sand.'

• AVOID 'NEUTRALISING' ADVERBS   Such phrases as *faintly repulsive, rather appalling, pretty meaningless, somewhat threatening* and *slightly lethal* cancel out the intended effect. Such an oxymoronic habit should be *gently stamped out*.

Grammatical Glue

This is something of a 'bits and pieces' chapter about those grammatical elements you remember vaguely but whose exact function you can't recall: determiners, conjunctions, prepositions and participles. When you see these terms translated into words you'll see how important they are:

DETERMINERS   *a, the, this, my, which, all*
CONJUNCTIONS   *and, but, or, if, because, like, whereas*
PREPOSITIONS   *with, at, to, for, on, in, around*
PARTICIPLES   *reading, growing, knocked, worked* and many thousands of words ending in *-ing* and *-ed*

Together, these words and their companions form a mass of grammatical glue with which we construct all our writing and speech. It is simply impossible to communicate without this glue. If anyone should attempt even a short passage of English without it, the passage might look like this:

> Windows room were wide open, Paris immense level abyss that itself foot house, built perpendicularly hill. Helene, out long chair, was windows.

It's a bit like one of those model kits in which all the pieces are present but none of it makes sense until you stick them all together. Here's the paragraph assembled and glued:

> Both windows of the room were wide open, and Paris unfolded its immense level in the abyss that hollowed itself at the foot of the house, built perpendicularly on the hill. Helene, stretched out on her long chair, was reading at one of the windows.

Obviously, we should know more about this useful stuff.

Determiners

Quite simply, determiners precede and determine certain qualities of nouns and noun phrases. In the attributive sense, they act as adjectives. Here, for example, is a partial list of the determiners we use most. The first four kinds are used to indicate that the noun is personal or specific, and are called *Definites*:

DEFINITE ARTICLE	I will buy *the* car. / He will see *the* car.
POSSESSIVE	It is *my* car. / It is *his* car.
POSSESSIVE PROPER	It is *Fred's* car. / It is *Lyn's* car.
DEMONSTRATIVE	I want *that* car. / He bought *this* car.
NUMBER	You have *two* cars? / No, just *one* car.

The next group of determiners are called *Indefinites* because they generalise or broadly qualify nouns:

INDEFINITE ARTICLE	I saw *a* great movie. / She ate *an* apple.
QUANTIFIER	She saw *every* movie. / I saw *most* movies.
EXCLAMATORY	*What* a movie! / It was *such* a great movie!
INTERROGATIVE	*What* movie? / *Whose* ticket did you use?

Once again, we find that we possess an easy familiarity with such words. We know not to use two determiners together: *I will buy the a car. Did you see some several movies?* We also learn to drop following nouns: *I saw them all* [movies]. *I bought both* [cars]. With ear and instinct most of us experience very few problems with determiners.

Conjunctions

Conjunctions are very strong glue because we use them to link parts of sentences together:

> She plays the violin *and* also the piano.

In this example, *and* is the conjunction that co-ordinates both parts of the sentence. It is the simplest kind of conjunction in that it is a link and nothing more; it adds nothing new to the sentence. In fact, you could turn it right round without altering the meaning:

> She plays the piano *and* also the violin.

But there are other conjunctions that, while gluing a sentence together, can also impart extra meaning:

> She likes the piano, *but* the violin is her favourite.

You'll note that this is not the same as *She likes the piano and the violin is her favourite*; the conjunction *but* promises an exception or a contrast. *And* is bland; *but*, *either/or*, *neither/nor* and *yet* offer more possibilities; but the strongest and most versatile conjunctions are the Subordinators. These conjunctions can provide quite a lot of information while still doing their joining job.

They are usually grouped according to the meaning they add to the join:

Expressing	Some examples	Typical usage
Time	*before, after, till, until, since, as soon as, while*	She'll come home *after* she's finished.
Place	*where, wherever*	I'll find out *where* he comes from.
Cause	*since, because, as, for*	I feel ill *because* I ate too much.
Condition	*if, although, unless, or, as long as*	I'll feel better *if* I lie down.
Comparison	*as, than, like, as if, as though*	It looks *like* it will rain.
Contrast	*although, while, whereas*	I'm good at English *while* she's good at maths.
Purpose	*so that, so as to, lest, in order that*	I must stop *so as to* allow others to speak.
Result	*so, so that, such that*	He shouted *so that* they could hear him.
Preference	*sooner than, rather than*	I'd eat worms *rather than* go hungry.
Exception	*except, except that, excepting that*	He'd play, *except that* he's torn a muscle.

Apart from this wide choice of hard-working conjunctions you can also dip into what are sometimes described as 'disguised conjunctions' like *considering, owing to, barring, provided* and *including*. These were formerly participles, which we'll look at after considering prepositions.

Prepositions – and Where to Put Them

About the only thing most of us know about prepositions is that they should never be used to end a sentence with! But this old rule hardly exists nowadays; instead, we are encouraged to use our own judgement on how we should end our sentences. But more of that later. Of greater importance is mastering the subtleties of this irksome but indispensable group of words.

A preposition usually acts as a linking word, like a conjunction, but it also relates one part of a sentence to the other:

We went	*to*	the beach.
She rose	*at*	dawn.

From just these two examples you will have noticed that prepositions have a particular ability to unite two elements in terms of space (*to*) and time (*at*). To clarify this point, here are some common prepositions:

SPACE	*between, above, over, into, near, beside, along*
TIME	*until, since, past, before, after, at, during*
OTHERS	*as, for, in, to, but, by, with, without*
MULTI-WORD	*instead of, other than, in front of, up to*

An interesting thing about prepositions is that when you use one in a sentence, it can only be replaced by another preposition:

She found a mouse *in* the house.
She found a mouse *near* the house.

She found a mouse *under* the house.

. . . and so on. You could substitute any number of prepositions – *beside, inside* – but only with some difficulty could you substitute any other class of words, say, adjectives, adverbs, determiners, conjunctions, nouns or verbs. You might say that a preposition is like a keystone in an arch; take it away, and . . .

There are really only three problems with prepositions. The first is that we tend to create long-winded ones when quite adequate short ones are freely available. In his *The Complete Plain Words*, Sir Ernest Gowers refers to these as verbose prepositions, and gives a list of them together with simpler equivalents. Here are a few worth avoiding:

> as a consequence of (*because of*)
> in the course of (*during*)
> in excess of (*more than*)
> for the purpose of (*to*)
> for the reason that (*because*)
> in the neighbourhood of (*about*)
> in the nature of (*like*)
> in addition to (*besides*)
> with a view to (*to*)
> in case of (*if*)
> prior to (*before*)
> subsequent to (*after*)
> in order to (*to*)
> in the event of (*if*)

The second problem with prepositions is the one already referred to. That is, like the last sentence, allowing a sentence to end with a preposition. A preposition pedant would have written, 'The second problem with prepositions is the one to which we've already referred.'

The reason for the objection can be traced back to the influence of Latin grammar on English; in Latin, ending a sentence with a preposition was frowned upon.

Generations of scholars upheld the rule, although when masters of the language like Shakespeare (In *Hamlet*: 'No traveller returns, puzzles the will,/ And makes us rather bear those ills we have / Then fly to others that we know not of?') started hanging them out to dry, the big rethink on prepositions began. The modern view is that unless they send jarring notes to the ear, let them stay. A sentence like, *That's the restaurant we ate in*, is perfectly acceptable. Quite often, extremely clumsy sentences result from straining to avoid finishing with a preposition; demonstrated neatly by Winston Churchill when, criticising some civil servant's prose, he commented, 'This is the sort of English up with which I will not put.' What we should be concentrating on, instead, is which prepositions should follow certain words. For example:

Do you	aim *for*	or	aim *at?*
Is it	disgust *over*	or	disgust *for?*
Is it	superior *than*	or	superior *to?*
Are you	oblivious *to*	or	oblivious *of?*

According to the great grammarian Eric Partridge, the latter choice is the correct usage. And there are dozens more; far too many to be listed here.

The third problem with prepositions is that the lazier among us tend to drop them altogether:

Defenestration means throwing someone out the window.

should read, *out of the window*. It is, needless to say, a habit to be discouraged.

Participles – Misplaced and Dangling

Participles are forms of verbs:

The horse *is galloping*.

76

The orchestra *is playing*.

When they are used to modify nouns they act like adjectives, as in *galloping inflation*. You can also see that the two examples above – *galloping* and *playing* – are simply verbs with *-ing* added. That's one form of participle, indicating the present, but there is another, indicating past tenses:

PRESENT add *ing*   *travelling, falling, telling, swimming*

PAST add *-ed*, *-en*, etc   *travelled, fallen, told, swum*

Here are some examples of a participle in use:

> *Travelling* back from Italy, she stopped in Paris.
> They *have travelled* constantly, staying at hotels.
> *Having travelled* for miles, he was tired and dirty.

Using participles like this adds interest and elegance to sentences. They are deceptively easy to use and we tend to launch them into our written and spoken sentences without so much as a thought. And that is the trouble, for every now and then we crash, brought down by a dangler.

Danglers and Manglers

- The exhibition features works by fashion photographers executed between 1940 and 1990.
- Being not yet fully grown, his trousers were too long.
- After descending through the clouds, London lay beneath us.
- If Swallowed, Seek Medical Advice. (poison label)

What's wrong with these sentences? What's wrong is that they have all been brought crashing down by danglers – dangling or disconnected participle phrases, participles that have lost their way or lost their noun. The result, in all cases, is ambiguity and even hilarity.

Were the photographers really executed? Of course not. Did London descend from the clouds? Have you ever seen growing trousers? And if you were swallowed, would you be in a condition to seek medical aid?

When this sort of thing happens, some rewriting is called for: (Notice the prepositional ending?)

- The exhibition features fashion photographers' works executed between 1940 and 1990.
- Because he was not yet fully grown, his trousers were too long.
- After we descended through the clouds, London lay beneath us.
- If Contents Are Swallowed, Seek Medical Advice.

The trick is, of course, to make sure that your participle is linked to its correct noun.

Mangled sentences like *Abraham Lincoln wrote the Gettysburg Address while travelling from Washington on the back of an envelope* are perhaps not as common as those habitually beginning with participles like *Speaking candidly . . .*

> Speaking as an old friend, there has been a disturbing tendency in statements emanating from Peking . . .

That was former US President Nixon addressing a Chinese trade delegation, which may have wondered who was doing the speaking. What the President should have said is:

> Speaking as an old friend, I have noted a disturbing . . .

Use participles by all means, but don't let your danglers do you in.

Punctuation: What's the Point?

Move a comma, as they say, and lose a friend; change a comma and save your life. Those dots, strokes and squiggles may be physically insignificant on the page and evanescent in our speech, but without them all would be chaos. Not knowing how to use them correctly can produce even more chaos. If you were to say to a person,

> I hate hypocrites; like you, I find them detestable.

that person would very likely agree. But imagine the reaction should you monkey slightly with the punctuation:

> I hate hypocrites like you; I find them detestable.

Old-time teachers were fond of quoting this chestnut: KING CHARLES I PRAYED HALF AN HOUR AFTER HE WAS BEHEADED. 'Jones at the back, there – where should the dot go?' Another well-known illustration recounts the fate of a warrior in ancient Greece who, on the eve of leaving for a war, visits the Oracle at Delphi. *Thou shalt go thou shalt return never by war shalt thou perish*, he was told. Mentally placing the commas after *go* and *return*, he left with great confidence. Unfortunately, he was killed in the first battle without realising that what the Oracle meant was, *Thou shalt go, thou shalt return never, by war shalt thou perish*. Less morbid are those gags that have a lady librarian placing an ad in a newspaper's personal classifieds: *Lonely librarian seeks a man who reads*. But the typesetter garbled the message and it appeared as: *Lonely librarian seeks a man. Who reads?*

> Sentences begin with a capital letter,
> To help you make your writing better.
> Use full stops to mark the end
> Of all the sentences you've penned.

runs an old rhyme. Seems absurdly basic, doesn't it, but you'd be surprised by the number of people who can interpret whole knots of complex road signs while driving at speed but cannot navigate their way through the grammatical equivalents.

Capitals and Stops

'Punctuation', *The Times* advises its journalists, 'is . . . not a fireworks display to show off your dashes and gaspers. Remember the first rule: the best punctuation is the full stop.'

A full stop (or stop, point or period) is used like a knife to cut off a sentence at the required length. The rule is that simple: where you place your stops is up to you, but generally it is at the point where your thought is complete, and the sentence looks and sounds right. When you are ready to embark on another thought, that's the time to think about a full stop. Master this, and you can then move on to using full stops stylistically, for emphasis:

> You couldn't get near Harry all day because he was constantly on the prowl, hunched in his greasy pants and dirty sweater, looking mean and taciturn and with his mind no doubt churning with murderous thoughts, for he had announced to too many people in too many places and in too loud a voice that he would kill Evans the instant he clapped eyes on him. And he did.

Commas

Commas are a little more complicated, perhaps because, although 'listening' to a sentence can be a good guide to comma placement, the pauses they create don't necessarily follow speech patterns. A comma's role is not to act as 'breath pauses' but to separate different thoughts within sentences.

> The snapshot with its naively honest images revolutionised our way of seeing the world.

Because this sentence would make essentially the same statement if it were written as *The snapshot revolutionised our way of seeing the world*, the incidental clause *with its naively honest images* is a relevant but separate thought, and should be separated from the main thrust of the statement by commas:

> The snapshot, with its naively honest images, revolutionised our way of seeing the world.

You'll notice that two commas are required to do this; a common mistake is to drop the second comma.

Here is a selection of typical comma placements:

BETWEEN ADJECTIVES	*It was a brash, garish, ugly painting. It was brash and garish, ugly and sloppy, and also quite worthless.*
BETWEEN VERBS	*He drank, swore, and abruptly departed.*
BETWEEN ADVERBS	*She crept down slowly, nervously, noiselessly, into the dark room.*
BETWEEN PREPOSITIONS	*The experience was for him, as for her, quite devastating.*
BETWEEN CONJUNCTIONS	*They wondered if, because the dogs were loose, they should venture in.*

In the last example you will see that a comma is almost always necessary between two conjunctions: *so that, while . . .; as, since . . .; because, in order that . . .* etc.

Apart from these semi-rules, placing commas is a judgmental matter. The fashion today (grammatical fashions change, albeit over centuries) is to do without them if the meaning remains clear, even to

saying *firm ripe bananas* in lieu of *firm, ripe bananas*.
Despite this, many people still insist on commas that
are decorative but redundant:

> Looking back, to the early days of the war, I
> sometimes think we were lucky.
> To the farmer it is a welcome sight, to see the
> stubble.
> The jay is a bird, that comes into the woods in
> June.

All three sentences would read better if the commas
after *back*, *sight* and *bird* were deleted.

Another common error is the comma used instead of
a linking conjunction to join two sentences:

WRONG   James took the car, it had an almost
             empty tank.
RIGHT   James took the car but it had an almost
             empty tank.

Semicolons

There is something about semicolons that can raise the
blood pressure. The writer George Orwell was so
against them that he wrote one of his novels, *Coming
Up for Air* (1939), without a single semicolon in it.
Actually, three crept in, only to be removed in later
editions. George Bernard Shaw complained of T. E.
Lawrence that while he threw colons about like a
madman he hardly used semicolons at all. Indeed, the
heat provoked by the anti-semicolonists some years ago
led to fears that it would become an endangered
species, and a Society for the Preservation of the
Semicolon was formed.

A semicolon is a pause somewhere between a strong
comma and a weak full stop. It is used to join phrases
and sentences which are related in theme but
independent and which would be disjointed if

separated by a full stop. This example by Partridge demonstrates it beautifully:

> If you can possibly do so, come; if you cannot come, write; if you haven't the time to write, send a telegram.

While it is true that semicolons are falling into disuse (from misuse?), they are very useful for joining phrases or sentences without recourse to conjunctions (*and*, *but*, *although*, etc.), and indispensable for separating matter which already contains commas:

> The speakers included Monica Watts, author of *The Autumn Triangle*; David Beardman, columnist, restaurateur and broadcaster; and Peter Tate, professional golfer.

Colons

The legendary grammarian Henry Fowler defined the function of the colon as 'delivering the goods that have been invoiced in the preceding words'. This might take the form of a conclusion, a summary, a list, or a quotation:

> There was one very good reason for his failure: *his right hand never knew what his left was doing.*
> She listened patiently for some minutes before her mind was made up: *she would go to Bath immediately.*
> Detective Stevens entered and took it all in: *the body, the still smouldering mattress, the fallen pipe.*
> Gradually, one by one, the words came back to me: '*And we forget because we must and not because we will.*'

In all four examples you will note that what precedes the colon is an otherwise complete sentence.

One final thought on the colon: It is *not* (like this

83

one) followed by a capitalised word in the same
paragraph.

Hyphens and Dashes

Except that they are little horizontal lines and one is
shorter than the other, hyphens and dashes are not
closely related. A hyphen joins two or more words
together, while a dash keeps them apart. What they
do have in common is that they are inclined to be
overused and abused.

The rules governing the use of hyphens are probably
the most complex and contradictory in grammar,
which is why their use is increasingly discouraged.
Generally, their chief use nowadays (which used to be
now-a-days) is to avoid ambiguity, and this is the line
we'll follow here.

When To Hyphen and When Not To Hyphen

Here are instances where hyphens are advisable or
unavoidable:

NOUNS AND PARTICIPLES USED AS ADJECTIVES	*hand-reared, bird-brained, weather-beaten, fact-finding*
ADJECTIVES AND PARTICIPLES USED AS ADJECTIVES	*bleary-eyed, good-looking, middle-aged, sour-tasting*
VERBS AND ADVERBS USED AS NOUNS	*passer-by, summing-up, break-in* (but *breakdown*!)
PHRASES USED AS ADJECTIVES	*door-to-door, good-for-nothing, open-air*
PHRASES USED AS NOUNS	*get-together, ne'er-do-well*
SOME PREFIXES	*ex-detective, pre-natal, vice-chancellor*

IDIOMATICS	*T-shirt, X-ray, U-turn*
NUMBERS	*twenty-one, ninety-nine* (but *three hundred and twenty-three*)
TO REDUCE CONFUSION	*re-cover* (if you mean to cover a settee) to avoid confusing with *recover*; *re-create*
LETTER COLLISION	*co-op, shell-like, de-ice*
PREFIXING PROPER NOUNS	*anti-Semitism, ex-British*
FAMILY COMPOUNDS	*mother-in-law, great-grandfather*

Such a catalogue could go on and on, each entry with its list of exceptions. A dictionary is essential to be absolutely sure, but even then some entries will be overtaken by current usage; not so long ago, words like *taxpayer* and *manpower* were hyphenated. When in doubt, leave it out. In his excellent *English Our English*, Keith Waterhouse warned that fruitless hours could be spent pondering hyphenating problems – like whether it should be *second-hand car salesmen* or *second-hand-car salesmen*. The unhyphenated *used car salesmen* seems to be the solution.

Dash It All

Advice on using dashes is rather more straightforward – don't! Or at least, use them sparingly.

Dashes are useful for inserting parenthetical statements into sentences.

> Mrs Owen immediately dived into the broom cupboard – *she was obsessive about crumbs on the*

85

lino – and emerged with the business end of a vacuum hose.

Such an aside or observation could have been enclosed within brackets, but the dashes (one at the beginning, and don't forget the one at the end) in this case were probably preferred because of their informality.

While dashes can substitute for colons, they should not be used in place of commas, which is considered to be a sign of sloppy writing. Nor should more than one pair of dashes be used in a sentence. But they can be effectively used for certain dramatic effects:

> In Hollywood if an actor's wife looks like a new woman – she probably is.

Brackets and Parentheses

What's the difference? Some confusion here, but parentheses usually refers to (round brackets), and brackets to [square brackets]. The latter are used for special purposes, so need not concern us. The words contained within the parentheses or round brackets are said to be in parenthesis.

Parentheses are discouraged by stylists who would rather have you reconstruct your sentence using commas instead. But they are useful for including explanations, comments and afterthoughts in sentences:

EXPLANATION   The films of Lloyd Hamilton (born 1891) constitute the bedrock of cinematic archaeology.

COMMENT   Cruelty to animals (I noted a scene in which a donkey's tail was tied to a post, and another where a jam tin with a firecracker in it was attached to a dog's tail) was a fairly common sight in children's comic papers in the 1920s.

Travel by car, choose the cross-channel route that offers best value for money, and look out for bargains (like newspaper tokens. Last summer we scored a free hotel in France).

There are two observations to be made on these examples. In the second example the matter in parenthesis is longer than the rest of the sentence, a situation to avoid. The third example illustrates a common error. Whatever is in parenthesis should be punctuated normally, i.e. as though the parentheses don't exist. Thus the full stop after *France* comes after a complete sentence and therefore should be *inside* the bracket: *Last summer we scored a free hotel in France.)*

Question Marks

Questions require question marks, but indirect questions do not:

DIRECT QUESTION   *Can I buy a ticket?*
INDIRECT QUESTION   *I asked if I could buy a ticket.*

Generally question marks come at the end of sentences but sometimes should be inserted within them:

Perhaps – who knows? – there may someday be some belated recognition for his services.

Don't forget that, no matter how long your sentence is, if there is a question in it, a question mark is still required:

Is it not curious that *Lourdes*, which within a year of publication sold over 200,000 copies, had critical acclaim poured over it like champagne and which caused such a furore that it was immediately placed on the Vatican's Index of prohibited books, is not still read today?

Exclamation Mark

These are probably the most overused of all grammatical marks, and are often served up in double, and even triple, doses:

> Sylvia went to Rome – again! That's the second time this year!!! And you'll never know who she met there!!

If that example isn't enough to put you off, nothing will. Use them only to express the strongest of feelings, and don't use them to cap jokes.

Quotation Marks

These inverted commas are used to enclose direct quotations and were once known as 'sixty-sixes' and 'ninety-nines' because of their resemblance to 66 and 99. In these days of typographical cleaning-up, however, you are more likely to see and use the simpler, single, '6' and '9', with the double marks reserved for quotes within quotes:

> 'I've always loved the White Garden,' she said, adding, 'but while Vita always maintained that it gave her the "most exquisitely lasting pleasure on a moonlit evening", it was during the day that it charmed me most.'

One of the more contentious points of punctuation is where the full stop should go – inside or outside the quotation marks. As with parentheses, if the stop (or comma, question mark or exclamation mark) relates to the quoted material, it should go *inside* the quotation marks, otherwise outside. The above is correct, as is:

> She remembered hearing Vita saying that it 'always gave her most pleasure on moonlit evenings'.

She asked, 'Did Vita say that the garden gave her most pleasure on moonlit evenings?'

Note that the quotation in the first example is not a complete sentence; the second example is.

You will have noted from your reading of newspapers and books that quotation marks are used for several other purposes, including idiomatic expressions (*He said the best thing for him would be to 'take a powder'*).

The Errant Apostrophe

Catastrophes with apostrophes are everyday occurrences. A flower stall offers *Lilie's*, *Anemone's* and *Mum's*; *bargain T-shirt's* and *shell suit's* are advertised in the local freesheet. A notice at a school announced: *This School and it's Playground will be Closed over Easter*. The confusion isn't helped, either, when a wordsmith of the stature of Tennyson leaves us with these immortal lines:

> Their's not to make reply,
> Their's not to reason why,
> Their's but to do and die: . . .

Their's? Their is? Their's is? Nobody has ever quite worked out what was on Tennyson's mind, but he certainly left us with a cute conundrum.

Actually, handling apostrophes is really a straightforward matter. But first, you must recognise that there are two kinds of apostrophes: one to indicate a contraction – that is, a word with some letters left out – and one to indicate possession of something:

> My God! Did you hear? London's burning!
> I hope London's fire services can cope!

In the first statement, the apostrophe is used to shorten the word *is* in *London is burning*; in the second, the apostrophe tells us that the fire services belong to London. Here are some simple examples:

POSSESSIVE APOSTROPHES	CONTRACTION APOSTROPHES
Michael's mountain bike	*She'll be here soon* (she will)
the girl's tunic	*It is six o'clock* (of the clock)
the girls' gym	*I won't do it* (will not)
St James's Square	*It's not fair* (it is)

So far, so good, but let's look a little closer at each kind of apostrophe in turn.

Possessive Apostrophes

To show that a noun possesses, has or belongs to something, an -*s* is usually added. In the case of singular nouns:

> *a dog's collar; a man's suit; that woman's dress; Beryl's garden; the country's problems; a day's work*

The same rule applies to plural nouns that don't end with an -*s*:

> *women's preferences; children's books; mice's tails*

Where common nouns, whether singular or plural, end with -*s*, we simply add an apostrophe after the -*s*. But with proper nouns we have the choice of adding -*'s* or an apostrophe without the extra -*s*, according to tradition or how it sounds. You won't see *girls's* as the plural form of *girl's*, but you will see *Charles's* and *Charles'*. Some more examples:

> *The Jones's house, Jesus' teachings, measles' after-effects, Glynis's career, teachers' meetings, Wales' ruggedness*

Sometimes the choice is arbitrary; you will probably see *Jesus's teachings* as often as the alternative.

90

Despite Tennyson, pronouns do not normally require apostrophes (an exception is one's):

its shadow, the car is theirs, the victory is ours

If you own a name you are entitled to do what you want with it, and many institutions and businesses are exercising this option and dropping apostrophes: *Missing Persons Bureau, Lloyds Bank, Gas Consumers Council, Womens Institute, Pears Soap*. And don't be caught out with James Joyce's *Finnegans Wake*, Thornton Wilder's *The Ides of March* and E. M. Forster's *Howards End*; they are titles, and none has apostrophes.

Contraction Apostrophes

The use of apostrophes for informal contractions is relatively straightforward:

hasn't	= has not	*I'm*	= I am
can't	= cannot	*it's*	= it is
there's	= there is	*let's*	= let us
mustn't	= must not	*I've*	= I have

Apostrophes are also used to concertina combinations like *shake'n'bake, sweet'n'low*; to drop the final letters of words like *finger lickin'* and *nuthin' doin'*; and to pluralise numbers and abbreviations: *1890's, MP's, CV's*, etc., although these are increasingly showing up without apostrophes: *1890s, MPs, CVs*.

But from all this, all you really need to remember is:

- *it's* is short for *it is*, and *its* indicates possession
- *who's* is short for *who is*; *whose* indicates possession

Twenty Sore Points

English grammar isn't like concrete which, once it hardens, never shifts. On the contrary, the language and its usage are always on the move. Arguments about its use erupt every day: in newspaper and publishing offices, in the law courts, in schools, at teachers' conferences, on trains, in pubs. You begin to wonder if the language and the rules that govern it were invented yesterday instead of several centuries ago.

The truth is that none of us always speaks and writes perfect, copper-bottomed English. Each of us has blind spots, rules we can never remember, concepts we never seem to understand, words of different meaning that sound the same or are spelt the same and which invariably confuse us.

Here are twenty 'sore points' of usage. There could be fifty, or fifteen hundred: the list could go on. But these have been selected for discussion because they seem to crop up so regularly.

-ISE OR -IZE   Although the *-ize* ending (derived from the Greek) is used in the US, in Britain there is a distinct preference for *-ise*. In this book, for example, *-ise* and *-isation* are used throughout. Many words, though, have always been spelt *-ise*: *advise*, *enterprise*, *despise*, *surprise*, etc. A few can look odd with the *-ise* ending (*capsise*) so are best left with *-ize*.

HOPEFULLY   The furore over the adverb *hopefully*, as used in sentences like

> Hopefully, the weather will improve this afternoon.

is based on a misunderstanding. In fact, the word, meaning *it is hoped*, has a perfectly legitimate parentage, albeit German. It began life as *hoffentlich*, meaning *I hope so*, and travelled with German immigrants to the US last century. During its stay there it was translated as *hopefully*, and now, as we all know, it is one of America's major exports to Britain, selling alongside the original adverb *hopefully*, meaning *full of hope*.

LAY AND LIE   The confusion between these verbs arises from the tenses:

lay	laid	laid
lie	lay	lain

The confusion is removed if you can remember that *to lay* is to put or set down something, while *to lie* is to recline. You *lay down the law, an egg is laid; you lie on the floor, she lay there and cried, she had lain there all night.*

DOUBLE NEGATIVES   Listen to this imaginary conversation:

> 'I didn't do nuffink, officer!'
> 'Well, if you didn't do nothing, you must have done something, right?'
> 'I didn't never do nuffink, honest!'
> 'That's all right, then. On your way!'

Here we have a double negative in the first line, which logically reverses the meaning, so the policeman is correct. But he is also correct – logically – in the last line, for he recognises that his would-be culprit has used three negatives, thus turning the double negative back to positive.

Why we should pick on this so-called uneducated usage is a mystery when educated French accepts and even requires it (*Je ne regrette rien: I don't regret nothing*) and educated English perpetrates double negatives (under the polite term of litotes) like *I'm not unhappy with the result*. But, in general, avoid.

WHILE AND WHILST   The latter is legitimate and means the same as *while*, but why use the longer word?

THAT, WHICH AND WHO   *That* can refer to persons, animals and things; *which* to animals and things; *who* and *whom* to persons only. There was a rule to use *that* to define the meaning or intention of the preceding word or phrase: *The car that Bruce drove down here has packed up*. *That* defines or identifies the car for us: the one he drove down here. The rule advised using *which* when the identifying information is already supplied in the sentence: *The old supercharged Bentley which Bruce drove down here has packed up*.

With persons, *that* is used to refer to any person, and *who* to a particular person: *The bloke that bought Bruce's Bentley lives in Birmingham. My cousin, who bought Bruce's Bentley, has money to burn.*

SPELLED AND SPELT   There are a number of verbs in this category:

> spell, dwell, smell, spill, spoil, kneel,
> lean, learn, leap, burn, dream

Although there is a strong and growing preference for *-t* endings, your options are still open. The *-ed* endings are almost universal in the US.

METAPHORICAL MIXTURES   *The manager of the football club admitted that he had several irons in the fire but he was keeping them close to his chest*. British Rail said that it has *a number of crossings in the pipeline, but these will now be put on ice*. A company chairman said that *they had stood on the edge of a precipice for too long and it*

94

was now time for a major step forward. A Radio 3 announcer: *The artist has given full reign to his marvellous ear for colour*.

These are mixed metaphors, and eternal vigilance is the price you must pay to avoid them. Always remember the famous utterance of British Leyland's Sir Alfred Sherman: *So long as there is a crock of gold at the end of the garden the spur to sink or swim is blunted*. Or read *Jeremiah, iv, 4 (Authorised Version)*.

LESS AND FEWER   Use *fewer* for numbers and plural nouns; *less* for size and non-count nouns: *At the festival, fewer pints were drunk and less beer was consumed*.

ONLY   This is a subversive word which, depending upon where it is placed in a sentence, can change its entire meaning. When we use *only* conversationally we use stresses to make our meaning clear; unfortunately we cannot do this when we use it in writing. For example:

A   I can only lend you £10.
B   I can lend you only £10.

Each of these two sentences means something different. **A** actually means I can't give you £10 but I can lend you that amount; while **B** means I can lend you £10 but that's the limit – I can't lend you any more.

Using *only* unambiguously requires care. The same goes for words like *merely, even, mainly, also* and *just*:

I just saw the film, not the play.
I saw just the film, not the play.

CAN AND MAY   *Can* relates to possibility, while *may* relates to permission. This was once taught with a scrap of dialogue which went something like this:

PUPIL:	Please, Teacher, can I go to the toilet?
TEACHER:	Yes, John, you can, because you know where it is and you have two legs and so you are perfectly able to go to the toilet. The question is, will I allow you to go?
PUPIL:	Oh, please, Teacher, may I go to the toilet?

The same shadings, of course, apply to *could* and *might*, but such distinctions have now become hopelessly blurred in everyday usage.

QUITE   This is a word to use carefully as it has two meanings:

> I'm quite certain that Paloma will win the Derby.
> He's great at swimming and quite good with the bat.

You can see why *quite* can play tricks. In the first example it qualifies and strengthens *certain* so that it means something like, *I'm absolutely certain* . . . But in the second example it weakens the word it qualifies, the resulting meaning being, *Well, he's good with the bat, but not that good* . . .

SPLIT INFINITIVES   Gallons of metaphorical blood have been spilt over this legendary grammatical no-no, rather pointlessly as it turns out. The situation today is that the careful user has nothing against the occasional split infinitive, but would prefer to do the splitting consciously rather than unconsciously.

Curiously, it is impossible to split an infinitive, which is the grammatical term for a basic verb like *grow* (from which spring *growing*, *grew* and *grown*). The so-called split infinitive results from an adverb or adverbial phrase being placed between to and the infinitive: *He wanted his son to confidently grow into the job he'd created for him.* A purist would either write *He wanted his son confidently to grow into the job he'd created for him,* or rephrase the sentence.

The trouble with many unsplit infinitives is that they can be grossly inelegant and very much out of whack with everyday speech. They can also sometimes result in ambiguity: *The Government is attempting dramatically to increase the number of people in higher education.* What is meant, presumably, is that the proposed increase will be dramatic, but here it looks as though it is the attempt itself that is full of drama. A split infinitive – *to dramatically increase* – in this case conveys the required meaning with precision.

If Elizabeth Taylor's intention is *to never drink again* or *never to drink again,* few people are going to split hairs over it. Glasnost has been declared on the split infinitive, but it is still way short of total freedom.

THAT   In the interests of economy it is acceptable to drop *that* from sentences providing the meaning remains clear:

> She sincerely believed that she was in love with him.
> She sincerely believed she was in love with him.

WHO AND WHOM   Many grammar books devote several pages to this perplexing pair, but for practical purposes a simple rule exists to keep you out of trouble. If you relate *he* to *who,* and *him* to *whom,* you are halfway there (it doesn't quite work with *she/who* and *her/whom*). When in doubt, simply substitute *he* or *him:*

> I couldn't find out who/whom had the tickets.

In this case, you wouldn't say *him might have the tickets,* but *he* (or, indeed, *she*) *might have the tickets.* Therefore *who* would be correct. Or:

Who/whom are you slagging off to your friends?

Here, we might ask, am I slagging *he* off? No, it must be, am I slagging *him* off?, so *whom* would be correct. It would also be pompous and pedantic to announce '*Whom are you slagging off to your friends?*', which is why, increasingly, people are confining themselves to safer *who* territory.

DIFFERENT TO, FROM, OR THAN The first two are acceptable, with a general preference for *from. Different than* is common usage in the US.

IF AND WHETHER *If* is a versatile word but its use to replace *whether* can lead to ambiguity:

Did you notice if he had dandruff?

places the emphasis on *noticing*; if the observer wasn't alert he or she wouldn't notice whether he even had hair. The question that should have been asked to get the required answer is:

Did you notice whether or not he had dandruff?

WHATEVER This word has been hijacked from its correct meaning, which is *no matter what*: *Whatever the difficulties, we will succeed.* Nowadays we are more likely to hear: *He's a real DIY nut, you know, laying tiles, plastering, painting, fixing windows, whatever* . . . It looks and sounds sloppy, and it is.

EACH AND EVERY Most of us know that *each* requires a singular verb because it concerns a single person. But so does *every*; when you talk about every person in the room you are really referring to each and every single one:

Each man, woman and child in there has some complaint.
Every man, woman and child in there has some complaint.

However, when *each* is preceded by a plural subject it needs a plural verb:

Their uniforms were each given a thorough going-over by the drill sergeant.

YOU AND I AND YOU AND ME   A rule that usually works for most people is to think of *you* and *I* as *we*, and *you* and *me* as *us*.

We are a terrific couple – *You and I* are a terrific couple.
They're calling *us* liars – They're calling *you and me* liars.

To test such statements:

You and me are going to be late – *Us* is going to be late.
You and I are going to be late – *We* are going to be late.

The second statement passes the test, and is correct.

Grammatical Gamesmanship

Here's a little reward for doing all that hard work: some amusing grammatical games and puzzles.
Answers on page 103.

A Pile of Pairs

Parts of the human body excepted, how many items can you list that are usually referred to as a pair, such as trousers, shoes and gloves? Try for twenty.

That's That!

This is considered to be the ultimate punctuation test. Try punctuating *That that is is that that is not is not but that that is not is not that that is nor is that that is that that is not.*

Be Your Own Subeditor

This report appeared in the Boston *Herald American*:

> By then, Mrs Costello will have shed 80 of the 240 pounds she weighed in with when she entered the Peter Bent Brigham hospital obesity program. A third of her left behind!

How would you rewrite this? Discuss with friends.

Prepositional Pile-up

From time to time readers of newspapers are challenged to invent a sentence ending in as many prepositions as possible. A string of five comes with this chestnut: 'The little girl complained to her mother about her bedtime storybook: "What did you bring that book that I didn't want to be read *to out of up for?*" ' This, in turn, was stretched to nine prepositions in Godfrey Smith's column in *The Sunday Times*: 'What did you want to bring that book, that I didn't want to be read *to from out of, about Down Under, up for?*'

This effort is, however, still well short of the world record, offered by an American woman living in Illinois: 'What did you turn your socks from *inside in to inside out instead of from outside out to inside in for?*' That's fourteen. Can you do better?

Punctuation Playtime

What are some well-known words that contain:
1. A hyphen and an apostrophe?
2. Two hyphens and an apostrophe?
3. Three hyphens and an apostrophe?
4. No hyphens but two apostrophes?

Selling Books to Old Children

Here's a book dealer's ad. Is he selling children's books that are old or books that appeal to older children? How would you rewrite it to make this clear?

OLD CHILDREN'S BOOKS/ANNUALS

Closing down sale, thousands to clear. List requirements with SAE please to: John, 88 Watford Road, Birmingham B30 1PD

Poetic Punctuation

Can you repunctuate this rhyme so that it makes sense?

> Every lady in the land
>   Has twenty nails upon each hand,
> Five and twenty on hands and feet.
>   This is true, and no great feat.

Answers to Grammatical Games

A PILE OF PAIRS Boots, cufflinks, leotards, mittens, pants, plimsolls, shorts, slacks, slippers, socks, stockings, suspenders, underpants, binoculars, eyeglasses, spectacles, bookends, chopsticks, earrings, pliers, skis, scissors, tweezers, tongs. Plus all the others you've thought of.

THAT'S THAT Follow this closely: *That that is, is; that that is not, is not; but that that is not is not that that is; nor is that that is that that is not.* No? Try again.

PUNCTUATION PLAYTIME Here are some of the words asked for, and there are doubtless others:

1. *bull's-eye cat's-eye* (wildflower) *cat's-tail* (species of reed)
2. *jack-o'-lantern*
3. *will-o'-the-wisp cat-o'-nine-tails*
4. *fo'c'sle* (forecastle of a ship)

POETIC PUNCTUATION With this punctuation, the poem makes sense:

Every lady in the land
    Has twenty nails. Upon each hand
Five, and twenty on hands and feet.
    This is true, and no great feat.

Read on

If this chapter

- has broken the grammatical ice for you;
- has made you aware of what you and others are doing when speaking, writing and reading;
- has helped you to correct and avoid grammatical mistakes;

and, especially,

- has interested and intrigued you to the extent that you wish to know more about using the English language,

then *Wordpower Guide* can ask for no more. But this book is only what its covers say it is: a quick trip through the timeless territory of language. It's a territory that's well worth exploring, and any of the books listed here will prove to be valuable and user-friendly guides. Most are available in cheaper paperback format.

Bryson, Bill. *Mother Tongue – The English Language*. London: Penguin Books, 1990
Cobuild (COLLINS Birmingham University International Language Database). *English Grammar*. London and Glasgow: Collins Publishers, 1990
Cobuild. *Student's Grammar*. London: Harper Collins, 1991
Crystal, David. *Rediscover Grammar*. London: Longmans, 1992
Crystal, David. *Who Cares About English Usage?* London: Penguin Books, 1984
Crystal, David (ed). *Eric Partridge in His Own Words*. London: André Deutsch, 1980
Fowler, H. W. *A Dictionary of Modern English Usage*.

(Revised by Sir Ernest Gowers). Oxford: Oxford University Press, 1965–1991

Gowers, Sir Ernest. *The Complete Plain Words.* London: Guild Publishing, 1986

Greenbaum, Sidney. *An Introduction to English Grammar.* London: Longman, 1991

Greenbaum, S. and Whitcut, Janet. *Guide to English Usage.* London: Longman, 1988

Howard, Philip. *The State of the Language.* London: Penguin Books, 1984

Leech, Geoffrey. *An A-Z of English Grammar & Usage.* London: Nelson, 1989

Partridge, Eric. *Usage and Abusage.* London: Penguin Books, 1990

Partridge, Eric. *You Have a Point There.* London: Routledge, 1983

Roberts, Philip Davies. *Plain English: A User's Guide.* London: Penguin Books, 1987

Thomson, A. J. and Martinet, A. V. *A Practical English Grammar.* Oxford: Oxford University Press, 1986

Times, The. English Style and Usage Guide. London: Times Books, 1992

Todd, Loreto, and Hancock, Ian. *International English Usage.* London: Routledge, 1990

Waldhorn, Arthur, and Zeiger, Arthur. *English Made Simple.* London: Made Simple Books (Butterworth-Heinemann), 1991

Waterhouse, Keith. *English Our English (and how to sing it).* London: Viking, 1991

Vocabulary

Introduction

THE GREATER THE CHOICE,
THE CLEARER THE VOICE

Here is art critic William Feaver describing an exhibition of paintings by Allen Jones:

> Allen Jones gives recitals of body-language (the jut of the silken bottom, the parting of the lips) and colour code (1,000-watt yellows, ice-maiden blue), tracing erotic lines that slither down the thigh and die away in drips and stains.

That verbal communication must surely be as vivid and exhilarating as the paintings it describes. In it, Feaver has obviously had at his elbow a formidable palette of words, none of them, incidentally, quaint or outlandish, but words ready to jump at his command to create a clear word-picture, yet also convey stimulating overtones of high excitement.

That is what communication, spoken or written, is about – clarity and colour: clarity to get your thoughts across unambiguously, and colour to attract attention and to 'sell' your message.

To help you achieve this you have all the advantages of the English language, which many regard as England's supreme gift to the world. Some 360 million people use its great lexicon of over 450,000 words, and a further 1.1 billion regard it as a second, official or dialect language. Only Chinese is used by more people, but as it is rumoured that more Chinese are currently learning English than the population of the United States, even that language may soon be eclipsed in global popularity.

As a very rough rule of thumb, the more words you

have available in your word bank, the more effectively you will be able to communicate. Shakespeare, who was no slouch when it came to communicating, possessed a vocabulary variously estimated at between precisely 17,677 words and approximately 30,000 words. At the other end of the scale, research on telephone calls in the US has revealed that 96% of all conversations were conducted with a vocabulary of only 737 words. In the middle, it is thought that an intelligent and reasonably well-read person in Britain has a word bank of between 7,000–15,000 words.

A 15,000-word vocabulary has many advantages over one of 7,000 words. If the essence of communicating is to convey what we mean with absolute clarity, then it is better to use words that express our thoughts precisely than words which merely approximate what we mean. In other words, the greater the choice, the clearer the voice. Inevitably, this calls for a vocabulary that recognises the differences between, for example, **flaunt** and **flout**, **parameter** and **perimeter**, **rebut** and **refute**, **saccharin** and **saccharine**, **turbid** and **turgid**, and so on.

Clarity, however, can go for naught if our efforts to communicate are flat and boring; nobody will want to listen to us. That's why we need even more words to colour our communicating, to make it flow, to sing, to captivate, to seduce, to sting. And there will also be times when the *mot juste* (*qv*) will not be found in our own language; so any serviceable vocabulary will include a selection of foreign words and phrases.

Word Bank is neither a dictionary nor a list of unusual and bizarre words, but a selection of words most people find useful, even essential, in their speech and writing. Many of them you will undoubtedly know; some of them you may think you know; while the balance will be new to you. Each entry is treated as a little puzzle or quiz, not to test your word power or IQ, but to help you commit the word, its spelling and meaning, to your memory.

Each time you do this, you are depositing a fresh word in your own word bank to be withdrawn when you need it. If you learn to use three new words a day, your vocabulary will have grown by 1,000 words at the end of a year. And the English language will be a little less like Flaubert's cracked kettle, 'upon which we beat out tunes for bears to dance to, while all the time we yearn to move the stars to pity'.

Word Bank

One of the best ways to expand your vocabulary is to
pause when you see a word, the meaning of which you
don't know or aren't too sure about, and look it up in
a dictionary. Often, however, you spot the word that
puzzles you on the train or tube or away from home,
and by the time you get anywhere near a dictionary
you've forgotten all about it. That's why it's a good
idea to build up your knowledge of words in advance.

Word Bank will help you do this with a selective list
of words of the kind that insinuate themselves into our
everyday conversation and reading. Only minimum
effort is required to choose or guess the correct
meanings of the words and to fix them in your mind;
but it's worth making the extra effort to look them up
in a good dictionary for the complete and detailed
definition or, in many cases, definitions.

A

Choose the correct meaning.

(*Answers page 190*)

abstruse	argumentative; hard to understand; scientific
accretion	increase by external growth; the components of concrete; the residue left by high tides
Achilles' heel	athlete's complaint; fashionable shoes by a Greek designer; vulnerable spot
acolyte	an attendant; oil lamp; rare mineral
acrimony	unclaimed treasure; bitterness; wild herb
actuary	hospital helper; insurance expert; part of a library where religious books are kept
acumen	pepper-like substance; penetrating insight; the ability to tolerate giddy heights
affidavit	a written statement made on oath; a solicitor's instruction; a judge's direction to a jury
aficionado	the sword thrust that kills in a bullfight; a keen fan or follower; a large wine barrel
agnostic	a religious hermit; a condition of the throat; a person who denies knowledge of God

agronomy	study of grasses; study of river pollution; study of soil
akimbo	hands on hips with elbows pointing away; legs wide apart; sitting with legs crossed
alfresco	famous New York salad; fizzy Italian wine; in the open air
alter ego	one's other self; slow opera movement; the membrane that encloses the yolk in an egg
amalgam	a compound of different metals; ash left from burnt ivory; fool's gold
amanuensis	a nurse specialising in tuberculosis care; a secretary; sewing machine mechanism
ambidextrous	ability to juggle with hands and feet; ability to jump long distances; ability to use both hands with equal facility
ambivalent	not complete; indecisive; unable to walk
amortise	to reduce or pay off a debt; to fix two pieces of wood together without nails or screws; to die leaving two or more wills
anachronism	type of lobster; collecting old clocks; a person or event misplaced in time
analogous	capable of being analysed; process for water-proofing shoes; similar in some respects
anathema	something hated; a love–hate relationship; a diagnostic technique for lung disease
angst	unfounded anger; mental instability; anxiety
annul	cancel; harden metal; every other year
animus	hostility; hairy; a spooky mist or fog
anosmia	inability to recognise the colour blue; inability to perspire; inability to smell
antipathy	hatred; aversion; fear

114

antonym	a word that makes sense when spelt backwards; a word of opposite meaning; a three-letter word
aperient	slow-working medicine; laxative; eye lotion
aphorism	a grammatical mistake; an embarrassing remark; a short, pithy saying
apiarian	relating to monkeys; animal rights; relating to bees
aplomb	poise and assurance; reckless abandonment; explosive anger
apocalyptic	prophesying ultimate destruction for all; semi-paralysed; denying religious freedom
apogee	edge of a plateau; tip of an iceberg; climax
apposite	directly behind; inappropriate; appropriate
apostasy	embracing several religions at once; renouncing one's religion or principles; returning to the Roman Catholic religion
appurtenance	an accessory; a boil on the neck; self-mockery
aquiline	green; smooth-surfaced; eagle-like
arachnid	spiny anteater; land crab; spider family
arbitrage	buying and selling securities on different markets to profit from differing rates of exchange; profiting from insider dealing; buying distressed futures of metals and commodities
arcane	rare and expensive; mysterious and secret; sweet and syrupy
argot	semi-precious stone; type of tobacco leaf; slang

How to use a dictionary

First, make sure you have a practical and up-to-date dictionary that you feel comfortable with. The 20-volume *Oxford English Dictionary 2* at £1,500 may be the ultimate in word reference books, but only a specialist would need it; at the other end of the scale there are mini and pocket-size dictionaries that can be worse than useless. Occupying the middle ground is a vast range of excellent dictionaries which in paperback can cost less than £5. Every bookstore and many large newsagents stock a selection (Oxford, Collins, Cassell's, Longmans, to name a few) so there is no excuse not to own this essential tool to help you expand your vocabulary.

A dictionary *defines* words; it does not usually explain how to use them. It describes, not prescribes. For guidance on how to use words there are books on English usage; for helping you find the word you want there are synonym dictionaries and the thesaurus.

An entry in a good dictionary offers quite a lot of compressed information. Let us analyse a typical entry (for the word *read*) in a typical dictionary (*Collins Paperback English Dictionary*, £4.99).

1. Main or Entry word, usually in bold type
2. Pronunciation, according to the International Phonetic Alphabet
3. Grammatical designation, in this case a verb
4. Participle forms of the main word
5. The first of fourteen different or differing meanings and usages of the word, often with examples

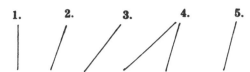

1. **2.** **3.** **4.** **5.**

read (riːd) *vb.* **reading, read** (rɛd). **1.** to understand (something written or printed) by looking at and interpreting the written or printed characters. **2.** (often foll. by *out*) to speak aloud (something written or printed). **3.** to interpret the significance or meaning of: *to read a map.* **4.** to interpret (signs, characters, etc.) other than by visual means: *to read Braille.* **5.** to have sufficient knowledge of (a language) to understand the written word. **6.** to make out the true nature or mood of: *she could read his thoughts.* **7.** to interpret in a specified way: *it can be read as satire.* **8.** to have a certain wording: *the sentence reads as follows.* **9.** to undertake a course of study in (a subject): *to read history.* **10.** to gain knowledge by reading: *he read about the war; a well-read young woman.* **11.** to register or show: *the meter reads 100.* **12.** to put into a specified condition by reading: *I read my son to sleep.* **13.** to hear and understand, esp. when using a two-way radio: *we are reading you loud and clear.* **14.** *Computers.* to obtain (data) from a storage device, such as magnetic tape. ~*n.* **15.** matter suitable for reading: *this book is a very good read.* **16.** a spell of reading. ~See also **read into, read out,** etc.

7.   **6.**

6. The same word but used, in this case, as a noun (15) and a participle form as a noun (16)
7. Cross reference to other forms and derivatives under separate entries

Some dictionaries also give the etymology of the word, explaining its derivation and evolution.

Armageddon	a class of battleship; a war that will end the world; the heavenly home for army generals
armoire	a lace shawl; a portable enamel bath; a large cupboard or wardrobe
arraign	to accuse before a court; to forcibly arrest; to hold under arrest pending bail
arriviste	a pushy self-seeker; a socialite thief; an immigrant refused entry to a country
asinine	haughty; darkly handsome; stupid
assuage	to irritate; to relieve; to roughen
atrophy	wasting away; malarial fever; blood clotting
attenuate	to lengthen; to make flat; to make thin
attrition	apologising to a court of law; the process of wearing away; automobile collision insurance
au fait	unacceptable; having expert knowledge; on the wrong side of the law
avuncular	like a kindly uncle; covered with pustules; good humoured only when under the influence of alcohol

B

Using the meanings given,
fill in the gaps.

(*Answers Page 190*)

bad _ _ age	Teasing banter and repartee
b _ _ chanalian	Riotous and drunken revelry
Bakel _ _ _	An early heat-resistant synthetic resin
ba _ _ ful	Full of evil, deadly intent
balus _ _ ade	A banister supported by balusters
b _ _ dolatry	Worship of Shakespeare
bar mit _ _ _ h	Jewish ceremony admitting a boy as an adult member of the faith
baro _ _ e	Extravagant style of decoration or architecture
b _ _ hos	Descent from the sublime to the ridiculous or commonplace
bay _ u	Marshy, slow-running stream in America
b _ _ titude	Heavenly bliss
behemo _ _	A huge person, animal or object
bel c _ _ to	Virtuoso singing
be _ _ icose	Aggressive and warlike
be _ _ wether	One who takes the lead or initiative
bem _ _ ed	Bewildered and confused
ben _ _ n	Kindly, gentle and genial
besmi _ _ h	To soil, or sully the good name of someone

bête n _ _ re	Someone or something regarded with fear and loathing
b _ _ elot	A small but often valuable article
bie _ _ ial	Occurring every two years
b _ _ urcate	To divide into two, or forked
bij _ _	A small, valuable jewel or trinket
bi _ _ teral	Relating to two sides or parties
bin _ _ _	System of numbers using 2 as its base
b _ _ psy	Removal of tissue from a body for examination
b _ _ sé	Indifferent, apathetic and unresponsive through over-indulgence
bl _ _ ch	To flinch, to shrink back from something
bli _ _ ely	Cheerfully carefree
b _ _ a fi _ e	Genuinely, in good faith
b _ _ homie	Good-natured friendliness
bon viv _ _ _	One who loves food and drink
b _ _ eal	Of the north; northern countries and peoples
bo _ _ y	Overgrown with trees and shrubs
bour _ _ oisie	The middle classes
b _ _ _ lerise	To cut words and passages from a book on prudish grounds
bra _ _ adocio	Bragging, boasting
br _ _ se	To cook slowly in liquid in a closed pan
Brob _ _ _ nagian	Of gigantic proportions, from the country of giants in *Gulliver's Travels*
brou _ a _ a	A fuss, an uproar
brus _ _ e	Blunt in manner; rough and abrupt
b _ _ olic	Pastoral; relating to the countryside

b _ _ imia	Abnormal craving for food with bouts of overeating followed by self-induced vomiting
bump _ _ ous	Excessively and unpleasantly self-assertive
b _ _ geoning	Sprouting; starting to grow
bur _ _ p	Very coarse canvas or sacking
b _ _ _ ish	To polish and make smooth and shiny
bus _ _ _	A waiter's assistant
B _ _ onic	Romantically melancholic

Lovely and unlovely words

You can't help liking and disliking certain words. The romantic novelist Barbara Cartland professes to love the words **shimmering, moonlight** (naturally!), **rapture, pure, innocent, divine** and **God**. A poll conducted by the *US Literary Digest* came up with **illusion, mirage** and **azure** as the top three, followed by **celestial, quintessence, ravish, whisper, twilight, meander, lovely, evanescent, taffeta** and **mellifluous**. In Britain, the learned journal *Logophile* published the words most loved by celebrities; these included **pellucid, aquiline, lily, silken, alembic** (Bernard Levin); **spume, vanilla, dingle, hellebore, dusk, murmur, heirloom, treacle, chocolate, flummery** (Posy Simmonds); **mandragora, valerian, polysyllable, adamantine** and **cellar-door** (Jilly Cooper). And the word most disliked by readers of *The Times*? **Chomp** – closely followed by **fax**.

C

Which of the two meanings
is correct?

(*Answers page 191*)

cabal	A group of plotters, or the brick lip on the top of a chimney stack
cabriole	A curved chair leg, or a horse-drawn carriage
cache	An old Indo-Chinese coin, or a hiding place
cajole	To persuade with flattery, or Indian cornmeal
calcareous	Containing calcium, or dental decay
callipygian	Ability to see in the dark, or having well-formed buttocks
callisthenics	Exercises for strength and beauty, or exercises to develop the lumbar muscles
calumny	A maliciously false statement, or a rude verse
camaraderie	A Parisian nightclub, or loyalty among comrades
campanology	The art of survival in the wilds, or the study of bell-ringing
canard	A false rumour, or a joke
candour	Openness and integrity, or hypocritical praise
cantankerous	Disagreeable and crotchety, or excessively cautious and thrifty

captious	Fearful of being imprisoned, or hard to please
carcanet	An inlaid jewel box, or a jewelled collar
carpal	Relating to the wrist, or relating to exotic fish
carte blanche	Advice to act quickly, or permission to act freely and unrestrained
cartel	An agreement between business interests to regulate output and prices, or an agreement between nations to exclude others
castellated	A special cigar wrapping, or castle-like
castigate	To chastise, or to beat severely
catalysis	Speeding up a chemical reaction with a substance that remains unchanged, or analysing the components of exhaust emissions
catamite	A boy prostitute, or the chief eunuch in a Turkish harem
catharsis	Curing medical problems by hypnosis, or purging emotional problems through dramatic re-enactment
catheter	A tube for draining fluids from the body, or a secret tunnel under a church
causerie	A chatty conversation or essay, or a group of people devoted to charity work
caveat emptor	Let the buyer have a choice, or let the buyer beware
cavil	To find fault, or to rush into things
celerity	Swiftness, or sourness
chancel	A circular window in a church, or the area around the altar reserved for the clergy
charlatan	An imposter, or a Scottish fortune-teller
chauvinism	Blind patriotism, or love of French art

chiaroscuro	Cherry brandy, or the visual effects of light and shade
chicanery	Coffee roasting, or trickery
chiffonier	A sideboard, usually with shelves and mirror above, or an elegant dressing-table, usually with a single drawer and oval mirror
chimera	An imagined monster or horror, or the patterns made by fire smoke
choleric	Tendency for chest complaints, or bad-tempered
chutzpah	A Hebrew lament, or cheerful audacity
cinéaste	A serious movie enthusiast, or a bitter taste
circa	Approximate, or 'within that century'
circumlocution	Travelling around the globe without crossing the equator, or a round-about way of talking
circumscribed	Removal of a toe, or to be restricted
clandestine	Love of bright lights and entertainment, or conducted in secrecy
clement	Mild and gentle, or wild and strong
cognoscenti	Connoisseurs, or principal male ballet dancers
colloquy	A dream that is remembered, or a dialogue
collude	To re-colonise a country, or to conspire, usually for dishonest purposes
comity	Friendliness, or extreme deviousness
complaisant	Freckled, or eager to please
concomitant	Partly incontinent, or in conjunction with
concupiscence	Sexual lust, or patronising
conflation	Blending two things together, or indigestion
consanguinity	Unlawful acts between humans and animals, or related by birth

contemn	To love nature, or to despise someone
contretemps	An awkward and embarrassing situation, or a contrary child
corpus delicti	The facts about a crime, or the preservation of a dead body for evidence

---

What is the longest word?

When Shakespeare used the word **honorificabilitudinitatibus** in *Love's Labour's Lost*, it held the record for the longest word in the English language for quite some time. It was overtaken in the 18th century by **floccinaucinihilipilification** (meaning the habitual estimation of the worthlessness of something) until challenged by the Mary Poppins' 34-letter **supercalifragilisticexpialidocious** in 1964, which even small children could get their tongues around. But both went down for the count in 1982 when the *Oxford English Dictionary* listed a lung disease calling for a 45-letter word: **pneumonoultramicroscopicsilicovolcanoconiosis**. Now it is reported that even **pn . . . osis** has been put in the shade by an 8,000-letter behemoth of a word that describes a protein derivative. Very impressive, but can it beat the word **smiles**? That's a word that has a mile between its first and last letters.

---

coruscate	To punish severely, or to glitter
costive	Cheating by altering prices, or constipated
coterie	An exclusive group of people sharing common interests, or a dance performed by four people
crapulous	Untidy, or given to overindulgent drinking and eating

crescendo	The loudest passage in a musical performance, or a gradual increase in sound and force
cruciform	Shaped like a cross, or crystalline
crustaceans	Oysters and mussels, or crabs and lobsters
cultivar	A plant originated by cultivation, or a Russian tea-drinking receptacle
cupidity	Dimpled, or inordinate desire to possess
cynosure	Centre of attaction, or justified cynicism
cytology	Study of the urinary tract, or the study of living cells

D

Choose the correct meaning.

(*Answers page 191*)

dado	early 20th-century surrealist movement; lower part of the wall of a room when differently decorated from upper part; a drink made from almonds
dalliance	flirting; sparkling; oratory
dearth	a plague; scarcity; frightening appearance
débâcle	an ornamented silver buckle; a large garden party; a complete rout and collapse
debilitate	to nourish; to wound; to weaken
déclassé	to come down socially; to act superior to one's status; to offer wine in the wrong glass
declivity	an abrupt drop; a gradual slope downwards; a sudden drop in barometric pressure
de facto	existing, though not legally; in defiance of the law; with the permission of the court
defalcate	to void; to misappropriate money; to sneeze
defenestration	to cut someone out of a will; to nullify an adoption; to throw someone out of a window

dégagé	free and easy; amorous; absentminded
déjà vu	old fashioned; a person acquainted with witchcraft; the illusion of having previously experienced a present event
deleterious	noxious; extremely sweet; wholesome
delphic	of dark appearance; always smiling; ambiguous
demagoguery	hatred of religion; emotional, prejudiced oratory; urge to degrade others
demi-monde	objects and clothing made in the 1920s; a woman of dubious character; a jewelled cloche hat
demotic	belonging to the common people; staring wildly; student of the black arts
demurrer	an objection; a writ; a demand for payment
dénouement	a foiled elopement; a military surrender; the unravelling and solution of a mystery
depilatory	for preventing bleeding; for removing hair; for reducing perspiration
de rigueur	required by etiquette; demanded by regulation; suggested by a close friend
desiccate	to chop finely; to dry; to shred
desultory	fish able to live in fresh and sea water; casual and unmethodical; to feel inferior
determinism	belief that determination will solve all tasks; belief that the father more than the mother determines their child's features; belief that external forces and not heredity determine an individual's actions and fate
dextral	left-handed; right-handed; colour blind

dialectic	patient with kidney failure; logical and analytical argument; a scientific religion
dichotomy	second hymn of a church service; operation on joints of the foot; divided into two
didactic	inclined to teach; inclined to avoid problems; inclined to depend on others
dilatory	slow; fast; standing immobile
dipsomaniac	pickpocket; cat burglar; alcoholic
discommode	to take another name; to inconvenience someone; to take away a person's passport
discrete	detached and separate; composed of a single substance; massive
disparage	discourage; destroy; depreciate
dissemble	to hide one's intentions; to hinder; to argue
distrain	to seize goods in payment for a debt; to obtain a legal claim on a person's wages; to purchase a distressed mortgage or lease
diurnal	pertaining to daytime; pertaining to the night; pertaining to leap year
divertissement	advertising that is repeated; a piece of music for the cello; an entertainment
doctrinaire	dogmatic devotion to a theory; a senior medical doctor; a training hospital
dolorous	indolent; boring; full of pain and grief
double entendre	two theatre tickets for the price of one; a *risqué* ambiguous statement or joke; highly gifted and artistic twins
doughty	formidably brave; glum appearance; very untidy
doyen	a Jewish professor; a folk music band; the senior member of a profession or group

draconian	breathing fire; harsh; death by quicksand
drugget	a coarse woven mat; a square-shaped pill; a parlour where opium is smoked
dudgeon	optimism; sullen resentment; disappointment
duodenum	a digestive gland; the hearing organ of the ear; the first portion of the small intestine

Johnson's dictionary

Although not the first, Dr Samuel Johnson's *A Dictionary of the English Language* was certainly the most influential dictionary until the appearance of the *New English Dictionary* – later called the *Oxford* – between 1884 and 1928. Nine years in the making with the combined labours of Johnson and six helpers, the massive dictionary defined 43,000 words and was published in 1755 to become the ultimate reference book on English for a century and a half. Yet Johnson's dictionary is far from being a dry academic tome; it positively bristles with its author's quirky personality, quite a few errors and inconsistencies, brilliantly concise definitions and – Johnson being Johnson – a few jokes. One of these was his definition of oats: '*A grain which in England is generally given to horses, but in Scotland supports the people.*' The Scots got their own back with the riposte: 'Johnson has explained why Scotland has the most beautiful women, and England the most beautiful horses.'

E

Using the meanings given, fill in the gaps.

(*Answers page 192*)

ebull _ _ nt	Full of high spirits and enthusiasm
e _ ful _ ent	Shining brightly
egal _ _ arian	One who believes in human equality
eg _ _ entric	Self-centred
egr _ gious	Flagrantly appalling
éla _	Panache
elegi _ c	Melancholic and mournful
ele _ _ antine	Huge, unwieldy
éli _ e	The best
El _ sian	Blissful, like a paradise
eman _ _ e	To issue or flow from
e _ _ ncipate	To set free
emas _ _ late	To weaken, to deprive of masculine properties
emb _ _ go	To restrict or prohibit
embolis _	The blocking of an artery or vein by a blood clot
embr _ onic	Undeveloped
eme _ date	To correct by removing errors and faults
emo _ _ ient	A preparation that softens and soothes
em _ lument	A payment for services

empa _ _ y	Identification with another's feelings
empiri _ _ l	Conclusions based on experiment, experience or observation
encom _ um	A citation of very high praise
en _ _ mic	Found in a particular place; indigenous
ener _ ate	To weaken
enf _ nt te _ _ ible	An embarrassing child
eng _ _ der	To cause or bring about something
enig _ _	Something unexplainable
en _ oin	To order or instruct someone to do something
en _ ui	Listlessness and boredom
enor _ ity	An atrocity of outrageous proportions
enunci _ _ e	To articulate clearly
e _ _ emera	Something short-lived
ep _ cure	A person devoted to sensual pleasures, especially eating and drinking
epig _ _ m	A witty saying or short verse
equit _ _ le	Fair and just
equi _ ocal	Ambiguous, uncertain
ergon _ _ ics	The study of working conditions and efficiency
ero _ enous	Sexually sensitive
ersat _	An artificial or inferior substitute
eruc _ a _ ion	Belching
er _ dite	Well-read and well-informed
eso _ eric	Something intelligible only to an initiated few
esp _ it de cor _ s	Spirit of loyalty and devotion to a group to which one belongs
et _ os	The inherent characteristics of a culture or organisation
etymol _ gy	The origin and history of words

132

e _ genics	The science of improving hereditary characteristics
e _ logise	To praise highly
eu _ _ emism	The substitution of a bland or pleasant expression for a disagreeable one

---

Word playtime

Expanding your vocabulary need not be drudgery: far from it. For about as long as words have existed we've played games with them – and as far as English is concerned, playing word games (crosswords, scrabble, puzzle books and all the rest) is an amusing way in which to put more muscle into your word power. Here are a couple of quickies:

- What do the words **cauliflower**, **behaviour**, **equation** and **mendacious** have in common?
- What single four-letter word is used in baseball, basketball, boxing, fishing, football, golf and hockey?

(*answers page 197*)

---

eupho _ i _	The heady feeling of supreme well-being
Eur _ _ ian	Of mixed European and Asian blood
e _ than _ sia	Painless killing of terminally ill or old people
evan _ _ cent	Fading away
exa _ erbate	To irritate and make worse
e _ coriate	To remove the skin
excul _ _ te	To free from blame
exe _ rable	Detestable
exeg _ _ is	A critical explanation
e _ emplary	Someone or something so good as to be worth imitating

exor _ ise	To drive out evil or evil spirits
expa _ iate	To speak or write at considerable length
expa _ _ iate	To expel someone from a country by force
exp _ _ te	To atone or make amends
expr _ pri _ te	To dispossess an owner of something, usually property, often for public use
ex _ ur _ ate	To remove supposedly offensive passages (from a book etc.)
ex _ irpate	To exterminate

F

Which of the two meanings
is correct?

(*Answers page 192*)

facile	Something accomplished easily but without depth, or a smooth liar
factotum	A 'jack of all trades' sort of servant, or the daily collection of workers' 'clock-on' cards
fait accompli	An accomplished fact, or a loyal but unwilling accomplice to a crime
fallacy	A Papal law, or a false belief or argument
farrago	An Indian grain, or a confused mixture
fascism	Authoritarian government, or an art movement
fastidious	Well-dressed, or hard to please
fatuous	Complacently stupid, or complacently overweight
faux pas	Cunning like a fox, or a social indiscretion
fealty	Bravery, or loyalty
febrile	Lukewarm liquid, or inclined to be feverish
feckless	A person without purpose or principles, or a horse impossible to train
fecund	fertile, or one-millionth of a minute

The Oxford English Dictionary – The OED

When Sir James Murray began to compile the first *OED* in 1879, he constructed in his garden an iron shed in which there were over 1,000 pigeonholes in readiness for several million slips of paper which would be stored in them. On these slips would be entered definitions and citations of words – the contributions of many thousands of amateur lexicographers from around the world. The marathon of compiling and defining, proofreading and publishing the dictionary occupied the rest of Murray's life; when he died in 1915 it had only reached the letter T. Another 13 years were needed to complete it and, with 16,000 pages in 10 volumes, it finally appeared in 1928, to be followed by the first supplement in 1933. Subsequently, other supplements were published, concluding with S–Z in 1986.

The new, *Second Edition* – the *OED2* – was published in 1989 with just under half a million words, illustrated by 2.5 million quotations,

felicitous	Charming and well-suited, or lit with a luminous glow
feral	Stained with iron, or in a wild state
fervid	Diseased, or impassioned
filibuster	A type of firework that ends with a cannonade, or the technique of delaying the progress of legislation by prolonged speechmaking
flaccid	Flabby, or milky
flews	The canals that feed a watermill, or the pendant jowls of certain breeds of dogs
flippant	Frivolous, or skipping
florescence	Blossoming of a plant, or glowing in the dark
florid	Ruddy or highly embellished, or the side of a coin which bears a date

packed into 20 weighty volumes. There, any similarities with Murray's dictionary end, for the *OED2* is a product of the computer age, and users possessing the right hardware can buy the entire work on CD–ROM for £500, or a third of the price of the books.

Capturing the original dictionary and the supplements electronically, while incorporating a further 30,000 new words and quotations, was an awesome undertaking requiring an estimated 500 person-years and an accuracy rate of just 4.5 errors per 10,000 keystrokes. The result is breathtaking; users can 'interrogate' the electronic version and extract complex information in seconds – information that might take days and even months to find in the book version. It can confirm, for example, that the only common English words ending in **-shion** are, astonishingly, **cushion** and **fashion**; and the only words ending in **-gry** are **angry** and **hungry**. Not many amateur lexicographers know that.

flout	To show off, or treat with contempt
foible	A small trinket, or a personal weakness
forensic	Pertaining to law courts, or pertaining to an autopsy
fortuitous	Ability to read future events, or accidental
fractious	Restless and irritable, or out of control
friable	Able to be cooked in oil, or crumbly
fulgent	Bright and dazzling, or the smell of death
fulminate	To explode, or a slow burning that causes fumes
fulsome	Gluttony, or excessive and insincere
fundamentalism	Belief in the literal truth of sacred texts, or belief that not only humans but all creatures have souls

furbelow	Flouncy trimming on clothing, or the line with which sailors measure the depth of water
furlough	Ten furlongs, or leave of absence

G

Select the correct usage.

(*Meanings page 192*)

gaffe	He finished off the shark with a gaffe. He later apologised for his gaffe.
gambit	Flashing a big smile at a man was her usual gambit. As he entered the cellar he had to stoop under the gambit.
gamut	His mind raced through the gamut of possibilities. The ugly little gamut came up and swore at me.
garrulous	Something she'd eaten made her queasy and garrulous. The more he drank, the louder and more garrulous he became.
gauche	The artist presented her with a framed gauche. The young girl was beautiful but gauche.
gazebo	He sat musing in the gazebo. At last he had the fleeing gazebo in his sights.
gefilte fish	They all congratulated her on her gefilte fish. He'd been fishing all day and had caught only three gefilte fish and a small salmon.
genuflect	As she entered, she genuflected

briefly towards the altar. The three-year sentence gave him ample time to genuflect upon his crime.

germane Her hair shone germane in the moonlight. He insisted that the financial situation was germane to the argument.

gerrymander The sitting candidate realised too late that the gerrymander would cost him the election. The gang boss threatened to gerrymander the FBI by fleeing to a neighbouring state.

gestation The average gestation time for a heavy meal is five hours. It was obvious that the mare's gestation was in its final weeks.

gesundheit *'Gesundheit!'* he said, raising his glass. *'Gesundheit!'*, he swore, and sat down, frustrated.

gigolo You could tell by his effeminate manner that he was a gigolo. She had plenty of money and a string of eager gigolos.

glutinous The plant trapped insects in its glutinous nectary. He came up and spoke to my aunt in his usual glutinous manner.

gobbet The starving prisoners clamoured for the gobbets of flesh. His body hung there for days beneath the evil, creaking gobbet.

gobbledegook Among Lewis Carroll's creations were the Snark, the Boojum, the Cheshire Cat and the Gobbledegook. The memo was utter gobbledegook.

gourmandise	The factory was built to gourmandise milk into cheese. Her dream was to gourmandise on fancy Swiss chocolates.
grandiose	The garden party was a grandiose affair. He was always grandiose with his money.

New words

The 'G' section might well have concluded with the word **gurney**, a wheeled stretcher used for transporting patients. **Gurney** is just one of an estimated 3,000 or so new words created every year, and after a decade or so its usage is sufficiently widespread as to guarantee a degree of permanence. Words are constantly joining and leaving the language. Words like **freet** (a proverb), **frim** (vigorous and healthy) and **frayne** (to ask or enquire) expire from under-use to make way for hundreds of new words on our lips like **bimbo** and **yobbo**, **gazundered** and **software**, **fax** and **filofax**. But not all new words make the grade; the square television aerial called the **squarial** had such a short life it could be termed an **emphemarial**, and terms like number-crunching and bean-counting are likely to remain in limbo for quite a while before acquiring lexical respectability. That need not prevent us using them, however; if we used only dictionary words in our everyday speech and writing our vocabulary would seem very stilted indeed. So *vivat* **pecs**, **bar code** and **couch potato**!

gratuitous	Not all the diners were gratuitous to the waiters. The movie was marred by the scenes of gratuitous violence.

gravamen	The gravamen of the case was the premeditated nature of the attack. The vicar finally delivered his gravamen to the happy couple.
gregarious	He was a gregarious person and invariably grew irritable when alone. When the gregarious mood hit him he would lie and wait for some casual prey.
gumption	The brick pillars were topped with weathered stone gumptions. The teacher told them that with a bit of gumption they could do anything.

Choose the correct meaning.

(*Answers page 193*)

habeas corpus	murder case lacking a body; demand for a prisoner to appear before the court; appeal to dismiss a case through lack of evidence
habitué	regular visitor; drug addict; well dressed
hackneyed	transported by horse-drawn carriage; stale and trite; tired and listless
hagiography	a stream of invective; a catalogue of complaints; a biography that regards its subject as a saint
ha-ha	a sunken fence; a fountain; a summer house
halcyon	peaceful and pleasant; a thick crayon used for stage makeup; the fringe on a carpet
halitosis	body odour; smelly feet; bad breath
hapless	clumsy; angry and irritable; unfortunate and unlucky
harbinger	someone or something that foretells an event; a rowing boat used for hunting whales; a species of honey-eating bird
hector	to shout; to act strangely; to bully

Homophones

When the crate was opened, out stepped a gnu, and the rest of the zoo wondered what the new gnu knew. The last three words are **homophones**: words pronounced the same but different in meaning and spelling. There are hundreds of them lying in wait for the unwary. Here are just a few to watch out for:

air, ere, heir, eyre	aisle, I'll, isle
born, borne, bourne	braise, brays, braze
by, buy, bye	cents, scents, sense
cord, cored, chord	eau, oh, owe
ewe, yew, you	flew, flu, flue
heal, heel, he'll	gnu, knew, new
holey, holy, wholly	knows, noes, nose
load, lode, lowed	meat, meet, mete
nay, née, neigh	oar, or, ore
pair, pare, pear	peak, peek, pique
prays, praise, preys	rain, reign, rein
road, rode, rowed	seas, sees, seize
teas, tease, tees	to, too, two
vain, vane, vein	

The different meanings of homophones and many other look-alikes and grammatical mischief-makers will be found in Chapter 4

hegemony	property passing from mother to children; the dominance of one country over another; the state's right to tax citizens
heinous	horse-loving; wicked; rural
hellebore	a rude and tiresome person; a group of plants; a type of ship's figurehead

heresy	an unorthodox belief; a wicked lie; a traitorous act
heterogeneous	of the same kind; of different kind; of either sex
heuristic	the capacity to inquire and find out; an obsession with time; lover of holy things
hiatus	a break or gap; a summer holiday; hiccups
Hibernian	pertaining to Scotland; pertaining to Ireland; pertaining to the Isle of Man
hindsight	all-round vision; the part of a gunsight nearest the eye; wise after the event
histology	study of organic tissue; study of ancient burial sites; study of hay fever
hogmanay	last day of the year; New Year's Day; a Scottish dance
hoi polloi	upper class; common people; high-brow
hologram	printing by means of gelatin; a ghostly vision of Christ; a three-dimensional photographic image
homogeneous	all the same kind; all different; mixed
honorarium	a minor award to civil servants; a payment; a collection of medals
hortatory	pertaining to clocks and time-keeping; sleepwalking condition; giving encouragement
hubris	arrogant conceit or pride; a sepia-like colour; an oil obtained from the sperm whale
humanism	a system concerned with kindness to animals; a system concerned with the needs of man; a system concerned with selective breeding
humdrum	an Indian grain; dull and tedious; irritating
hydrology	the study of water; the study of ferns; the study of the upper atmosphere

hygrometer   measures moisture in the air; measures air pressure; measures impurities in the air

hyperbole   exaggeration; a huge arena; hypnotherapy

Using the meanings given, fill in the gaps.

(*Answers page 193*)

icono _ _ ast	One who attacks established doctrines and beliefs
i _ iomatic.	Speech and expressions characteristic of a region or country
idios _ ncrasy	A personal habit or peculiarity of manner
id _ _ atry	Worship of idols and images
ignom _ _ y	Disgrace and dishonour
imbrogl _ _	A complex and confused state of affairs
imm _ late	To kill by sacrifice, usually by fire
immu _ ed	Imprisoned, walled in
im _ utable	Unchanging and unalterable
i _ passe	An insurmountable obstacle or situation
implac _ ble	Unrelenting and not to be appeased
imp _ _ tune	To demand urgently and persistently
imprimat _ r	A mark of approval
improm _ tu	Off hand, without preparation
impu _ n	To dispute the validity or truth of an argument, or challenge the word of someone
in _ _ vertent	Unintentionally careless

147

incip _ ent	In the first stages
incogni _ o	Avoiding recognition by disguise or by assuming another name
incul _ ate	To impress on the mind by repetition or force
inc _ mbent	The holder of a position or office; a moral obligation under the circumstances
ind _ _ nity	Security against damage or loss
indigen _ _ s	Native to a particular country or region
indig _ _ t	Destitute
ineffab _ _	Too overwhelming to be expressed in words
inel _ ctable	Inevitable and unavoidable
ine _ orable	Unmoved, unbending and unyielding
in _ ra dig	Beneath one's dignity
in _ énue	A naive and artless yong girl
ingen _ ous	Open, candid and frank
ini _ ical	Hostile and behaving like an enemy
inna _ e	Inborn
inno _ uous	Harmless
innuen _ o	An oblique hint or suggestion, usually derogatory
insa _ ubrious	Unhealthy
ins _ dious	Subtly intent on deceiving or betraying
insouc _ ant	Careless and unconcerned
inter ali _	Among other things
interdi _ t	To authoritatively forbid
interne _ ine	Mutually destructive
inter _ tice	A small space or crack between two things
int _ ansigent	Uncompromising and irreconcilable
intr _ _ sic	Essential, inherent

in _ _ overt	Someone interested in his own thoughts, feelings and actions
invei _ h	To verbally denounce
invi _ ious	Provoking anger and resentment
i _ ascible	Easily excited and angered
i _ _ evocable	Incapable of being revoked or repealed

Janus words

What's the difference between dusting tomato plants for mildew and dusting the grand piano? The same word is describing two completely opposite actions: adding dust and removing it. **Dusting** is known as a Janus word – a verbal hermaphrodite that can have either of two opposite meanings. Such words are fascinating: think about **sanction, fast, handicap, cleave** and **draw** (when you draw the curtains are you opening them or closing them?) – all of them have opposite meanings.

Close cousins of Janus words are words that appear to be opposites but which share the same meaning: **inflammable** and **flammable, bend** and **unbend, passive** and **impassive**. You might also like to ponder such contradictory terms as **getting up** and **getting down** from the dinner table; and **slowing up** and **slowing down** in a car.

J

Which of the two meanings
is correct?

(Answers page 193)

jaundiced	A prejudicial attitude, or an untrue statement
jejune	Bright and sparkling, or immature, insipid and uninteresting
jeopardy	Exposure to danger or loss, or a pattern with wide stripes used for camouflage
jeremiad	An extremely unlucky person, or a lament
jettison	To throw things overboard, or to crash a boat into a dock
jihad	A crusade for or against a belief or faith, or the ruling council of a Muslim state
jingoism	A compulsion to tell jokes, or aggressive patriotism
jocose	Humorous and facetious, or red-faced
joie de vivre	Joy of being alive, or a delight in aggression
junta	A ruling council, often dictatorial, or a South American dictator
juvenescence	Loss of memory, or becoming young again
juxtapose	To place something against something else, or to cover something up with something else

Know what I mean?

'Er . . . you know . . . those silver things you put three candles in . . . ummm . . .' **Candelabra,** of course! How many times do we accurately describe something but can't remember its name? Here are some definitions of fairly common things; see if you can supply their names.

1. The plaster moulding used to disguise the join between wall and ceiling
2. The pedal you push when you change gear in a car
3. The raised-dot alphabet for the blind
4. Those timber or concrete walls that run across the foreshore down to the sea
5. The small Victorian lady's writing desk with drawers down one side
6. The theory that divides the brain and skull into sections denoting mental and emotional characteristics
7. The heavy farm horse that is dark brown with white markings
8. The signs much used by astrologers
9. The craze in pubs for singing popular songs to taped musical accompaniment
10. Those men that wave frantically at horse races

(answers page 197)

K

Select the correct usage.

(*Meanings page 193*)

karma
He lay on the ground, wrapped in a bright red karma. He sat there, dejected, convinced his karma was not good.

kibbutz
She looked healthy and radiant after her year at the kibbutz. The Prime Minister's problem was that he could not control the ruling kibbutz.

kitsch
It was well known that as an artist he produced nothing but kitsch. As a family friend, he undertook to act as the children's kitsch.

kleptomaniac
After a dozen convictions for theft she was finally diagnosed as a kleptomaniac. His sleepwalking confirmed him as a kleptomaniac.

kosher
The new woollen kosher fitted her perfectly. Three passengers on the flight had ordered kosher meals.

kowtow
He had never seen a Chinese person with the traditional kowtow. He hated to kowtow to his employers in the big house.

kudos
They would spend hours playing kudos. His sales figures brought him plenty of kudos.

Litotes

Litotes (pronounced *ly-to-tees*) is an ancient rhetorical device used to express understatement, as in: 'He was not totally displeased', meaning 'He was very pleased'. Another common example is 'not bad', meaning 'pretty good'. Litotes are also useful for expressing a 'not-completely-opposite' thought; to say that someone is 'not unhappy' means not that they are happy, but that they are content and satisfied. Litotes you'll constantly come across include 'not unwelcome', 'not unlike' and 'not a few': all part of our rich but often contradictory vocabulary.

L

Choose the correct meaning.

(*Answers page 194*)

lachrymose	oversweet; ready to weep; muscular
laconic	economical (of speech); casual; given to boasting
lacuna	a gap or blank; the centre of a lens; the hazy ring around the moon
laity	clergy; laymen; male members of a choir
laissez-faire	restricting immigration; over-willingness to accept harsh laws; policy of non-intervention
lambent	easily bent; softly flickering; blue-tinted
lampoon	ship's lantern; a satiric attack; a whale
languor	lack of energy and enthusiasm; a sexually inviting look; semi-consciousness
largess	water that gathers in the hull of a ship; a type of peach; a generous gift, usually money
lascivious	lustful; given to laughter; blood-red
latent	existing but not noticeable; just prior to boiling point; triangular sail
lateral	towards the top; towards a bottom edge; to or from the side
laudable	sanctified; praiseworthy; drugged with opium

154

legerdemain	folklore; sleight of hand; deep knowledge
leitmotif	a recurring theme; German subway system; a motiveless crime
lèse-majesté	royal divorce; bending the knee; high treason
lethargic	lead poisoning; drowsy and apathetic; shortage of breath
libido	Italian teenager; the sexual drive; a wash basin used for shampooing hair
libretto	text of an opera or vocal work; soprano section of an operatic choir; interval during an opera
licentious	sexually unrestrained; operating without a licence; involved in piracy
lickerish	inspired playing of the clarinet; wet and sloppy; lustful and lecherous
lionize	to threaten; to treat someone as a celebrity; to covet the adulation of crowds
lissom	persuasive speech; golden haired; supple
locum tenens	a professional substitute; an alcoholic delirium; a woodworker's tool
logorrhea	disease of the gums; abnormal talkativeness; theory of numbers
longueur	train of a wedding dress; a vain person; a tedious passage in a book or play
loquacious	talkative; semi-naked; having red-rimmed eyes
Lothario	seducer of women; swarthy; extremely strong
louche	charming; effeminate; shady and devious
lubricious	charming in manner; outrageously effeminate; oily and lecherous
lugubrious	mournful; lewd; vain
lumpen	people who are overweight; deprived and degraded; gentlemen farmers

Which of the two meanings
is correct?

(*Answers page 194*)

macerate   To regurgitate food, or to soften by
soaking

Machiavellian   Unscrupulous scheming, or achieving
political ends by use of explosives

Mallemaroking

For a ship to be icebound these days is something
of a rare event; either that, or the newsworthiness
of icebound ships is rated about zero. But if, say,
a ship *were* icebound, one would think that the
sailors on the unfortunate vessel would be a
downcast lot, glumly counting off the weeks and
months to the arrival of the thaw. However, a
word exists that suggests we are wrong. That
word is **mallemaroking**, meaning the carousing of
seamen aboard icebound ships. Alone among
dictionaries, it seems, *Chambers Twentieth Century
Dictionary* has carried the word over many years
through several editions, so there must be a use
for it. Perhaps a clandestine but booming travel
business exists, flying tourists to ships icebound
in the Arctic Circle for a good old mallemaroking.
Or perhaps *Chambers* is having us all on.

macrocosm	A universal whole, or a thin sliver of tissue for microscopic examination
magisterial	Dictatorial, or a liking for legal robes
magnum opus	A champagne bottle which holds 6 magnums of champagne, or the greatest work of an artist, composer or writer
maladroit	Awkward and clumsy, or a love of reptiles
malaise	A tropical disease, or a vague feeling of uneasiness and discomfort
malapropism	Using the wrong cutlery, or misusing words
mal de mer	A sea delicacy, or sea sickness
malfeasance	Lying under oath, or official misconduct
Malthusian	The theory that populations will always outstrip the food supply unless checked, or that the world consumes resources faster than it can create or replace them
maudlin	Tearfully sentimental, or easily convinced
maunder	To receive alms on Maundy Thursday, or to wander incoherently
mea culpa	'The drink is poisoned', or 'It's my fault'
megalomania	Fear of spots, or delusions of grandeur
megrim	A severe headache and depression, or a horrific dream
mélange	A mixture, or a milk jelly dessert
mêlée	A lady's long silk dressing gown, or a confused fight
mellifluous	Sweet to the taste, or sweetly flowing
ménage	A household, or a stable of horses
mendacious	Prone to lying and deception, or miserly
mendicant	A holistic doctor, or a beggar

mephitic	Offensive to the nose, or a substance that makes the eyes water
meretricious	Annoyingly repetitive, or vulgarly attractive
mesmerise	To hypnotise, or to cure illnesses by immersing in ice or icy water
metabolism	The bodily process that converts food to energy, or the theory that base metals like lead can be converted to gold
métier	One's natural vocation, or a group of art students
metronymic	Music with a steady beat, or a name or qualities derived from a maternal ancestor
micron	A unit for measuring the weight of stars, or one-millionth of a metre
micturate	To preserve crystals in oil, or to urinate frequently
milieu	Environment, or large, ornate wardrobe
millennium	One thousand years, or the year o
minatory	Threatening, or abnormally tall
misanthropy	Compulsive hoarding, or hatred of mankind
miscegenation	Lack of birth control, or racial interbreeding
misnomer	A mistaken or wrongly applied name, or an unnamed child
misogyny	Hatred of women, or fear of marriage
mnemonic	An eight-line poem, or a device to help the memory
moiety	A half share, or prone to subservience
moiré	A unit of radioactivity, or a wavy-patterned fabric
monograph	A black and white computer screen, or a treatise on a single subject
moratorium	A temporary suspension of an activity, or a burial ground for non-believers

moribund	Coming to an end, or highly fertile
mot juste	A misleading summing up by a judge to a jury, or the perfectly fitting word or phrase
mufti	A very hot curry, or ordinary clothes worn by a serviceman off duty
mundane	Ordinary and matter-of-fact, or a person who has a deficient sense of humour
myocardiogram	A record of waves from the frontal lobe of the brain, or a record of the muscular activity of the heart
myopia	A propensity to weep, or short-sightedness

N

Using the meanings given,
fill in the gaps.

(*Answers page 194*)

nad _ r	The lowest possible point
n _ scent	Beginning to exist or develop
nebul _ _ s	Vague and indistinct
n _ crop _ y	Examination of a dead body
ne _ arious	Wicked and evil
neg _ s	A drink of wine, hot water, sugar and spices
n _ m _ sis	Retributive justice
neol _ _ ism	The coining of a new word or giving a new meaning to an existing word
neoph _ te	A novice or beginner
ne _ hritis	Inflammation of the kidneys
nepoti _ _	Favouring one's relatives, especially in relation to jobs and positions
ne _ us	Something that joins or links
nih _ lism	A doctrine that holds that nothing has value or meaning, and rejects all traditional values, beliefs and institutions
n _ _ some	Offensive and disgusting, especially a smell
no _ age	The period of legal minority

The nous on dous

How many words end in **-dous**? Surprisingly, less
than a dozen. But if you leave out the rare
(**nefandous** – unmentionable), the archaic
(**plumbous** – resembling lead) and the scientific
(**steganopodous** – webbed toes) there are only
four in common use. See if you can identify them:

The climb up Everest was h _ _ _ _ dous
The weather, though, was h _ _ _ _ _ dous
The views were simply s _ _ _ _ _ dous
And the thrill of it all was t _ _ _ _ _ dous

(*answers page 198*)

non _ _ alant	Indifferent, calm and cool
non se _ _ itur	An illogical conclusion or statement
nost _ um	A dubious cure-all
n _ bile	A woman of marriageable age
nug _ _ ory	Unimportant, and not worth anything

O

Choose the correct meaning.

(*Answers page 194*)

obdurate	determined; stubborn; pleasant and obliging
obeisance	a gesture of homage; traitorous; obstinate
obfuscate	to paint in bright colours; to swear; to confuse or obscure
obloquy	a prayer for the dead; evasive language; abusive and reproachful language
obsequious	loyal; servile; gentle
obsolescent	becoming outdated; obsolete; easily broken
obstreperous	unruly and uncontrollable; untrustworthy; making slanderous statements
obviate	to speed things up; to criticise harshly; to make unnecessary
occidental	an oriental; a westerner; a South American
occlude	to mist over; to shut out; to ooze out
odium	hatred; a very bad smell; a rare metal
odontologist	cares for the feet; cares for the nose; cares for the teeth

oenologist   an expert in conversion of crude oil; an expert in wine and winemaking; an expert in soapmaking

oeuvre   a dish of quails' eggs; a list of soldiers killed in a battle; the whole work of a writer or artist

oligarchy   an unbroken line of female descendants; a government controlled by a privileged few; a communal olive grove in Greece

omniscient   knowing everything; being ruled by astrology; fear of the dark

opprobrium   disgrace; a dark place; an eye disease

oracular   roughly elliptical; prophetic; squinting

orotund   of spherical proportions; pertaining to apes and monkeys; eloquent and pompous speech

ossified   turned into paste; into bone; into rubber

ostensibly   seemingly; obviously; incautiously

ostentatious   silent and secretive; pretentious and showy; using bright, dazzling colours

osteopathy   treatment using water and sea products; treatment using nerve stimulation; treatment using massage and bone manipulation

otiose	useless and futile; fat and lazy; slow and lumbering
outré	mannish; fashionable; eccentric
overt	hidden and secret; open and public; shy and retiring

Pairs – of the dangerous kind

The word that is emerging for words that are easily confused is, not surprisingly, **confusables**. A common practice seems to be, 'when in doubt, leave them out', which is a pity because many so-called **confusables** are decidedly useful in everyday speech and writing. Here are just a few:

compulsive, compulsory	deprecate, depreciate
enormous, enormity	flout, flaunt
implicit, explicit	ingenious, ingenuous
loan, lend	militate, mitigate
licence, license	noisome, noisy
obsolete, obsolescent	official, officious
parameter, perimeter	perquisite, prerequisite

and the list goes on. Even **its/it's** is these days regarded as a dangerous pair. An important aspect of building a more muscular vocabulary is to know the precise meanings of words, especially confusables. See Chapter 4 for further guidance.

P

Which of the two meanings is correct?

(*Answers page 195*)

paediatrician	A specialist in bone diseases, or a specialist in children's diseases
palaver	A drawn-out discussion, or a Mexican-Indian woven cape
palpable	Evident and obvious, or barely eatable
panacea	A universal remedy, or wishful thinking
panache	Dash and verve, or a vague ache
Panglossian	Optimistic, or self-defeating
panegyric	Any bitter medicine, or an elaborate and very flattering expression of praise
panjandrum	A Punjabi feast, or a self-important official
pantheism	The doctrine that the universe is a manifestation of God, or the theory that all souls exist until eternity
paparazzi	A long row of marble columns, or tenacious freelance photographers of celebrities
paradigm	A model example, or a tongue-twisting phrase
paragon	A person held up to ridicule, or a model of excellence

parameter	An outermost limit, or variable constants used to determine a mathematical problem
paramour	An occasional lover, or the lover of a married man or woman
paranoia	Fear of criticism or attack, or delusions of persecution or grandeur
paraphrase	A restatement in different words intended to clarify, or a passage rewritten to hide its true meaning
pariah	Head of a tribe, or a social outcast
pari mutuel	A banking system that guarantees depositors a fixed interest rate, or a betting system that divides the total stakes among the winners
parlous	Embittered, or perilous
parsimony	A church endowment, or stinginess
parvenu	A newly rich social upstart, or a leading patron of the arts
passé	Up to the minute, or behind the times
pastiche	A work that imitates the style of another, or a slow movement for orchestral strings
paterfamilias	Male head of a household, or the collective uncles of a family
pathogenic	Pertaining to autopsies, or capable of causing disease
patina	Circumference of the retina of the eye, or an oxidised layer
patisserie	A shop selling pastries, or preserved meats
patrial	Pertaining to a person's country of birth, or a person with an unknown father

patrician	A fluent speaker of French, Italian and Spanish, or an aristocrat
Pecksniffian	An admirer of the works of Charles Dickens, or a hypocrite who advocates moral behaviour but who acts otherwise
pectorals	Chest muscles, or stomach muscles
pedagogue	A windy orator, or a schoolteacher
pedantry	Excessive attention to rules and details, or the relentless pursuit of debtors
peignoir	A clasp to pull a woman's hair back, or a long, loose woman's negligee or dressing gown
pejorative	Disparaging and derogatory, or pompous
pellucid	Clear and transparent, or pearl-like
percipient	Rude and abrupt, or quick to see and understand
peregrination	A journey, or travelling in circles
peremptory	Cautious and hesitant, or decisive and final
perennial	Annually, or everlastingly
perfunctory	Careless and half-hearted, or vigorous
peripatetic	Prone to indigestion, or always travelling
periphrasis	Roundabout speech or writing, or obsession with words
pernicious	Irritating, or harmful
peroration	A memorial address, or the summing up at the end of a speech

perquisite	Unearned money or benefit, or a service that is required before a payment is made
persiflage	Frivolous banter, or embarrassing flattery
perspicacious	Unduly suspicious, or having the ability to understand things clearly
pertinacious	Cheeky, or stubbornly persistent
philanderer	A womaniser, or a travelling salesman
philistine	A person indifferent to the arts and learning, or someone who attacks established values
phlegmatic	Pessimistic, or stolidly calm and unexcitable
physiognomy	The study of cranial bumps and depressions, or a person's facial features
picayune	Petty and niggling, or bright and sparkling
pied-à-terre	A temporary or secondary apartment, or a dish featuring snails
pinnate	A flagless flagpole, or having the shape and arrangement of a feather
pixilated	Slightly dotty, or obsessed with garden gnomes
placebo	A substance given in place of real medicine, or a glass-walled garden summer house
plagiarism	Falsely attributing modern imitations as works of the old masters, or stealing and using another's ideas, inventions or writings and passing them off as one's own work

plangent	A deep and resounding noise, or a small, square-shaped pill
Platonic	A blood-bond between two men, or spiritual and non-sensual
plebeian	One who pleads before a court, or common and vulgar
plenary	Complete and absolute, or intermediate
plethora	Superabundance, or an operation for gallstones
plutocracy	Rule by the wealthy, or rule by the ignorant
podiatry	The art of speech-making, or the treatment of disorders of the feet
poignant	Sad looking, or penetrating and affecting
poltroon	A person of mixed race, or a craven coward
polymath	A systematic mathematician, or a person versed in many areas of learning
potable	Suitable for drinking, or easily carried
preciosity	Excessive refinement of speech, or effeminate mannerisms
predicate	To assert as a fact, or to firmly predict
predilection	A vague dislike, or a special liking
prehensile	In a primitive state, or capable of grasping
prescient	Having foresight, or easily irritated
prevaricate	To evade and mislead, or to argue fiercely
prima facie	Unfounded allegations, or self-evident
probity	Serious and analytical, or proven integrity

proclivity	A strong and natural tendency, or rising ground in a landscape
prolapse	A recurrence of a disorder, or the downward displacement of an organ
prolix	Tediously long-winded, or the centre of an ellipse
propinquity	Warning signals, or nearness
propitious	Subject to loss of balance, or favourable
pro rata	Payment for professional duties, or in the same proportion
proscribe	To forbid, or to prescribe under duress
proselytise	To translate thoughts into words, or to convert someone from one opinion or belief to another
prosthesis	Replacement of a body part with an artificial substitute, or an unwelcome medical opinion
protean	Versatile and changeable, or of vast girth
provenance	Certificate of proof of authenticity, or place of origin
prurient	Pure in thought and deed, or inquisitive about the smutty and obscene
psychosomatic	Physical disorder caused by or influenced by the emotions, or terminal
puerile	Silly and childish, or offensively smelly
puissant	Self-mocking, or powerful
pukka	Genuine and reliable, or a show-off
pulchritude	Innocence and reverence, or physical beauty
pullulate	To vibrate and sway, or to breed rapidly

punctilious	Paying strict attention to details of conduct, or having an obsession with time
purlieus	The fashionable clothes of high society, or the outskirts and boundaries of a neighbourhood
pusillanimous	Meanfisted, or timid and cowardly
putative	Supposed or reputed, or emerging
putti	A soldier's leggings, or the naked cherubs in art and sculpture
Pyrrhic victory	A victory that is costly and fruitless, or a victory that has emerged from the ashes of defeat

Q

Select the correct usage.

(*Meanings page 195*)

quasi-	A quango is a quasi-autonomous national government organisation. The room featured a quasi-patterned wallpaper in blues and reds.
querulous	The matron was fed up with her querulous attitude. The teacher was delighted with her querulous approach to difficult problems.
quiddity	They were amused by the poor man's quiddity. The quiddity of a pun is its wit.
quidnunc	The position of desk clerk at the Grand Hotel was ideal for a quidnunc like Mr Peters. After losing so much money he felt like a quidnunc.
quietus	The assassination and its bloody aftermath were followed by the long-awaited quietus. The bell tolled its long and lonely quietus.
quixotic	His face reddened with quixotic anger. Charging at the defenders, he shot for goal in true quixotic style.

Questions! Questions!

What's that, Mummy? Dad – what's that thing called? Most children's requests for names are easily satisfied, but occasionally they catch us out. What do you answer when a child asks . . .

- What's that fringed bit of paper wrapped round the end of the cutlets?
- When you went and had your ring valued, what was that magnifying thing the jeweller wore on his eye?
- What's the place called where they keep and breed cats?
- When they cut hedges into all those funny shapes, what's it called?
- What are those holes called that separate postage stamps?
- When you go up stairs you step on the treads, but what are the upright bits that keep the treads apart called?

(*answers page 198*)

quondam	He met his quondam secretly each Saturday. The horse ran up to and nuzzled its quondam owner.
quorum	The conductor surveyed the vast quorum of singers. Satisfied a quorum was present, the chairman announced the start of the meeting.
quotidian	The neighbours were maddened by the quotidian uproar from the boarding house. He was a polished quotidian from Shakespeare to Keats.

R

Using the meanings given, fill in the gaps.

(*Answers page 196*)

R _ belaisian	Extravagant and boisterous
racont _ _ r	An expert story-teller
ra _ _ ish	Flashy and disreputable
rail _ ery	Good-natured teasing
r _ ison d'être	Reason for existing
ranc _ _ r	Deep-seated hatred and resentment
r _ pport	Harmonious relationship
rappr _ chement	Restoration of friendly relations after some disagreement
rara a _ is	Someone or something very unusual
rati _ cination	Reasoning by the use of logic
r _ _ cous	Harsh-sounding
react _ _ nary	A person hostile to change or progress
re _ arbative	Repellant and forbidding
recalci _ rant	Stubborn and uncontrollable
rec _ _ t	To formally retract a belief or opinion
re _ herché	Rare, strange and exquisite
recidiv _ sm	Habitual relapse into criminal behaviour
rec _ _ dite	Obscure, profound and little-known

Roget's Thesaurus

Opinion is divided over *Roget's Thesaurus*, which, with some 100,000 words grouped under 1,000 headings, has been consulted over the past century and a half by many millions of word-stuck writers in search of suitable synonyms and apt antonyms. But how useful (**Utility: useful, of use, serviceable, usable, proficuous, good for, subservient**, etc) is *Roget's*, really? Despite some updating – the last in 1987 – it remains a sort of bluffer's guide, and with its jarring mix of the trendy and archaic, compositions cobbled together from its pages must look and sound very stilted indeed. By all means browse through *Roget's* for fun and even enlightenment, but for that elusive *mot juste* your best bet is a plain dictionary of synonyms.

recru _ esce	To break out afresh
rectit _ _ e	Moral integrity
red _ lent	Smelling of something that stirs the memory
redou _ table	Formidable and commanding respect
ref _ _ endum	A vote by the electorate to ratify or reject a particular issue
refra _ tory	Resistant and troublesome
reful _ ent	Shining brightly
ren _ ge	Break a promise or fail to fulfil an undertaking
rep _ eh _ nd	To criticise or blame
repudi _ te	To reject and disown
r _ trograde	To go backwards; deteriorate
retrou _ sé	Turned up
rhetor _ _ al	Concerned with effect rather than content
ri _ tus	A gaping open mouth

ripar _ _ n	Pertaining to river banks
ri _ oste	A quick and clever reply
risib _ e	Inclined to laughter
ro _ o _ o	Highly elaborate and florid 18th-century French style of decoration
r _ ué	A dissipated lecher
rum _ ustious	Boisterous and unruly

Sozzled, sloshed and squiffy

After what must have been a marinated marathon, the American wordsmith Paul Dickson came up with 2,231 words, phrases and slang expressions for intoxication. Here are just a few of them:

aced	aglow	banjanxed
besotted	bibulous	blasted
blimped	blitzed	blotto
bombed	bunnied	cockeyed
corked	crapulous	ebriose
flummoxed	embalmed	floored
gaga	fogmatic	frazzled
lathered	gone	half-sprung
non compos	lushed	motherless
overloaded	obfuscated	out to lunch
sauced	plastered	roostered
totalled	schnoggered	shellacked
zippered	umbriago	varnished

S

Which of the two meanings is correct?

(*Answers page 196*)

salacious	Obscene and lustful, or obsessively jealous
salient	Highly conspicuous, or with a following wind
salutary	Formal, or beneficial
sang-froid	Haughty manner, or coolness and composure under pressure
sardonic	Sneering and scornful, or shy and retiring
Sassenach	An English person, or a Scot
saturnine	Having a mane of black hair, or melancholic
savoir-faire	Extremely witty, or having a fine sense of what's right and wrong socially
scaramouch	A boastful buffoon, or a young beggar
scatology	Having a great knowledge of trivia, or an unhealthy interest in excrement
Schadenfreude	Delight in another's misfortunes, or to remain calm in a heated argument
scintilla	A group of bright stars, or the tiniest, most minute particle
scrivener	A clerk who writes up documents, or an official who supervises patients' debts to hospitals
scut	A rabbit's tail, or a short levering tool
sebaceous	Prone to skin complaints, or fatty

177

secular	Pertaining to sacred things, or pertaining to worldly things
sedulous	Persistent and diligent, or casual
semantics	Concerned with the sounds of words, or concerned with the meanings of words
semiotics	The study of signs in communications, or the study of Indian languages
senescent	Becoming young again, or growing old
sententious	Self-deceiving, or pompous moralising
sequestered	Cut out of an inheritance, or secluded
serendipitous	The inclination to find things unexpectedly, or the ability to make others happy
serrated	Saw-toothed, or rough like sandpaper
shibboleth	A password, gesture or mark that distinguishes a group of people, or a perpetuated untruth
sibilant	A silently sounded letter in a word, or the sound of a hiss
silviculture	Silkworm farming, or forestry
similitude	Resemblance, or the feeling of weightlessness
simony	False accusation, or trading in sacred objects
simulacrum	A shadowy, deceptive likeness, or a recurring nightmare
sinecure	A well-paid cushy position, or the inability to bend an arm at the elbow
sinistral	A hot wind that blows from the Mediterranean, or left-handed
skulk	To lurk unseen with wrongdoing in mind, or to run away from trouble
sobriquet	Flowers presented to a singer after a performance, or a nickname
sodality	Malicious scheming, or companionship
soi-disant	Devil-may-care, or 'self-styled'
soigné	Elaborately well-groomed, or a jewelled clasp for the hair

soirée	An evening of conversation and music, or a gathering of female friends
solecism	A recorded sun-spot, or a grammatical mistake
solipsism	The theory that only the self is real and knowable, or an unforgivable social gaffe
sommelier	A brandy warehouse, or a wine waiter
somnambulism	Talking to the spirit world, or sleepwalking
sonorous	Giving out a full, rich sound, or a person with a knowledge of the Mexican language
sophistry	The use of fallacious and deceptive argument, or having a preference for one's own sex
soporific	Oily, or sleep-inducing
sotto voce	Slightly inebriated, or in an undertone
spavined	Worn out and broken down, or split in two
specious	Seemingly right and correct but actually not, or undersized
splenetic	Tendency to be constantly ill, or bad-tempered
sporadic	At regular intervals, or occurring occasionally
stasis	A static state, or an irregular heartbeat
stentorian	A strict teacher, or loud and powerful
stultify	To make something appear foolish and absurd, or to check growth
stygian	Bottomless depths, or impenetrably dark
subliminal	Something perceived below the threshhold of consciousness, or thought transference
subsume	To include or absorb into, or to reduce
succinct	Easily dissolved, or sharp and concise
supercilious	Grossly superficial, or arrogantly indifferent

179

supernumerary	Superfluous, or every hundredth person or object in a group
suppurate	To vibrate, or to fester
surrogate	An appointed substitute, or a person dependent upon public funds
svelte	Slim and graceful, or superbly groomed
sybaritic	A worshipper of Satan, or indulging in sensual pleasures
sycophantic	Servile flattery, or complaining about details
symbiosis	Mutually advantageous partnership of two dissimilar organisms, or the ability of some fluids to permeate through others without being absorbed
synergy	Artificially induced energy, or co-operative activity to produce enhanced benefits
syntax	The rules of grammar that arrange the words in a sentence, or the accents in speech

T

Choose the correct meaning.

(Answers page 196)

tachometer	measures distance; forward speed; speed of rotation
tacit	surly; implied; obvious
tactile	pertaining to sense of sight; pertaining to sense of touch; pertaining to sense of hearing
talisman	a charm; a potion; a blood-bond
tangible	chewy; ethereal; real
taupe	pale purple; grey-brown; silvery
telekinesis	ability to hear unearthly voices; ability to spin the head around; ability to move things without touching them
temerity	boldness; meekness; harshness
temporal	spiritual; official; earthly
temporise	to delay; to half-finish something; to gloat
tendentious	boring; biased; cautious
tenet	a sharp lesson; a belief; a criticism
tenuous	flimsy; extremely long; complicated
tercentenary	an anniversary of 200 years; an anniversary of 300 years; an anniversary of 400 years
tessellated	chequered; fringed; stepped

theism	belief in rule by religion; belief in one God; belief in existence of many gods
thrall	excitement; bondage; fear
timorous	fearful; tiny; loud-voiced
tinnitus	disease of the skin; inflammation of the knee joint; ringing in the ears
tocsin	an alarm; a virulent poison; an antidote
torpid	sluggish; warm; slithery
tort	a junior judge; a private or civil wrong; a criminal offence
tractable	easily traced; easily swallowed; docile
traduce	to defame; to seduce; to persuade
tranche	to simmer; to multiply; a portion
transcend	to rise beyond; to disappear; to go across
transient	speedy; fleeting; a lover of travel
travail	painful toil; uncomfortable travelling; wailing at a funeral

tremulous	lisping; singing in low register; trembling
trenchant	cutting and forceful; eating with gusto; living underground
trichology	study of shells; study of combustible matter; study of hair
tridactyl	having a long tail; having three fingers or toes; having armoured scales
triptych	a painting on three panels; a religious sculpture; a three-handled vase
triumvirate	a gathering of cardinals; a group of three people wielding power; a three-cornered hat
troglodyte	a gargoyle; a large toad; a cave dweller
trompe l'oeil	lavender bath oil; a painting that gives the illusion of reality; a resounding victory
trope	a figure of speech; a malarial infection; a woman's pith helmet
truncate	to cut off the top; to cut off the bottom; to cut off the sides
tumescent	decaying; dozing; becoming swollen
turbid	cloudy; distended; sexually aroused
turpitude	inherent depravity; moral uprightness; strength of character
tyro	a seducer; a good-for-nothing; a beginner

U

Select the correct usage.

(*Meanings page 197*)

ubiquitous	In summer the ubiquitous dandelions dazzle the eye. The ubiquitous landlord extracted ferocious rents from his tenants.
ullage	The shipowner was fined for tipping ullage into the river. The wine merchant complained about the excessive ullage in the barrels.
ululate	He watched as the dancer ululated her body. As darkness approached he waited for the wolves to ululate.
umbrage	She took umbrage at the slightest criticism. The cellar was damp and reeked of umbrage.
unconscionable	He took an unconscionable time to walk to the rostrum. On several occasions during the day she would lapse into unconscionable dreams.
unctuous	After the sermon everyone felt decidedly unctuous. He addressed them in unctuous tones.
unilateral	The convoy steered a unilateral course. The governor made a unilateral decision to suspend the constitution.

Usage

Roughly speaking, there is **Correct English** and there is **Usage**. Usage is what the majority of people do with the language, and it is often at odds with what is considered to be correct. It sometimes happens that people will begin to use a word wrongly, and soon almost everyone is doing the same. When this happens, some linguists say that the wrong usage then becomes the right usage. If, for example, most people say and believe that the **hoi polloi** are the toffs (it actually means the common people) then that becomes the accepted meaning. If people believe that **lemmings** are little rodents that follow each other into the sea in large numbers and drown (which they do only exceedingly rarely) then that is the correct definition. **Aggravate** is another case. It means to worsen, but many people think it means to annoy (confirmed by research polls), and this belief is growing. So in your lifetime you may witness one of the wonders of English: a word that, through incorrect usage by ordinary speakers, changes its meaning.

urbane	She arrived with her rich, urbane escort. He looked utterly urbane in his string vest and seedy jacket.
usurious	The upheaval left them anxious and usurious. He had no alternative but to borrow the money at usurious rates.
uxorious	Fred's wages were completely at the mercy of his uxorious nature. She loved the room, with its faintly uxorious atmosphere.

V

Using the meanings given, fill in the gaps.

(*Answers page 197*)

vaci _ _ ate	To waver, or sway this way and that
valetu _ inarian	A chronic invalid
vapi _	Insipid, dull and flat
v _ nal	Unprincipled and ready to accept a bribe
vende _ _ a	A long-lasting blood-feud
ve _ acity	Honesty and truthfulness
verba _ im	Word for word
verisim _ litude	Appearance of being true
ver _ acular	The native language, habits or activities of a locality
ve _ nal	Pertaining to spring
vertig _ nous	Whirling round at a dizzy rate
vic _ _ ious	Experienced or imagined through the words or deeds of another
vicen _ ial	Every twenty years
vici _ _ itude	A change or variation
v _ lify	To defame
vir _ u	A taste for the rare, curious and beautiful
vis- _ -vis	In relation to
vis _ eral	Arising from the viscera, or from deep feeling
vitia _ e	To corrupt or spoil

186

v _ treous	Of glass or glasslike
vi _ uperation	Abuse in harsh language
volit _ on	Free exercise of the will
volte-f _ ce	Reversal of point of view or attitude
v _ luptuary	A person devoted to self-indulgence and luxury
vouch _ afe	To grant with condescension

Vowels

As languages go, English is not over-endowed with vowels; one Vietnamese language has 55. On the other hand, some 80,000 Abkhazo speakers in the Caucasus Mountains manage with only two. In the English language it is not unusual to find words containing all five vowels, but finding words with vowels only is rather more difficult. One of them is **euouae**, a term used in Gregorian music; another is **aiaiai**, the roseate spoonbill. And, cheating a bit, there is the ancient Tuscan city of **Oueioi**, and Circe's fabled island of **Aeaea**.

W

Which of the two meanings is correct?

(*Answers page 197*)

wagon-lit	A coach lamp, or a sleeping car on a continental train
wizened	Dried and shrivelled, or very learned
wraith	A ghostly apparition of a living person or someone who has just died, or a phosphorescent mist rising from swamp water
wrangler	One with first class mathematical honours at Cambridge University, or same at Oxford University
wunderkind	The doctrines of the Lutheran Church, or a child prodigy

---

Webster's 'dirty' dictionary

When *Webster's Third International Dictionary* was published in 1961 it caused a storm by listing such no-no's as **ain't** [Contraction of am not: 'I'm going too, ain't I?'] and **piss-poor** – which brought upon Webster's the ire of a bishop, who wrote, 'The greatest of all American dictionaries has been corrupted at the center.'

X, Y and Z

Which of the two meanings
is correct?

(*Answers page 197*)

xanthic	Ability to survive with little moisture or water, or yellowish
yahoo	Brutish half-human creature, or a type of monkey found in Madagascar
yashmak	Cheese made from yak's milk, or the veil worn by Muslim women in public
zealot	A fantatic, or an ornamental brass tray
zeitgeist	The spirit of an age, or the collective spirits of the dead
zenith	The lowest point, or the highest point
ziggurat	A terraced, pyramidal temple, or an experimental airship of the 1930s
zwieback	A wild boar, or a type of sweet cake

Answers

Where words were followed by two or three possible definitions, the definitions are identified here in order by the letters a, b and c. For example, the first word below is **abstruse**; of the three definitions, the correct one is the second one, 'hard to understand', which is identified as **b**.

A abstruse, b; accretion, a; Achilles' heel, c; acolyte, a; acrimony, b; actuary, b; acumen, b; affidavit, a; *aficionado*, b; agnostic, c; agronomy, c; akimbo, a; alfresco, c; *alter ego*, a; amalgam, a; amanuensis, b; ambidextrous, c; ambivalent, b; amortise, a; anachronism, c; analogous, c; anathema, a; *angst*, c; annul, a; animus, a; anosmia, c; antipathy, b; antonym, b; aperient, b; aphorism, c; apiarian, c; aplomb, a; apocalyptic, a; apogee, c; apposite, c; apostasy, b; appurtenance, a; aquiline, c; arachnid, c; arbitrage, a; arcane, b; argot, c; Armageddon, b; armoire, c; arraign, a; *arriviste*, a; asinine, c; assuage, b; atrophy, a; attenuate, c; attrition, b; *au fait*, b; avuncular, a

B *badinage*; bacchanalian; Bakelite; baleful; balustrade; bardolatry; bar mitzvah; baroque; bathos; bayou; beatitude; behemoth; *bel canto*; bellicose; bellwether; bemused; benign; besmirch; *bête noire*; bibelot; biennial; bifurcate; *bijou*; bilateral; binary; biopsy; blasé; blench; blithely; bona fide; *bonhomie*; bon vivant; boreal; bothy; bourgeoisie; bowdlerise; braggadocio; braise; Brobdignagian; *brouhaha*; brusque; bucolic; bulimia; bumptious; burgeoning; burlap; burnish; busboy; Byronic

C cabal, a; cabriole, a; cache, b; cajole, a; calcareous, a; callipygian, b; callisthenics, a; calumny, a; camaraderie, b; campanology, b; canard, a; candour, a; cantankerous, a; captious, b; carcanet, b; carpal, a; *carte blanche*, b; cartel, a; castellated, b; castigate, a; catalysis, a; catamite, a; catharsis, b; catheter, a; *causerie*, a; *caveat emptor*, b; cavil, a; celerity, a; chancel, b; charlatan, a; chauvinism, a; chiaroscuro, b; chicanery, b; chiffonier, a; chimera, a; choleric, b; chutzpah, b; cinéaste, a; *circa*, a; circumlocution, b; circumscribed, b; clandestine, b; clement, a; *cognoscenti*, a; colloquy, b; collude, b; comity, a; complaisant, b; concomitant, b; concupiscence, a; conflation, a; consanguinity, b; contemn, b; contretemps, a; *corpus delicti*, a; coruscate, b; costive, b; coterie, a; crapulous, b; crescendo, b; cruciform, a; crustaceans, b; cultivar, a; cupidity, b; cynosure, a; cytology, b

D dado, b; dalliance, a; dearth, b; débâcle, c; debilitate, c; *déclassé*, a; declivity, b; *de facto*, a; defalcate, b; defenestration, c; *dégagé*, a; *déjà vu*, c; deleterious, a; delphic, c; demagoguery, b; *demi-monde*, b; demotic, a; demurrer, a; dénouement, c; depilatory, b; *de rigueur*, a; desiccate, b; desultory, b; determinism, c; dextral, b; dialectic, b; dichotomy, c; didactic, a; dilatory, a; dipsomaniac, c; discommode, b; discrete, a; disparage, c; dissemble, a; distrain, a; diurnal, a; divertissement, c; doctrinaire, a; dolorous, c; double entendre, b; doughty, a; doyen, c; draconian, b; drugget, a; dudgeon, b; duodenum, c

E ebullient; effulgent; egalitarian; egocentric; egregious; *élan*; elegiac; elephantine; élite; Elysian; emanate; emancipate; emasculate; embargo; embolism; embryonic; emendate; emollient; emolument; empathy; empirical; encomium; endemic; enervate; *enfant terrible*; engender; enigma; enjoin; ennui; enormity; enunciate; ephemera; epicure; epigram; equitable; equivocal; ergonomics; erogenous; ersatz; eructation; erudite; esoteric; *esprit de corps*; ethos; etymology; eugenics; eulogise; euphemism; euphoria; Eurasian; euthanasia; evanescent; exacerbate; excoriate; exculpate; execrable; exegesis; exemplary; exorcise; expatiate; expatriate; expiate; expropriate; expurgate; extirpate

F facile, a; factotum, a; *fait accompli*, a; fallacy, b; farrago, b; fascism, a; fastidious, b; fatuous, a; *faux pas*, b; fealty, b; febrile, b; feckless, a; fecund, a; felicitous, a; feral, b; fervid, b; filibuster, b; flaccid, a; flews, b; flippant, a; florescence, a; florid, a; flout, b; foible, b; forensic, a; fortuitous, b; fractious, a; friable, b; fulgent, a; fulminate, a; fulsome, b; fundamentalism, a; furbelow, a; furlough, b

G gaffe [b] = tactless remark or blunder; gambit [a] = an opening move; gamut [a] = a whole range; garrulous [b] = talkative; gauche [b] = awkward and socially graceless; gazebo [a] = a small summerhouse with a view; gefilte fish [a] = fish meal and eggs, shaped into balls and poached; genuflect [a] = to bend the knee; germane [b] = relevant; gerrymander [a] = manipulation of electoral boundaries to give a candidate an unfair advantage; gestation [b] = the period from conception to birth; *gesundheit* [a] = 'Good Health!'; gigolo [b] = a paid male escort, or kept man; glutinous [a] = sticky; gobbet [a] = a lump or piece; gobbledegook [b] = pompous jargon; gourmandise [b] = to eat excessively; grandiose [a] = impressive, perhaps pretentiously so; gratuitous [b] = uncalled for; gravamen [a] = the key point or gist of a legal action; gregarious [a] = one who enjoys company; gumption [b] = energetic initiative

H habeas corpus, b; *habitué*, a; hackneyed, b; hagiography, c; ha-ha, a; halcyon, a; halitosis, c; hapless, c; harbinger, a; hector, c; hegemony, b; heinous, b; hellebore, b; heresy, a; heterogeneous, b; heuristic, a; hiatus, a; Hibernian, b; hindsight, c; histology, a; hogmanay, a; *hoi polloi*, b; hologram, c; homogeneous, a; honorarium, b; hortatory, c; hubris, a; humanism, b; humdrum, b; hydrology, a; hygrometer, a; hyperbole, a

I iconoclast; idiomatic; idiosyncrasy; idolatry; ignominy; imbroglio; immolate; immured; immutable; impasse; implacable; importune; imprimatur; impromptu; impugn; inadvertent; incipient; incognito; inculcate; incumbent; indemnity; indigenous; indigent; ineffable; ineluctable; inexorable; *infra dig*; *ingénue*; ingenuous; inimical; innate; innocuous; innuendo; insalubrious; insidious; insouciant; *inter alia*; interdict; internecine; interstice; intransigent; intrinsic; introvert; inveigh; invidious; irascible; irrevocable

J jaundiced, a; jejune, b; jeopardy, a; jeremiad, b; jettison, a; jihad, a; jingoism, b; jocose, a; *joie de vivre*, a; junta, a; juvenescence, b; juxtapose, a

K karma [b] = destiny; kibbutz [a] = an Israeli community farm; kitsch [a] = sentimental, garish or pretentious (usually art); kleptomaniac [a] = obsessive thief; kosher [b] = food prepared in accordance with Jewish dietary laws; kowtow [b] = to behave in a servile way; kudos [b] = praise and credit

L lachrymose, b; laconic, a; lacuna, a; laity, b; *laissez-faire*, c; lambent, b; lampoon, b; languor, a; largess, c; lascivious, a; latent, a; lateral, c; laudable, b; legerdemain, b; leitmotif, a; *lèse-majesté*, c; lethargic, b; libido, b; libretto, a; licentious, a; lickerish, c; lionize, b; lissom, c; locum tenens, a; logorrhea, b; *longueur*, c; loquacious, a; Lothario, a; *louche*, c; lubricious, c; lugubrious, a; lumpen, b

M macerate, b; Machiavellian, a; macrocosm, a; magisterial, a; *magnum opus*, b; maladroit, a; malaise, b; malapropism, b; *mal de mer*, b; malfeasance, b; Malthusian, a; maudlin, a; maunder, b; *mea culpa*, b; megalomania, b; megrim, a; *mélange*, a; mêlée, b; mellifluous, b; ménage, a; mendacious, a; mendicant, b; mephitic, a; meretricious, b; mesmerise, a; metabolism, a; *métier*, a; metronymic, b; micron, b; micturate, b; milieu, a; millennium, a; minatory, a; misanthropy, b; miscegenation, b; misnomer, a; misogyny, a; mnemonic, b; moiety, a; moire, b; monograph, b; moratorium, a; moribund, a; *mot juste*, b; mufti, b; mundane, a; myocardiogram, b; myopia, b

N nadir; nascent; nebulous; necropsy; nefarious; negus; nemesis; neologism; neophyte; nephritis; nepotism; nexus; nihilism; noisome; nonage; nonchalant; *non sequitur*; nostrum; nubile; nugatory

O obdurate, b; obeisance, a; obfuscate, c; obloquy, c; obsequious, b; obsolescent, a; obstreperous, a; obviate, c; occidental, b; occlude, b; odium, a; odontologist, c; oenologist, b; *oeuvre*, c; oligarchy, b; omniscient, a; opprobrium, a; oracular, b; orotund, c; ossified, b; ostensibly, a; ostentatious, b; osteopathy, c; otiose, a; *outré*, c; overt, b

P paediatrician, b; palaver, a; palpable, a; panacea, a;
panache, a; Panglossian, a; panegyric, b; panjandrum, b;
pantheism, a; paparazzi, b; paradigm, a; paragon, b;
parameter, b; paramour, b; paranoia, b; paraphrase, a;
pariah, b; *pari mutuel*, b; parlous, b; parsimony, b;
parvenu, a; *passé*, b; pastiche, a; paterfamilias, a;
pathogenic, b; patina, b; patisserie, a; patrial, a; patrician, b;
Pecksniffian, b; pectorals, a; pedagogue, b; pedantry, a;
peignoir, b; pejorative, a; pellucid, a; percipient, b;
peregrination, a; peremptory, b; perennial, b;
perfunctory, a; peripatetic, b; periphrasis, a; pernicious, b;
peroration, b; perquisite, a; persiflage, a; perspicacious, b;
pertinacious, b; philanderer, a; philistine, a; phlegmatic, b;
physiognomy, b; picayune, a; *pied-à-terre*, a; pinnate, b;
pixilated, a; placebo, a; plagiarism, b; plangent, a;
Platonic, b; plebeian, b; plenary, a; plethora, a;
plutocracy, a; podiatry, b; poignant, b; poltroon, b;
polymath, b; potable, a; preciosity, a; predicate, a;
predilection, b; prehensile, b; prescient, a; prevaricate, a;
prima facie, b; probity, b; proclivity, a; prolapse, b;
prolix, a; propinquity, b; propitious, b; pro rata, b;
proscribe, a; proselytise, b; prosthesis, a; protean, a;
provenance, b; prurient, b; psychosomatic, a; puerile, a;
puissant, b; pukka, a; pulchritude, b; pullulate, b;
punctilious, a; purlieus, b; pusillanimous, b; putative, a;
putti, b; Pyrric victory, a

Q quasi [a] = having the semblance of, not quite, querulous
[a] = of a complaining disposition; quiddity [b] = the essence
or uniqueness of something; quidnunc [a] = a gossip; quietus
[a] = final conclusion; quixotic [b] = possessing high but
impractical aims; quondam [b] = former; quorum [b] = an
agreed number of people required to be present before a
meeting can be held; quotidian [a] = occurring daily

R Rabelaisian; raconteur; raffish; raillery; *raison d'être*; rancour; rapport; *rapprochement*; *rara avis*; ratiocination; raucous; reactionary; rebarbative; recalcitrant; recant; recherché; recidivism; recondite; recrudesce; rectitude; redolent; redoubtable; referendum; refractory; refulgent; renege; reprehend; repudiate; retrograde; *retroussé*; rhetorical; rictus; riparian; riposte; risible; rococo; roué; rumbustious

S salacious, a; salient, a; salutary, b; sang-froid, b; sardonic, a; Sassenach, a; saturnine, b; *savoir-faire*, b; scaramouch, a; scatology, b; *Schadenfreude*, a; scintilla, b; scrivener, a; scut, a; sebaceous, b; secular, b; sedulous, a; semantics, b; semiotics, a; senescent, b; sententious, b; sequestered, b; serendipitous, a; serrated, a; shibboleth, a; sibilant, b; silviculture, b; similitude, a; simony, b; simulacrum, a; sinecure, a; sinistral, b; skulk, a; sobriquet, b; sodality, b; soi-disant, b; *soigné*, a; soirée, a; solecism, b; solipsism, a; sommelier, b; somnambulism, b; sonorous, a; sophistry, a; soporific, b; *sotto voce*, b; spavined, a; specious, a; splenetic, b; sporadic, b; stasis, a; stentorian, b; stultify, a; stygian, b; subliminal, a; subsume, a; succinct, b; supercilious, b; supernumerary, a; suppurate, b; surrogate, a; svelte, a; sybaritic, b; sycophantic, a; symbiosis, a; synergy, b; syntax, a

T tachometer, c; tacit, b; tactile, b; talisman, a; tangible, c; taupe, b; telekinesis, c; temerity, a; temporal, c; temporise, a; tendentious, b; tenet, b; tenuous, a; tercentenary, b; tessellated, a; theism, b; thrall, b; timorous, a; tinnitus, c; tocsin, a; torpid, a; tort, b; tractable, c; traduce, a; tranche, c; transcend, a; transient, b; travail, a; tremulous, c; trenchant, a; trichology, c; tridactyl, b; triptych, a; triumvirate, b; troglodyte, c; *trompe l'oeil*, b; trope, a; truncate, a; tumescent, c; turbid, a; turpitude, a; tyro, c

U ubiquitous [a] = existing everywhere; ullage [b] = the space in a container not taken up by its contents; ullulate [b] = to howl or wail; umbrage [a] = a sense of slight or injury; unconscionable [a] = going beyond reasonable bounds; unctuous [b] = excessively suave and moralising; unilateral [b] = something done or undertaken by a single person or party; urbane [a] = polite and polished; usurious [b] = extortionate interest on loans; uxorious [a] = excessive doting on a wife

V vacillate; valetudinarian; vapid; venal; vendetta; veracity; verbatim; verisimilitude; vernacular; vernal; vertiginous; vicarious; vicennial; vicissitude; vilify; virtu; vis-a-vis; visceral; vitiate; vitreous; vituperation; volition; volte-face; voluptuary; vouchsafe

W wagon-lit, b; wizened, a; wraith, a; wrangler, a; wunderkind, b

X, Y and Z xanthic, b; yahoo, a; yashmak, b; zealot, a; zeitgeist, a; zenith, b; ziggurat, a; zwieback, b

Word playtime The four words each contain all five vowels. The four-letter word common to all the sports listed is *hook*.

Know what I mean? 1. cornice   2. clutch pedal
3. Braille   4. groynes   5. davenport   6. phrenology
7. Clydesdale   8. zodiac   9. karaoke   10. tic-tac men

The nous on dous hazardous, horrendous, stupendous and tremendous

Questions! Questions! 1. papillote 2. loupe
3. cattery 4. topiary 5. perforations 6. risers

Two or more of a kind 1. A *pack* of hounds 2. A
murder of crows 3. A *covey* of partridges 4. A *business* of
ferrets 5. A *dray* of squirrels 6. A *pride/troop* of lions
7. An *exaltation* of larks 8. A *chattering* of starlings
9. A *herd* of whales 10. A *mustering* of storks

Spelling

One in ten is a dunce at spelling

One in ten adults who took a simple spelling test for a survey failed to provide a single correct answer. Only one in six scored full marks.

One thousand people were asked by Gallup to spell necessary, accommodation, sincerely, business, separate and height. Women performed better than men, with more than 40 per cent scoring at least five compared with 30 per cent of the men. Only 27 per cent of those tested could spell accommodation.

The findings were disclosed yesterday at the launch in London of two video films aimed at improving spelling and grammar. Alan Wells, of the Adult Literacy and Basic Skills Unit, said the survey highlighted a "sad state of affairs" with more than four million adults estimated to be struggling to read and write.

The Times, 12 November 1992

Introduction

Perhaps there are people who are always one hundred per cent sure of their spelling, but you won't meet them often. More likely, they could be fooling themselves.

On the spur of the moment, how many of us can write down words like abrogate, afficionado, anomalousness, apophthegm and abysmal (Oops! One of those was misspelled) with the absolute assurance that they are all spelled correctly? Or the names of the famous Mogul temple at Agra in India, or the French national anthem, or the title of the Persian poem which contains the line, 'A jug of Wine, a Loaf of Bread – and Thou'? How about the President of Libya? Citizens of Monaco? Never mind that it's Magdalen College in Oxford and Magdalene College in Cambridge; the Colosseum in Rome and the Coliseum in London; a good many of us get stuck at Piccadilly and Marylebone!

Bad spelling isn't necessarily a sign of illiteracy or lack of intelligence; it's an indication that we're only part-way through the task of mastering the vast lexicon of words in the English language. A faulty memory, poor word or letter recognition, even basic human laziness can all contribute to standards of spelling ranging from the unreadable, inarticulate and sloppy to the occasional but embarrassing lapse.

The difficulty begins with the way in which written English handles the sounds of the language. We use around forty different sounds to express ourselves, yet have only twenty-six letters in our alphabet with which to write them down. This means that certain letter combinations have to double for different sounds, which enabled George Bernard Shaw to demonstrate that *fish* could be spelled as *ghoti*: *gh* as in *cough*, *o* as in *women* and *ti* as in *nation*.

It is also a fact that whatever it is, English has a word for it; so it is no surprise that against the Russian language with some 130,000 words and the French with around 150,000, the complete English dictionary will contain between 400,000 and half a million words. That's a lot to learn and remember, so you are excused the occasional slip-up.

We must also grapple with the problem that almost half the words we use are not English at all. From the Vikings on, we have begged, borrowed and stolen words (and have had a good many thrust upon us), few of which follow the rules of spelling, such as they are. All these rules seem to have inconvenient exceptions – the 'i' before 'e' except after 'c' rule is an instance of this. So the spelling of English is a real minefield, not rendered any less hazardous by the pernicious habit of modern commerce of introducing non-words like *pak*, *kool*, *kleen*, *arrid* and *squeez-ee*.

On the plus side, however, the English speller does not have to cope with funny little strokes, eyebrows and dots over the letters, nor with having to remember whether a word is masculine or feminine. Its rules, however complex they may seem, are child's play compared with many other languages.

English is a rich and bubbling brew, at the same time wild and disciplined, reinventing itself constantly, and capable, almost, of expressing the inexpressible. That is probably why, today, it is held in the highest esteem as an instrument of international communication, of learning, of creative vision. It is already the first language of 350 million people and the official language of a billion more. You can't beat it, so why not join it – and improving your spelling skills would make a good start.

One Thousand Most Misspelled Words

(Plus a sprinkling of real stinkers and foreign words)

abate, abatable
abattoir
abbreviate
abdominal
aberration
abrogate
abscess, abscesses
abstemious
abyss, abysmal
accelerate, accelerator
accessory
acclimatize
accolade
accommodate, accommodation
accompanist
accrue
achievable, achievement
acknowledgement
acolyte
acoustic
acquaintance
acquiescence
acquire
acquittal, acquitted
acumen
acupuncture
addressee
adenoid

adieu [in Spanish, *adios*]
adjunct
admissibility
adolescence
ad nauseam
adulatory
advantageous
adventitious
aegis
aerial
aesthete, aesthetic
aficionado
a fortiori
ageing
agent provocateur
agglomeration
aggrandize
aggrieve
agribusiness
aide memoire
à la carte
alienation
alimentary
allege, alleging
alter ego
amanuensis, amanuenses (pl)
ambidextrous
amoeba
amortization
amphibious
anachronism
anaemia
anaesthetic, anaesthesia, anaesthetize
analytical
anathema
ancillary
androgynous
animadvert
annihilate, annihilation

annotate, annotator
annulment
anodyne
anomalous
anomie
anonymous, anonymously, anonymity
antecedent

If This Student Received a 'B' in GCSE English, Does it Make You Feel Like a Genius?

A few gems from the English paper of a 16-year-old that earned a B grade: cuircus, headake, bargin, libray, coushon (cushion), safaty, pationt, earlyst, simaler (similar), equaly, mearley (merely), appreachiate, familer, imeadiate, brouch, matiri (materially), cemitry, leasure, frerternali (fraternally), misalanios (miscellaneous) . . .

---

antediluvian
antenna
antipodean
aphrodisiac
apocalypse
apophthegm
apoplectic
apostasy

Majority of illterates live in Third World

From the newspaper *The Muslim on Sunday*

---

apostrophe
appal, appalled, appalling
apparel
apparently
appellant, appellate
appendectomy
appliqué
apposite
approbate
appurtenance
arbitrage, arbitrary
arboretum
archetypal
archipelago
areola [human tissue]; aureola [halo]
armadillos
armoire
arpeggio
arraign
arriviste
arrondissement
ascendancy
asphyxiate
asphalt
assassin, assassination
assuage
asthma, asthmatic
atelier
attenuate
aubergine
auxiliary
avocado
awesome

baccalaureate
bacchanalian
bacillus

'Ullo, 'Ullo! Wot's This 'Ere Then?

The following is a sampling of language misdemeanours committed in a London police station's crime reports. Articles reported stolen included a four birth tent, a Ford Cubrololey (Cabriolet), an Alpha Romeo, several garden gnombs and a carkey jacket. Offences were committed at Hybry (Highbury) Corner and Sidnum (Sydenham), and one suspect, who gained entry by forcing a skylark, was described as wearing a pale blue suite. Another was probably a Frenchman, as he was wearing a leather berry. Fair cop, guv?

baguette
bailiff
balalaika
balletomane
ballot, balloted, balloting
balustrade, banister
barbiturate
baroque
barrel, barrelled
bas-relief
bayonet, bayoneted
beatitude
belligerent
benefice, beneficence, beneficial
biannual (twice yearly); biennial (every two years)
bias, biased
bijou
bilingual
bilious
billet-doux
bimetallism
biopsy

bituminous
bivouac, bivouacking
blancmange
bogie (under-carriage); bogey (golf); bogy (ghostly)
bonhomie
bon vivant
bouillabaisse
boule
bourgeois, bourgeoisie
braggadocio

Twenty Most Misspelled Words

Early in 1992 *The Sunday Times* commissioned a
leading UK examination board to test a sample
of 1,500 secretaries, clerks, administrative and
office trainees for ability to spell everyday words.
Four words were misspelled by more than half
the sample. Here are the full results, showing the
percentage getting each word wrong:

Word	%	Word	%
practice/practise	54	competent	37
withhold	52	calendar	35
occurred	52	warranty	35
innovate	52	acquire	34
benefited	48	liaise	34
principal/principle	45	truly	34
incur	44	expedite	33
grievance	40	discrete/discreet	33
concede	40	affect/effect	32
transferred	39	accommodation	32

With the word pairs, the percentages are those
who could not identify or spell the correct word
in sentences such as, 'the principle/principal of
the college visited the faculty'. Worse, 11% got
'secretary' wrong, and 7% could not spell 'train'.

bric-à-brac
broccoli
brougham
brusque
budgerigar
bulrush
bureaucracy, bureaucrat

cabriolet
cachet
caesarean
caffeine
caique
calendar (of days, weeks, months)
calibre
callisthenics
calypso
camaraderie
camellia
carburettor (carburetter also acceptable)
carcass
caress
carat (fineness of gold; weight of precious stones)
carpeted, carpeting
carte blanche
casualty
cataclysm
cataloguing
catarrh
catechism
cauliflower
caveat
centenary, centennial
cerebellum
cerebrum
chaise longue
champignon
chandelier
changeable, changeability

chargé d'affaires
charismatic
chauffeur
chauvinism
chiaroscuro
chiffonier
chihuahua
chinoiserie
chlorophyll
cholesterol
chromosome

Howlers

Poor spelling is not always a serious matter. Try keeping a straight face through these student howlers:

- Russians use the acrylic alphabet
- Daniel Defoe wrote simply and sometimes crudly
- At Nelson's funeral, fifty sailors carried the beer after laying in state on a catapult
- Paris was once haunted by many cortisones
- Thomas Gray wrote the *Alergy in a Country Churchyard*
- Before a caterpillar becomes a butterfly it is a syphilis
- Alfred Tennyson was England's famous poet lariat
- I enjoy being embossed in a good book

---

cicada
cirrhosis
clairvoyant, clairvoyance
clandestine
clarinet, clarinettist
cliché

climacteric
clique, cliquish
cloisonné
coalesce
cognoscente (plural is cognoscenti)
coleslaw
colitis
colloquial, colloquy
colonnade
coloratura
colossal, collosus
combated, combating, combative
commemorate
commensurate
commiserate
commissary
committed, committal
commodore
communiqué
complaisant
concomitant
concours d'élégance
concupiscent
condominium
confrère
connoisseur
connubial
consanguinity
conscientious
consensus
consummate
contemporaneous
continuum
contractual
contretemps
cordon bleu
cornucopia
coronary
corpuscle

correlate
corrigendum
coup (takeover); coupé (car)
crèche
crochet (knitting); crotchet (music)
croupier
cuisine
cul-de-sac
cystitis (bladder); cytitis (skin)

> **STRONG MEDICINE:** The results of the office workers' spelling test do not astonish me. When my son started at his comprehensive school in 1972, I was told by the teachers of the English department that spelling was not taught because it did not matter.
>
> A teacher at my daughter's primary school took a different view. He thought spelling did matter. Encountering "medycine", so spelled, in my daughter's work, he sternly amended it to "medecine".

This letter to *The Times* from a reader indicates that not all teachers, despite the best intentions, get it right!

dachshund
débâcle
début, débutante
deceased (dead, follows being diseased, or ill)
deciduous
décor, decorum
deleterious

delicatessen
delirium
demonstrable
deodorize, deodorizer
dependence, dependent, dependency
de rigueur
desiccate
détente
deter, deterring, deterrent
diabetes
diaphragm
diarrhoea
dichotomy
dilettante
dinghy
diphtheria
dismissible
dissimilar
dissociate
divertissement
domino, dominoes
double entendre (rarely double entente)
drachma
duodenum
dysentery

ebullient
ecclesiastical
echelon
ecstasy
eczema
edge, edging
effervescence
effloresce
effrontery
egalitarian
eighth
eisteddfod
electrolysis

elegiac
embryo, embryos
emolument
enamel, enamelled, enamelling
enfant terrible
enforceable
ensuing

entrée
entrepreneur
envelop (to wrap); envelope (for letters)
epitome
equivocal
erroneous
estrangement
eulogize; eulogy
euthanasia
exaggerate, exaggeration
exculpate
exegesis
exhilarate, exhilaration
exhumation
expatriate
extirpate
extrasensory

facetious
facia (also fascia)
fahrenheit
fait accompli
fallacy, fallible, fallibility
faux pas
fiasco, fiascos
flamboyant
fledgeling
fluorescence
focus, focused, focusing
foetus
forbade, forbid
forbear (patience; also ancestor), forbearance
forebode, foreboding
forego, foregone (to go before); *see* forgo
foreman
forewarn
forfeit
forge, forging
forgo, forgone (to go without); *see* forego
fortieth
fortuitous
Fräulein
fuchsia
fugue
fulfil, fulfilled, fulfilling, fulfilment
fullness
fulsome
furore
fuselage
fusilier, fusillade

gallop, galloped, galloping, galloper
gargantuan
garnishee
garrulous
gaseous
gasoline (increasingly used over gasolene)

gastric, gastritis
gay, gaily, gaiety
gelatinous
gemmology
genius, geniuses (the plural is not genii!)
geriatric
germane
gerrymander
gesundheit
geyser
ghoul
gigolo

More on (or Moron) GCSE Grades

Asked to describe the landing of an aircraft, a young student was awarded a D grade in GCSE English for this effort: 'A preuer shape was apporching from the southern valley graerly they disitusis recililly design aeroplane cirlcing above'. Another student did rather better and was given a C grade: 'The machine touched down with prissision in the rough mountqiness regane, with out even scraping its' serface'. Other candidates got C grades despite these minor transgressions: polosy (policy); amitter (amateur); ensiatic (enthusiastic); morage (mortgage); headech (headache) and carm (calm).

gladiolus, gladioli (plural)
glassful, glassfuls (plural)
glaucoma
glutinous
gnome, gnomic
gonorrhea
gouache
goulash
gourmet (appreciates food); gourmand (glutton)
grammar
grandeur
grandiloquent
gratuitous
grievance, grievous
groin
guarantee, guarantor
gubernatorial
guerrilla (warfare)
guillotine
gymkhana
gymnasium
gynaecology

habeas corpus
habitué
haemoglobin
haemorrhage, haemorrhoids
halcyon
handful, handfuls
hara-kiri
harangue
harass
hashish
hausfrau
hauteur
heinous
herbaceous
hereditary
hermaphrodite

herpes
heterogeneous, heterogeneity
heterosexual
hiatus
hiccup
hierarchy
hirsute
histamine
histrionic
hoeing
holocaust
hombre
homoeopath
homogenous, homogeneity
homo sapiens
honorarium, honorary, honorific
hors-d'oeuvre
humerus (arm bone)
hullabaloo
humour, humorous, humorist
hundredth
hyacinth

Enquire or Inquire: Enquiry or Inquiry?

Although, by a fine margin, the *Oxford English Dictionary* prefers INquire, it still remains a free choice. ENquire is the Old French and Middle English form, while INquire is the Latinized version. Caxton (inquyred), Spenser (inquere), Bacon and Tennyson plumped for the IN prefix, while Chaucer (enquyrid), Shakespeare and Milton preferred the EN style. Some draw the fine distinction between enquire (to ask a question) and inquire (to investigate). In America it is inquire, as it always is in *The Sunday Times*.

hydrangea
hyperbole (exaggeration); hyperbola (curve)
hypnosis
hypochondria
hypocrisy
hypotenuse
hypothesis, hypotheses (plural)
hysteria, hysterical

ichthyosaurus
idiosyncrasy
imminent (impending) – not to be confused with
    eminent (important) or immanent (inherent or
    permanent)
immeasurable
immense, immensely
immobile
immovable
impassable, impasse
impeccable
impresario
impressionism
imprimatur
impromptu
incandescent
incidentally
incisor
incognito
incumbent, incumbency
indefatigable
indefensible
independent, independence
indict, indictment
indigenous
indigestible
indispensable
indivisible
inexhaustible
inexpressible

infinitesimal
inflammation, inflammable, inflammatory
inflatable
ingenious (inventive); ingenuous (naive)
inherit, inheritance, inheritor
inimical
innocuous
innuendo
inoculate
inquire (*see* 'Enquire or Inquire', p. 218)
insolvent, insolvency
insouciant, insouciance
install, installation, instalment
insular
insure (to secure); ensure (to make certain)
insurrection
intelligent, intelligence, intelligible, intelligentsia
intercede
intermezzo
internecine
inter, interred, interment
interrogate, interrogation
interrupt, interrupter
intransigent
inveigle
irascible
iridescent
irreconcilable
irreparable
irrestible
irretrievable
irrevocable
isosceles
isotype
itinerant, itinerary

jamb
jardinière

Letters to *The Times*, 1991

Geometric change
From Mr Colin Dixon

Sir, Having just completed the marking of GCSE mathematics papers for a national examining group, I am fully convinced that the silly season is upon us once more. From the first 100 scripts marked the following spellings of a well-known triangle were gleaned:

Isocilies, isosoles, isosceleses, isoseles, iscoseles, iscoseles, iscocelles, isoceles, isosoclles, isoscles, isocoles, isoscoles, isocelesse, issocelles, isosales, isosalies, isosceles, icosolese, issoles, isosillies, issocelles, isoscellies, iscolesces, iscosles, iscoelise, iscocelleses, iscosoleses, iscolilis, ososellese.

On the assumption that words change by popular demand, then change is inevitable, but to which spelling?

Yours sincerely,
COLIN DIXON

Geometric change
From Mr Andrew Ashton

Sir, I read with interest the letter from Mr Colin Dixon (July 4) concerning the spelling of isosceles. He counted 29 different spellings in marking 100 examination scripts.

It reminded me of an excellent mnemonic, that would have been of use to his candidates. I learnt it in my school days at Newcastle Royal Grammar School and have used it ever since: 'I saw our Sherpas climb Everest last Easter Sunday'.

I wonder how many versions of the word 'parallel' Mr Dixon found.

Yours sincerely,
ANDREW ASHTON

From Mrs Anne Mathews

Sir, Mathematics pupils have to be taught the meaning of the word 'isoceles' before they can use it: if a teacher explains that 'iso' comes from 'isos', Greek for 'equal' and 'sceles' from 'skelos', Greek for 'leg', surely the pupils will have a better chance of remembering both meaning and spelling. They will also realise that there is both interest and practicality in knowing a little Greek.

Yours sincerely,
ANNE MATHEWS

jejune
jewel, jeweller, jewellery
jocose, jocund
jodhpur
joie de vivre
judgement (judgment in legal works)
juggernaut
juicy, juiciness
jurisprudence
juvenilia
juxtapose, juxtaposition

kaleidoscope
khaki
kleptomania
kohlrabi (the vegetable)

label, labelled, labelling
laboratory
laborious
labyrinth, labyrinthine
lackadaisical
lacquer
laissez faire
lama (Buddhist priest); llama (S. American animal)
languor, languorous
largess (although the French, largesse, is often used)
larrikin
laryngitis, larynx
lascivious
lassitude
lasso, lassoed, lassoing
laudable, laudatory
legitimize
leitmotiv (sometimes hyphenated: leit-motiv)
leprechaun
lèse-majesté
leukaemia
level, levelled, levelling

liaise, liaison
licence (a permit or authorization)
license (to permit or allow), licenser or licensor,
    licentiate
lieutenant
like, likeable
likely, likeliest
lineage (ancestry); linage (number of lines)
lingua franca
liquefy, liquefaction
liquorice
littérateur
locum-tenens
longevity
loquacious
louvre
lustre, lustrous

macabre
mackerel
mackintosh
maelstrom
maestro
maharajah
mahogany
maisonette
majolica
mal de mer
manage, manageable, management
manikin
mannequin
manoeuvre, manoeuvred, manoeuvrable
manqué
maraschino
mariage de convenance
marijuana
marriageable
marvel, marvelled, marvellous
masochism

massacre, massacred, massacring
massage, masseur, masseuse
matriarch, matriarchal
mayonnaise
menagerie
meretricious
meringue
metamorphosis

From Bad to Worse A large sample of schoolchildren was given a spelling test in 1984, which was repeated with a similar sample in 1989. During the intervening five years, the percentage increase of misspelled words rose markedly:

	1984	1989
bargain	14%	25%
library	14%	21%
merely	26%	39%
politician	33%	41%
exaggerate	43%	56%
committee	57%	75%
leisure	22%	33%
sufficient	29%	38%
appreciate	24%	30%
permanent	45%	51%

---

mezzanine
migraine
mileage (although milage is acceptable)
milieu
millennium, millennial
minuscule
mischievous
misfeasance
misogyny
misspelt (misspelled is a longer alternative)
mistakable

mnemonic
moccasin
model, modelled, modelling
monastery
moratorium
moustache
myopia
myxomatosis

nadir
narcissus, narcissi, narcissistic, narcissism
nascent
neophyte
nephritis
neuralgia
neurasthenia
niece
noblesse oblige
noisome
non sequitur
nouveau riche
nuptial

oasis, oases (plural)
obbligato
obdurate
obeisance
obfuscate
obnoxious
obsequious
obsolete, obsolescent, obsolescence
obstetrics, obstetrician
obstreperous
occur, occurred, occurrence, occurring
octogenarian
odyssey
oesophagus
offence, offensive
olympiad

omniscient, omniscience
omnivorous
onerous
opaque
opportunely
opportunity
opprobrium
orthopaedic
oscillate, oscillating, oscillatory, oscilloscope
osmosis
outré
overall
overrate; overreach; override; overrule; overrun

paean
page, paging, pagination
palaeontology
palate, palatable
palette
palliasse
panacea
panache
pancreas
pandemonium
papier-mâché
papyrus, papyri (plural)

High IQ Doesn't Mean Good Spelling

A recent study of 114 pupils at Strode sixth-form
college in Surrey found that although their IQs
were above average, their scores in spelling tests
were below the standard expected of the average
16-year-old in 1977. Fewer than one in five could
spell words such as erroneous, accommodate,
allegiance, eligible and villainy. One in three
misspelled the words foreign and initials.

paraffin
parallel, paralleled, parallelogram, parallax
paralyse, paralysis
paraphernalia
parenthesis, parentheses (plural)
pari-mutuel
paroxysm
parquet, parquetry
pass, passable
passé
pasteurise
pastiche
pâté de foie gras
pavilion
peccadillo, peccadilloes
pedal, pedalled, pedalling
pejorative
pelargonium
pencil, pencilled, pencilling
penicillin
peninsula
penitentiary
penny, penniless
perceive, perceiving, perceivable
peremptory
perennial
periphery
permissible
perorate, peroration
perquisite
personnel
perspicacious
phantasmagoria
pharmacopoeia
phenomenon, phenomena (plural)
phlebitis
phlegm
phonetic
phosphorescence

phosphorus (the element), phosphorous (the adjective)
phylloxera
physique
pibroch
picket, picketing
picnic, picnicked, picnicking, picnicker
pièce de résistance
pied-à-terre
pituitary
pity, pitied, pitiful, pitiable, pitiless
plateau, plateaux (plural)
playwright
plebeian
plethora
pneumatic
pneumonia
poliomyelitis
polythene, polyurethane
pomegranate
poseur
posthumous
potato, potatoes (plural)
preciosity
predecessor
predilection
prefer, preference, preferred, preferring
premiere
prescience
presentient
preventive
prima facie
primordial
principal (the chief)
principle (the code of conduct)
profit, profited, profiting, profiteer
promiscuous
promissory
pronounce, pronounceable, pronouncement,
    pronunciation

The Prevalence of Preventative

Why use preventative when the shorter preventive means exactly the same? Mr V Edwards, of Sittingbourne, Kent, admonishes users of the former with this little rhyme:

> Who coined the word preventative?
> Was there an incentative
> For someone so inventative?
> And could we hear of villains held
> In custody detentative?

propeller, propelled, propelling
prophecy (the forecast); prophesy (to forecast)
prophylactic, prophylaxis
proprietary
proselyte, proselytism, proselytize
prosthesis

Ptantalizing Ptongue Ptwisters

The English language abounds with words containing 'silent letters' (doubt, psalm, knot, sword, solemn, etc) but perhaps none so strange as the 'pt' words. Here are a few:

ptarmigan – a mostly white, grouse-like bird
pterodactyl – extinct featherless flying reptile
pterylology – the study of birds' feathers
ptilosis – a disorder of the eyelashes
ptisan – a barley water drink
Ptolemy – the Greek astronomer and
     mathematician
ptomaine poisoning – from eating putrefied food

protégé, protégée (feminine)
pseudonym
psoriasis
psychology; psychoanalysis; psychiatry; psychopathy;
    psychosomatic; psychotic
puerile
pulchritude
punctilious
purée
pusillanimity, pusillanimous
pyjamas (pajamas in the US)
pyrrhic

quadruped
quarrel, quarrelled, quarrelling, quarrelsome
quatrefoil
quay, quayside
questionnaire
queue
quietus
quixotic
quotient

rabbi, rabbis
racoon (raccoon in the US)
radius, radii (plural)
raison d'être
rancour, rancorous
ranunculus
rapprochement
rare, rarefy, rarefaction
rate, rateable, rating
rationale
recalcitrant
receivable
recherché
reciprocal
recognise, recognisable, recognisance
recommend, recommendation

recondite
reconnaissance, reconnoitre
recumbent
redundant
refer, referred, referring, reference, referendum
régime
rehabilitate
reiterate
rejuvenescence
reminiscence
remonstrate, remonstrator
renaissance
repellent
repertoire
replace, replaceable, replacement
reprehensible
reprieve
repudiate

The 'Bad Spelling' Syndrome

In the 1980s it was not uncommon for some
parents, perhaps in despair, to wonder if there
was a 'bad spelling' syndrome running in the
family – the members of which (grandparents,
parents, children) were intelligent but simply
couldn't spell. Experts soon raced to the rescue
with the theory that such people were sinistrocular
(a tendency to use the left eye rather than the
right) and were not taught to read phonetically
but by 'look and say word sheet' methods –
wonderful for the majority who are dextral (right-
handed) and able to combine word recognition
with reading. The left-handers, it is claimed, have
difficulty with the word recognition method,
retaining only a hazy recollection of the correct
order of letters. The jury's still out on this one.

rescue, rescued, rescuing, rescuable
resplendent
restaurant, restaurateur
resurrection
resuscitate
retroactive
rheumatism
rhinoceros
rhododendron
rhubarb
ricochet, ricocheted, ricocheting
riposte
risqué
riveted, riveting
rotisserie
roughage

sabbatical
saccharin (the substance)
saccharine (sugary)
sacrilege, sacrilegious
sacrosanct
sagacious
salubrious
salutary
samurai
sanatorium (plural sanatoria or sanatoriums); often
    sanitarium in the US
sanctimonious
sanguine, sanguinary
sapphire
sarsaparilla
satellite
sauerkraut
savoir faire
schnapps
schooner
sciatica
scimitar

scintillate
sclerosis
scurrilous
scythe
seance
secateurs
secretary, secretariat, secretaire
seismic
seize
sepulchre, sepulchral
serendipity
shibboleth
shillelagh
siege
silhouette, silhouetted
sinecure
siphon, siphoning
sirocco
sizable
smorgasbord
sobriquet
soliloquy
somersault, somersaulting
sommelier
somnambulism
sophomore
soufflé
soupçon
sphagnum moss
spontaneous, spontaneously, spontaneity
staccato
stalactite (hanging); stalagmite (rising)
stationary (still, fixed); stationery (paper)
stiletto, stilettos (plural)
story (tale); storey (floor of building)
straight (line); strait (sea channel); strait-laced
strychnine
stupefy, stupefied, stupefying
subpoena, subpoenaed

subterranean
succinct
suffrage, suffragette
sulphanilamide
sumptuous
superannuation, superannuated
supercilious

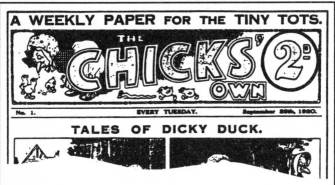

Ask Mum-my to buy 'Chicks' Own' ev-er-y Tues-day

When the children's comic paper *Chicks' Own* was launched in 1920 it became the world's first comic to be entirely printed in hyphenated syllables. It, and its later rivals, also became the vehicle by which hundreds of thousands of young children learned to read. A reader of *The Sunday Times*, Jennifer Gilbert, remembered how 'my mother's finger traced below the words and helped me assemble longer ones by building up the clearly separated syllables. As a result, I was an efficient reader when I went to school at four. The comic was an excellent example of the old-fashioned syllabic method of learning to read, and I owe my lifetime devotion to the printed word to it.' Reading was hy-phen-a-ted fun for ev-er-y one!

superintendent
supersede
suppository
suppress, suppression, suppressor
surrealism
surreptitious
surrogate
surveillance
sycophant, sycophancy
syllabub
syllabus, syllabuses (plural)
symmetry
synchronous
syncopate, syncopation
synonymous, synonymously
synopsis, synopses (plural)
synthesis, synthetic
syphilis
syringe, syringeing
syrup, syrupy

The Wurd Burglrs Ar At It Agen

Once a year, it seems, there is a fresh effort to
simplify spelling, and to introduce words like
'naw' (gnaw), 'dum' (dumb) and 'det' (debt).
Speling made eezy sounds like a good idea, but
so far every effort has finished on the junk pile.
Even the Simplifyd Speling Society (for that is
how they spell it) has difficulty getting its message
across. One of their press releases began,
'Aulmoest evrithing that we reed iz tiypskript at
sum staej . . .' Well, bak to the droring bord . . .

---

tableau, tableaux (plural)
table d'hôte
tachometer

tacit, tacitly
taciturn
taipan
tarantula
tattoo, tattooed, tattooing
telecommunications
temperance
tendentious
tepee
terrazzo
tête-à-tête
therapeutic
thesaurus
thief, thieves, thieving, theft
thyroid, thyroidectomy
timpani
titillate, titillation
toboggan, tobogganing
tomato, tomatoes (plural)
tonsillitis, tonsillectomy
toque (woman's hat); torque (rotational force)
tornado, tornadoes (plural)
torpedo, torpedoes (plural)
totalisator
touché
toupee
tourniquet
trauma, traumatic, traumatise
tranquil, tranquillity, tranquillise
triptych
trousseau, trousseaux (plural)
tuberculosis
tunnel, tunnelled, tunnelling
tyranny, tyrannical

ubiquitous, ubiquity
ultramarine
umbrella
unanimous, unanimously

unctuous
unguent
utility, utilitarian

vaccine, vaccination
vacillate, vacillation
vacuum
variegated, variegation
vehicle, vehicular
velodrome
vendetta
venereal
veranda
verbatim
verisimilitude
vermilion
verruca
veterinary, veterinarian

The ITA – Initial Teaching Alphabet

One of the most controversial methods of teaching
spelling was introduced in the 1960s: the *Initial
Teaching Alphabet*. Essentially but only
approximately phonetic, it had a 45-letter
alphabet which was described by one critic as 'a
cross between upside-down Serbo-Croat and
Greek'. Instruction in the nue speling went
something like this: 'You can spell "fox" *focks* or
foks but it doesn't matter because eventually we
will tell you that it is really spelt "fox".' While
it had its stout defenders among educators, others
pronounced the results of ITA 'catastrophic'. Or,
in ITA-ese, *kataestrofic*. Strange, but true.

vicarious
vicissitude

victuals, victualling, victualler
vinaigrette
vin ordinaire
vis-à-vis
viscous, viscosity
vituperate, vituperation
volcano, volcanoes (plural)
voluntary, volunteer
voluptuous, voluptuary

weather (climate); wether (sheep); whether (question)
werewolf
whereabouts
whereas
wherein
wherewithal
whitlow
whole, wholly
withhold
woe, woebegone, woeful, woefully
wool, woollen, woolly

yashmak
yoghourt, but increasingly, yoghurt
Yom Kippur

zeitgeist

I Before E Except After C.
Who Sez?

Of all the rules of spelling, none is more capricious than the 'i' before 'e' except after 'c' rule, or, as the old jingle had it:

> I before E
> Except after C,
> Or when sounded as A,
> As in *neighbour* or *weigh*.

And of course most words do follow this rule:

- achieve, brief, fierce, niece, relieve, shield, shriek, thief and yield
- conceivable, deceive, perceive, receive
- beige, feint, freight, reign, rein, skein, veil

But, hold on! you shout. What about *either*? And *heifer*, *weird*, *sovereign* and *foreign*? It is true; these are all 'ei' words in which there is no 'c'. Nor is the 'ei' pronounced to sound like 'ay'.

To deal with some of these troublesome words, someone invented another rule: 'i' before 'e' except after 'c' and before 'g'. This effectively takes care of words like *foreign* and *sovereign*, and also of words like *sleight* and *height*, especially if you remember this addition to the original rhyme:

> I before E
> Except after C,
> Or when sounded like A,
> As in *neighbour* or *weigh*,
> Or when sounded like 'ite',
> As in *height* or *sleight*.

And everyone went home happy. Or did they? Because still lurking in the dictionary were such outlaws as *either*, *seize*, *seizure*, *weird* and *heifer*. To our knowledge they are still there, still untamed by any rule or guideline, except perhaps by that of the fondly remembered schoolmistress Miss Hall, who insisted her pupils learned the following:

'Neither leisured foreign neighbour seized the weird heights during the reign of the sovereign king who forfeited the reins of government. The heir feigned that the neigh of either reindeer was due to the weight, which was eighty skeins of yarn in the sleigh.'

Has Miss Hall collared the lot?

Rules to Retain, Remember, Refine or Reject

There are many more spelling rules besides Miss Hall's homilies; unfortunately many are so cumbersome as to be self-defeating:

> 'Words of more than one syllable, ending with a single consonant preceded by a single vowel, if accented on the last syllable usually double the final consonant before a suffix beginning with a vowel, as in commit/committing, excel/excelled, occur/occurrence, regret/regrettable.

Did you follow that? Could you remember it? Worse, there are some nasty exceptions to this rule: transfer/transferable and chagrin/chagrined, to name just two.

Nevertheless, here are a few fairly simple rules that may be found useful:

- Drop the silent 'e' when adding endings that begin with a vowel, like *able*, *ance*, *ed*, *er*, *ible*, *ing*, *or*, *ous* – as in love/lovable, persevere/perseverance, hope/hoped, write/writer, sense/sensible, come/coming, create/creator, grieve/grievous.

- Keep the silent 'e' when adding endings that begin with a consonant, like *ful*, *less*, *ly*, *ment*, *ness* – as in care/careful, tire/tireless, love/lovely, move/movement, like/likeness. Unfortunately you must also remember the few exceptions to this rule: argue/argument, due/duly, true/truly and whole/wholly. You can make your own judgement/judgment on judge.

- Keep the silent 'e' when adding the endings *able* and *ous* to words that end in *ce* or *ge*, as in notice/

noticeable, marriage/marriageable, advantage/
advantageous.

- Words that end in 'l' keep it when adding *ly*, as in
cool/coolly, local/locally, poetical/poetically.

- With words ending in 'c', add a 'k' before endings
like *ed*, *ing*, and *y*, as in mimic/mimicked/
mimicking, panic/panicky, traffic/trafficking, frolic/
frolicking.

- With words ending in 'n' keep the 'n' when adding
ness, as in clean/cleanness, thin/thinness, sudden/
suddenness.

- When a word ends in *ee* or *oo*, keep the letter pairs
whatever you are adding, as in see/seeing, glee/
gleeful, woo/wooed/wooing.

There is obviously a limit to the number of such rules
that the average speller can absorb, remember and
apply quickly when required. For most of us,
unfortunately, spelling consists of two choices: learning
the hard way, or, as Mark Twain put it, 'I don't give
a damn for a man that can spell a word only one way.'

Word Imperfect

Hemingway Jones was a brilliant novelist, yet no
publisher had yet accepted his work. The trouble was,
Hemingway couldn't spell. If only he had someone to
correct his spelling, he'd be a famous writer in no time!
So why not help him? Here are the opening paragraphs
of his new novel, *The Biege Bhudda of Bagdhad*:

The old vetrinarian paused under the verandah,
perspiring in his kakhi jacket. It was at least ninety
farenheit. Mosquitos wirred over his head and,
crouching under the fuchsia, an iguano flickered its
evil tongue at him, iridescent in the flourescent glow of
the parrafin lamp.

It had been a long day. First, he'd vacillated Mrs
Horner's chihwahwa for diptheria and pneumonia. The
poor animal had squirmed and writhed so much that
the needle had perpetrated Mrs Horner's prosterior
instead; now he could look forward with certainety to
a lawsuite. Then there was that hysterical hippo-
potomus with a predeliction for *homeo sapiens*. And,
finally, the marahraja's pink parrakeet with the swollen
proboscis and a fine vocabluary of words not suitable
for the ears of young ladies.

The vet sank wearily down on the chaise longue near
the rhododendhrons, poured himself a generous shot
of Irish whisky, and considered his dilemna. Would he
continue here and risk a coronory, or take up the more
congenial post at the armadillo park in the Carribean?

[Answers over page]

Problem Proper Nouns

For every word we use in the course of an average day, we probably use five times as many proper nouns or names. Many of these are commonly misspelled, too, so here is a short list of those likely to cause trouble. The names of people – surnames and given names – are covered in another volume in the **One Hour Wordpower** series, *The Name Book*.

Abergavenny, Gwent, Wales
Aberystwyth, Dyfed, Wales
Abyssinia
Aldeburgh, Suffolk
Appelation Controlée
Archimedes
Achilles tendon
Aer Lingus
Afghanistan

Answers to Word Imperfect

If Hemingway Jones used the following spellings, his novel might stand a better chance:
beige/buddha/Baghdad/veterinarian/veranda/
khaki/fahrenheit/ Mosquitoes/whirred/iguana/
fluorescent/paraffin/vaccinated/ chihuahua/
diphtheria/penetrated/posterior/certainty/lawsuit/
hippopotamus/predilection/*homo sapiens*/
maharajah's/ parakeet/vocabulary/
rhododendrons/dilemma/coronary/Caribbean.
Twenty correct is a reasonable score. There is no such thing as Irish whisky, by the way; whisky is exclusive to Scotland. It should be Irish whiskey.

Agamemnon
Aladdin
Aldwych
Algonquin Hotel, New York
Alsace-Lorraine
Alzheimer's disease
Amontillado sherry
Annunciation
Anorexia nervosa
Apache
Aphrodite
Apocalypse
Appalachia
Arbroath, Tayside
Arc de Triomphe
Aristotle
Armageddon
Art nouveau
Ascension Day
Ashby-de-la-Zouch, Leicestershire
Athanaeum Club
Aubusson carpets
Audubon Society
Augean stables
Auld Lang Syne
Auld Reekie
Aurora Borealis
Auschwitz
Axminster carpets
Azerbaijan

Babylon
Baccalauréat
Bacchus
Baedeker (travel guides)
Baghdad
Baha'i (faith)
Bahrain

Balthazar
Bannockburn
Barabbas
Bathsheba
Bayreuth Festival
Béarnaise sauce
Beau Brummell
Beaufort scale
Beau Geste
Beaujolais
Beaulieu Castle, Hampshire
Bechuanaland
Beelzebub
Belshazzar's Feast
Berchtesgaden
Betws-y-Coed
Bishop's Stortford
Blenheim Palace, Oxfordshire
Bletchley
Boadicea
Bohème, La (opera)
Bohemian
Bokhara rugs
Bordeaux
Boris Godunov (opera)
Boughton Monchelsea
Bouillabaisse
Bourgogne, France
Bovey Tracey, Devon
Braille
Brechtian
Brightlingsea, Essex
Britannia
Brittany
Brummagem
Buchenwald
Buddha
Bundestag

The Ligature Untied

Caesar, manoeuvre, aesthetic, oenology, mediaeval, encyclopaedia and archaeology are words that once contained a ligature, either a joined ae (æ) or a joined oe (œ). The trend today is to separate them – very few typewriters and computer keyboards accommodate ligatures, anyway – and to further simplify the word by squeezing out one of the letters, resulting in esthetic, medieval, maneuver, primeval, and so on. This process is rather more advanced in America than it is in Britain.

Caernarfon (not Carnarvon), Gwynedd
Caerphilly, Glamorgan
Caesar, Caesarian
Camembert
Cape Canaveral
Capodimonte porcelain
Caribbean
Casablanca
Casbah
Cerebral thrombosis
Cerne Abbas, Dorset
Chapel-en-le-Frith, Derbyshire
Chardonnay
Charlemagne
Chartreuse
Chateaubriand
Château d'Yquem
Cheyenne
Chianti
Cincinnati
Cinque Ports
Cirencester, Gloucestershire
Coq au vin

Coquilles St Jacques
Coliseum (London)
Colosseum (Rome)
Comanche
Comédie-Français
Comédie humaine
Compton Wynyates, Warwickshire
Connecticut
Cosa Nostra
Così fan tutte
Courtauld Institute
Crème brûlée
Crêpe suzette
Criccieth, Gwynedd
Curaçao
Czechoslovakia

Dadaism
Daguerrotype
Dail Eirann (Republic of Ireland parliament)
Daiquiri
Dalai Lama
Daphnis and Chloe
Dardanelles
Darjeeling
Déjà vu
Déjeuner sur l'herbe (Manet's painting)
Delhi
Demoiselles d'Avignon (Picasso's painting)
Deuteronomy
Deutschland
Diaspora, The
Dien Bien Phu
Dionysus
Disraeli
Djibouti
Dobermann pinscher
Dolgellau, Gwynedd
Domesday Book

Don Juan
Don Quixote
Doppelgänger
D'Oyly Carte Opera Company
Dungeness, Kent

Ebbw Vale, Gwent
Ecclesiastes
Ecumenical Council
Edinburgh
Eichmann Trial
Eisteddfod
Élysée Palace, France
Emmentaler cheese
Encyclopaedia Britannica
Entre-Deux-Mers
Eustachian tube
Evangelicalism
Excalibur
Existentialism
Ezekiel

Fabergé (jewelled eggs)
Faerie Queene, The
Feock, Cornwall
Fernet Branca
Fledermaus, Die (Strauss opera)
Folies-Bergère
Forsyte Saga
Führer, Der
Fu Manchu, Dr (Chinese movie detective)

Gallipoli
Gandhi
Gethsemane
Gewürztraminer
Gioconda, La (Mona Lisa)
Givenchy (fashion house)
Glyndebourne Festival

Gobelins tapestry
Godalming, Surrey
Gondoliers, The (Gilbert and Sullivan opera)
Goonhilly Downs
Gorgonzola
Götterdämmerung
Graf Zeppelin
Gruyère cheese
Guggenheim Museum, New York
Guinness
Gujarati
Gulbenkian Foundation
Gurkha

Habeas Corpus
Hallelujah Chorus
Hanukkah (sometimes Chanukkah)
Hawaiian
Heraklion, Crete
Herstmonceux, Sussex
Hippocratic Oath
Hiroshima
Houdini
Houyhnhnms (breed of horses in *Gulliver's Travels*)
Huguenots

Iago
Ightham, Kent
Immelmann turn
Indianapolis
Innisfail, Ireland
Inveraray Castle
Iolanthe (Gilbert and Sullivan opera)
Izvestia (Russian newspaper)

Jakarta, Indonesia
Jeroboam
Jodrell Bank
Juilliard School of Music, New York

Jungian psychology

Kafkaesque
Kama Sutra
Keynsian economic theories
Khartoum
Khmer Rouge
Kirkcudbright
Kirkintilloch
Kirriemuir
Knaresborough
Kubla Khan
Ku Klux Klan
Kyrie eleison

The Pitfalls of Word Recognition

Just as it's not uncommon to mistake a person for someone else, we can all fail to recognise words at times. Often, a single misplaced letter is all it takes to transform a simple statement into an unfortunate pun. Here is a small collection contributed by the public.

His record high jump was sheer poultry in motion.
It is true that no man is in Ireland.
He immediately flew into a high dungeon.
Unfortunately, his father died interstate.
I wouldn't touch it with a ten-foot Pole.
After the storm the beach was covered with jellyfish testicles.
A strange child, and old beyond her ears . . .

La donna è mobile (aria from *Rigoletto*)
La Guardia Airport, New York
Lalique glass
Lascaux Caves, France

Lausanne, Switzerland
Legionnaires' disease
Leicestershire
Leighton Buzzard
Leipzig
Lichtenstein
Liebfraumilch
Lilliputian
Lindbergh baby kidnapping
Lindisfarne, Holy Island off Northumberland coast
Linlithgow
Linnean Society
Llandrindod Wells, Powys
Llandudno, Gwynedd
Llanelli, Dyfed
Llangollen, Clwyd
Llareggub (the town in Dylan Thomas's *Under Milk Wood*)
Lohengrin
Looe, Cornwall
Louis Quinze
Lourdes, France
Lucia di Lammermoor
Luxembourg
Lyonnaise
Lysistrata (Aristophanes' comedy)

McCarthyism
Machiavellian
Machu Picchu, Peru
Magdalen College, Oxford
Magdalene College, Cambridge
Mahabharata (Hindu epic poem)
Mahatma Gandhi
Mahdi (Muslim messiah)
Maigret, Inspector
Maitre d'hôtel
Majolica (opaque glazed pottery)
Malagasy Republic (Madagascar)

Malawi (formerly Nyasaland)
Malthusianism
Mancunian

Lost Beauties In 1874 the lexicographer Charles
Mackay published *Lost Beauties of the English
Language*, in which he bemoaned the fact that
several thousand words in the language had fallen
out of use. For bad spellers, this was good news,
but on the other hand many of the lost words
were colourfully expressive, as these few examples
show:

benothinged	*annihilated*
drouthy	*thirsty*
jobbernowle	*thickhead*
maw-wallop	*badly cooked*
wowf	*bonkers*
spousalbreach	*adultery*
tapsalteerie	*topsyturvy*
unbuxom	*scraggy*
wanchancie	*unlucky*
shoon	*plural of shoe*

Manon Lescaut (novel and opera)
Manzanilla dry sherry
Mao Tse-tung, or Mao Zedong
Maraschino cherry
Marseillaise, The
Marylebone, London
Massachusetts
Mau Mau (Kenyan nationalist movement)
Meccano
Mediterranean
Meissen porcelain
Mennonite religion
Mephistopheles
Mesopotamia
Messerschmitt

Methuselah
Meursault, Burgundy white wine
Michaelmas
Milwaukee, Wisconsin, USA
Minneapolis, Minnesota, USA
Minotaur
Misérables, Les (Victor Hugo's 1862 novel)
Mississippi
Missolonghi, Greece
Missouri
Mistinguette (Paris music-hall star)
Mitsubishi
Möbius loop
Mogadishu, Somalia
Mohammed
Mohave Desert, USA
Mohican Indians
Monégasque (citizen of Monaco)
Montaigne, French essayist
Montessori teaching system
Montezuma
Montmartre, Paris
Montparnasse, Paris
Montreux Festival
Montserrat
Morocco
Morte d'Arthur
Moulin Rouge
Münchausen, Baron
Mustapha Kemal (Turkish leader)
Mycenaean civilisation

Narcissus
Nassau, Bermuda
Navaho Indian tribe
Neanderthal Man
Nebuchadnezzar
Nehru
Nefertiti (Egyptian queen)

Beware Welsh!

In the Principality of Wales there is still a considerable amount of Welsh spoken, and even more written. Names that English-speakers know and love – Brecon Beacons, Snowdonia, Cardiff and Holyhead, for example, can, on a signpost or a map, change in a flash to Bannau Brycheiniog, Eryri, Caerdydd and Caergybi respectively. The Welsh are always sympathetic to the vain efforts of outsiders trying to master the language, and you will earn extra kudos by being able to correctly spell at least a few of the names important to their history and culture. Try these:

> Cymru (Wales)
> Dewi Sant (St David, patron saint of Wales)
> Rhodri Fawr (ninth-century king who united Wales)
> Llywelyn the Great (King of Wales who died 1240)
> Dafydd ap Gwilym (famous Welsh poet, died fourteenth century)
> Owain Glyndŵr (creator of the first Welsh parliament)

Plaid Cymru (Welsh nationalist party)
Pleiades galaxy
Pleistocene
Portuguese
Poseidon
Poughkeepsie, New York
Presbyterian
Ptolemy
Pygmalion
Pyongyang, North Korea
Pyramus and Thisbe
256

Pyrenees
Pythagoras

Qaddafi, Muammar el–
Qantas
Qatar
Quattrocento
Quirinale, Rome

Rabelaisian
Ranunculus
Rashomon (classic 1951 Japanese movie)
Rastafarian
Rechabites (Friendly Society)
Reichstag
Renaissance
Reykjavik, Iceland
Rhesus (Rh) Factor
Rievaulx Abbey, Yorkshire
Riyadh, Saudi Arabia
Roget's Thesaurus
Roosevelt
Roquefort cheese and dressing
Rorschach Test
Rosencrantz and Guildenstern
Rosenkavalier, Der (Strauss opera)
Rosh Hashanah (Jewish New Year)
Rosicrucians
Rothschild
Rubáiyát of Omar Khayyám, The (Persian poem)
Rwanda

Sagittarius
Salzburg Festival
Sarajevo, Bosnia
Sartor Resartus
Saskatchewan, Canada
Savile Club, London
Saxmundham, Suffolk

Scheherazade
Schweppes
Scylla and Charybdis
Sequoia
Sèvres porcelain
Shepheard's Hotel, Cairo
Shoeburyness, Essex
Sicily
Siegfried
Sikhs
Sinai
Sinn Fein
Sioux Indians
Slivovitz (plum brandy)
Sohrab and Rustum

Grass Roots Spelling

Non-gardeners never fail to be perplexed, even
irritated, by the fluency with which the most
threatening botanical names trill from the tongues
of the professionals. They can spell them, too!
Here are some tricky ones you might like to sow
in your spell-check memory:

Agapanthus, Amaranthus, Amaryllis, Anemone,
Antirrhinum, Aquilegia, Aspidistra, Aubrietia,
Bignonia, Bougainvillea, Buddleia, Calycanthus,
Camellia, Ceanothus, Chrysanthemum,
Convolvulus, Cotoneaster, Cyananthus,
Cymbidium, Cytisus, Dahlia, Deutzia,
Dryopteris, Eucalyptus, Freesia, Fuchsia,
Gypsophila, Hyacinth, Impatiens, Liquidambar,
Narcissus, Nymphaea, Pelargonium,
Philodendron, Phlox, Pieris, Pyracantha,
Rhododendron, Stephanotis, Tradescantia,
Weigela, Yucca.

Sophocles
Sorbonne, The
Struwwelpeter (children's storybook character)
Sturm und Drang
Sudetenland
Sumer is icumen in
Sylphides, Les (ballet)

Taj Mahal
Tammany Hall
Tannhäuser (Wagner opera)
Tecumseh (Shawnee Indian chief)
Tennessee
Thermopylae
Tiffany
Tipperary, Ireland
Toynbee Hall, London
Transcendentalism
Trovatore, Il (Verdi opera)
Tschiffeley's Ride
Tutankhamen

Ulysses
Unter den Linden, Berlin
Utilitarianism

Valkyries
Velázquez
Venezuela
Versailles
Viet Minh
Vieux Carré, district of New Orleans
Vladivostok
Vlaminck, Maurice (French painter)

Wedgwood pottery
Wehrmacht
Welwyn, Hertfordshire
Wenceslas

Wickambreaux, Kent
Wilhelmstrasse, Berlin
Witwatersrand, South Africa
Woolf, Virginia
Wooloomooloo, New South Wales
Wootton Bassett, Wiltshire
Wroxeter, Shropshire
Wynken, Blynken and Nod

Xanadu (fabled city in Coleridge's poem, *Kubla Khan*)

Yangtze Kiang, China
Yom Kippur (Jewish Day of Atonement)
Yosemite, US national park

Zaire
Ziegfeld Girls
Zeppelin
Zimbabwe
Zinoviev Letter
Zoroastrianism

Spelling Test

The craft of spelling, as indicated earlier, is less a matter of rules and more a matter of remembering. Every word is different in some way, and many people do well by remembering these differences; simply by looking at a word they are able to tell if it looks 'right' or 'wrong'. If you have spent an hour browsing through this book, try this test. About half the words in this list are correct.

1. playright _____
2. accelerate _____
3. Luxembourg _____
4. biassed _____
5. diaphram _____
6. Portugese _____
7. repellent _____
8. surreptitious _____
9. suprintendent _____
10. Picadilly Circus _____
11. sizable _____
12. ricochet _____
13. permissable _____
14. conoisseur _____
15. Mitshibusi _____
16. fulsome _____
17. pavillion _____
18. personnel _____
19. titillation _____
20. neice _____

(*Answers over page*)

Answers to Spelling Test

1. playwright
2. correct
3. correct
4. biased
5. diaphragm
6. Portuguese
7. correct
8. correct
9. superintendent
10. Piccadilly Circus
11. correct
12. correct
13. permissible
14. connoisseur
15. Mitsubishi
16. correct
17. pavilion
18. correct
19. correct
20. niece

Scores: 20 correct – top of the class
15–18 – above average
14 – average
below 14 – browse for another hour and try again.

Usage

Introduction

If we are what we say and write, what are we to make of the author of this?

> 'Reference your contract proposal we except all those items within the parameters we discussed, but its neither fair or acceptable to insist on a delivery date prior to April. We could have had agreement months ago if you had not made the order dependant on such unrealistic delivery dates.'

The paragraph contains five examples of words used incorrectly, and a further example of indecorous usage.* It is taken from a letter written (or dictated) by a young middle-management sales executive of a London firm **which** (not **that**) supplies industrial cleaning materials.

But before we start gleefully gloating over the young man's linguistic lapses, we might be wise to ensure our own houses are in order. Are we all confident about using **lay** and **lie**, **who** and **whom**, **shall** and **will**, **that** and **which**, **its** and **it's**? Is it **try and** or **try to**? **Compare to** or **compare with**?

Are the kids **noisy** or **noisome**? Is petrol **flammable** or **inflammable**? What's the difference between **manslaughter** and **murder**? **Perennial** and **annual**? **Peremptory** and **perfunctory**? **Perspicacity** and **perspicuity**?

Does it really matter? Well, a man who confuses **prostrate** with **prostate** is just as likely to knock on the door of a **proctor** as a **proctologist**. Apart from being downright embarrassing, using words incorrectly

*All the answers will be found in this chapter.

can transform what you say, write and mean into garbage and gobbledegook.

Few of us are ever free from doubts over the proper use of words. Many of us go through life blithely unaware that we are using certain words or expressions wrongly, and feel puzzled and resentful when we are misunderstood.

It need be neither difficult nor time-consuming to improve our understanding and use of 'difficult', look-alike and chronically misused words. The aim of this chaper is to provide the means to achieve this, concisely and invitingly. Many of the black holes in our usage of certain words arise from complex rules; in this book, however, you will search in vain for these, as you will for terms such as predicate nominative complement and non-restrictive personal relative pronoun.

This chapter on Usage will relieve anxieties about **among** and **amongst, hiccup** and **hiccough, on** and **upon**. It will explain the subtle differences between **obsolete** and **obsolescent, obligate** and **oblige, relatively** and **comparatively**. It will explain the true meanings of **burgeoning, decimate, empathy** and **quantum leap**. It will introduce you to the Hemingway mnemonic to help you choose between **who** and **whom**. And it will gently lead you away from clichés and vogue words like **hopefully, viable, debrief** and **utilise**. Browse through this book with pleasure; refer to it for ever (not **forever**).

Word Check

a, an

Use **a** before words beginning with consonants (a book, a glass, a TV) and **an** before words beginning with vowels (an apple, an egg, an ice-cream, an omelette, an undertaker). There are some exceptions, however: the word one, because of the way it is pronounced, demands an **a** (a one-horse town); words beginning with a soft h need an **an** (an heiress, an habitual liar) but words that sound the h don't (a horse, a hospital, a hotel); and certain words beginning with the long u which is pronounced 'yew' need an **a** (a ukelele, a uniform).

accent, dialect

An **accent** is a variation of pronunciation from the standard language; a **dialect** also strays from standard pronunciation but in addition uses a different vocabulary and grammar.

accept, except

To **accept** is to receive something; **except** means to exclude, omit, leave out, reject.

accident, injury

An **accident** is an unforeseen event but which need not necessarily result in **injury**: 'It was a spectacular accident and it was amazing that nobody was injured.'

actually, virtually, really

Actually and **really** mean in fact, but both words are much abused and over-used. 'Did he actually say that?' is legitimate; 'Well, actually, I wouldn't mind a drink' is abuse. **Virtually** means in effect, substantially, mostly, for all practical purposes, not quite.

advantage, benefit

An **advantage** is a situation that favours success; a **benefit** is a form of help that is earned, paid for or given.

adversary, opponent

Both are interchangeable, a fine difference being that **adversary** has a hostile and antagonistic ring to it, while **opponent** has sportier, friendlier connotations.

adverse, averse

They look and sound similar but are used in very different ways. **Adverse** means hostile and damaging: 'The adverse conditions wrecked their holiday.' **Averse** indicates disinclination and reluctance: 'She is averse to dishing out favours.'

affect, effect

These two words have a profusion of meanings that produce a rash of confusions! To **affect** is to influence or to cause something to happen: 'Smoking can adversely affect your health.' An **effect** is a result: 'One effect of smoking is lung cancer.' Other meanings are close, but not the same: 'The burglar effected entry by the skylight'; 'The third movement of the symphony always affected him greatly.' Remember that:
- **affect** – cause – usually a verb
- **effect** – result – usually a noun

affecting, affection, affectation

A troublesome trio! An **affecting** play is one that touches the emotions; **affection** describes the act or state of fondness and attachment; while an **affectation** is a pretence.

after, afterwards

'He ran after the robber' means to pursue or seek, but **after**, like **afterwards** (and **afterward** – American) also means following in order or later in time. **Afters** are desserts or puddings.

aggravate, exasperate

Aggravate means to make a condition worse; it does not mean to annoy. If you want to **exasperate** someone, try teasing, irritating or provoking them, which could **aggravate** their ill-temper.

agree with, agree to

One usually **agrees with** a person but **agrees to** a proposition or an idea. 'I agreed with him about using the car but couldn't agree to his taking it for a week.'

A letter or two is all it takes

A changed letter in a word can make a lot of difference, and most of us make malapropian slips from time to time. Witness these:

- He's in hospital in the expensive care ward
- When it comes to marriage, Western people believe in the principle of monotony
- She went off in high dungeon
- He was proud to have at last entered the portholes of fame
- Although he's old he still has all his facilities
- Superman was supposed to have had X-rated vision

all right

If we accept **already**, **altogether** and **almost**, why not **alright**? Sorry, **alright** is all wrong, and although you'll see it in countless novels and magazine articles the authorities insist it doesn't exist.

alter, altar

As the builder said to the bishop: 'I'm sorry, but I can't alter the altar.'

alternate, alternative

Alternate means one after the other, to take turns or to substitute. An **alternative** is a choice, usually restricted to only one other option. The same applies to **alternately** and **alternatively**. 'You can work alternately, that is on alternate days, or alternatively you might prefer to work one week on and one week off.'

America, American

What is **America**? Does it mean North America, including Canada; or the Americas, which might include Central America, the Caribbean and even South America? Do **Americans** include native Indians and Nicaraguans along with citizens of the Bronx and Brooklyn? The sheer weight of usage now defines **America** as the **United States of America**, and **Americans** as citizens of that nation, and it's bad luck for the rest. If you wish to be both clear and fair, use the **United States**, the **United States of America**, the **USA** or the **US**. Where the term **US citizen** is cumbersome, there is little alternative but to use **American**: 'The current record is held by an American.'

although, though

Fairly interchangeable. **Though** means 'despite the fact that . . .'; **although** means 'even though'. It's a matter of what looks and sounds right: 'Although it was a mongrel, I bought the dog anyway'; 'I bought the dog, though it was a mongrel.'

amateur, novice

An **amateur**, as opposed to a **professional**, indulges in an activity as a pastime. A **novice** is a beginner, while a **tyro**, a word rarely used now, is an awkward, untrained novice.

American English

Most of us are familiar with those words that in the US have different spellings than they have in Britain: **tire/tyre, sulfur/sulphur, center/centre, color/colour** and so on. Americans also use different words to describe similar things: **elevator/lift, vacation/holiday, sidewalk/footpath, diaper/nappie, candy/sweets** are just a few. No offence or embarrassment is caused if we get these wrong, but watch out for words like **fanny** (which denotes two completely different parts of the anatomy), **pecker** (Americans have been known to fall down in shock when exhorted to 'keep your pecker up'), and **knock up**, which can have the same effect when, for example, a hotel receptionist is asked for an early morning call: 'Can you knock me up at half past six?'

---

among, amongst, between

Use **between** to connect two persons, objects or ideas: 'There is little difference between the two of them.' **Among** is used in connection with several things: 'There is little difference among all five candidates.' **Amongst** means the same, but why not use the shorter, simpler **among**?

amoral, immoral

Amoral means unconcerned with morals, an unmoral person, someone without a moral code. To be **immoral** is to act against a moral code, to be licentious, to offend an existing moral code.

analysis, synthesis

Analysis is to take apart, to examine, to reduce something to its elements; **synthesis** is the opposite, to put things together, to combine, to build something from various elements.

anticipate, expect, hope

The traditional meaning of **anticipate** is foresee or 'think of beforehand': 'He anticipated the cyclone by putting into the nearest harbour.' Many people mistakenly use **anticipate** for **expect**, which means to look forward to something that is certain or very likely: 'I expect you to be in early on Mondays.' It is interesting that Nelson exhorted his men with 'England expects . . .' rather than 'England hopes . . .'; **hope** is an altogether more wishy word meaning to desire something with confidence but with an uncertain expectation of fulfilment: 'I hope the neighbour's party won't be too noisy.'

anxious, eager

'She was anxious to get home' is wrong; what is probably meant is, 'She was anxious (about walking in the dark) and eager to get home.'

Anxious implies a degree of fear or apprehension, while to be **eager** is to be impatient, keen, enthusiastic.

anybody, anyone

These are interchangeable, and singular. 'If anybody/anyone is there, will he please answer the doorbell?' is correct. However, with objections nowadays to the 'he', and with the questioner not knowing the gender of the person on the other side of the door, it is now acceptable to use 'they' or 'their': 'Will they please answer the doorbell?' **Anyone** is split into two words when single persons or objects are being described: 'Anyone can eat any one of these cakes.'

any more

Try saying **anyway, anyhow, anyone, anything**; now say, 'He doesn't live here anymore'. It comes out as two words, doesn't it, with the stress on 'more'? That's why there is no such word as 'anymore'. So don't write it that way any more.

apparent, evident

Apparent means seeming to appear; **evident** means conclusive, clear to one's understanding. **Manifest** is the strongest term, which means clear to both sight and understanding.

appraise, apprise, assess, evaluate

To **appraise** is to estimate the worth of somebody or something; to **assess** is to estimate the value of something, usually property, for tax purposes; to **evaluate** is to determine the numerical and monetary value of something; to **apprise** is to inform: 'The waiter quietly apprised him of the size of the bill.'

around, round, about

Using these words is largely a matter of taste. 'I have **about** 100 LPs in my collection' is usually preferred to **around**, and 'I walked **round** the city' is preferable to **around**.

assume, presume

One meaning of **assume** is unambiguous: to undertake something, as in, 'He arrogantly assumed the role of leader.' The other meaning, to suppose, to take for granted, is often confused with **presume**, which means to take for granted without any reasoning or proof. Should Stanley have said, 'Dr Livingstone, I assume?' A fine difference.

assurance, insurance

Assurance is life insurance in the form of a policy that assures an eventual financial benefit. **Insurance** is a guarantee of payment for damage through fire, accident or some form of misfortune.

assure, ensure, insure

To **assure** somebody is to give them confidence; to **ensure** is to make certain; to **insure** is to protect financially.

authentic, genuine

Authentic is usually applied to something that is produced by someone, about which there is no doubt; it is the opposite of **counterfeit**: 'The expert agreed that the painting was an authentic Goya.' **Genuine** has a wider range of meanings and is generally used to imply some innate or original quality: 'The handbag was genuine leather.'

average, ordinary

To say someone lives in an **average** home is meaningless; the person lives in an **ordinary** home. **Average** should only be used in its mathematical sense and even then there can be different meanings. If five individuals are aged 5, 11, 14, 20 and 25, their **average** (mean) age is the total 75 divided by the number 5 = 15.

back, behind, backward, backwards

Back is a true all-purpose word describing a position at the rear, away from you, reversed or returning, and, with its other meanings, is used in an amazing number of ways (**quarterback, backchat, backslider, back-seat driver**). But if we say '**in front of**', why can't we say '**in back of**' like the Americans? Well, it isn't done in Britain, where we say **behind**. **Backward** is an adjective: 'He was a backward child'; 'It was a backward step'; but it can also be used adverbially along with **backwards**. As adverbs, either **backward** or **backwards** may be used: 'He stepped backward/backwards.'

baited, bated

Bated means restrained or diminished; **bait** is food used as a lure to catch something: 'He stood there with bated breath while his wife baited the hook.'

balcony, circle, dress circle, gallery, stalls

In most theatres, the **stalls** are at floor level, with the **circle**, usually divided into **dress circle** and **upper circle**, on the next level. Above the circle is the **balcony**, with the **gallery** at the very top.

baring, barring, bearing

These derive from **bare**, **bar** and **bear**, meaning respectively: to uncover, to obstruct, and to carry.

because, since, on account of, owing to, due to

Some tough decision-making here! **Because** means 'for the reason'; **because of** means 'by reason of': 'He had to buy a new car because the other one packed up'; 'He had to return his new car because of a faulty gear box'. **On account of** is used to qualify a phrase: 'He can't drive the car on account of the gear box.' Use **since** to imply a time lapse: 'He's been walking to work since his car broke down.' **Owing to**, **on account of** and **because of** are for all practical purposes synonymous; the odd man out is **due to** which strictly speaking means **caused by** and should always link the result with the cause: 'His failure with girls was due to not having a car.' Careful users will not use **due to** as a substitute for **because**.

begin, commence, initiate, start

Although these words have much the same meaning, they are used differently. **Initiate** and **inaugurate** are mostly used to describe the origination of a specific undertaking, like a building project or the foundation of an association. **Commence** is interchangeable with **begin**, except that it is rather more formal, while **start** implies a certain abruptness: 'Drivers, start your engines!'

believe, feel, think

The usage of these words follows this logic: you **believe** with faith, you **feel** with your senses and emotions, and you **think** with your mind: 'I believed he was telling the truth but felt he was hiding something, and I now think he was lying all the time.'

beneath, under

Beneath and **below** mean 'lower than' and are the opposite of **above**; they all describe a position but without reference to any scale. **Under** (and **underneath**) is the opposite of **over** and both suggest a sense of position and proximity: 'His exam marks were well below mine'; 'She slid eagerly under the blankets.' As you can see, the differences are extremely subtle.

benefit

See **advantage, benefit**

beside, besides

Beside means next to, or by the side of. **Besides** means in addition to, or moreover: 'She wanted me to sit beside her; besides, there were no other vacant seats in the room.'

between

See **among, amongst, between**

biannual, biennial

Biannual is twice a year; **biennial** is once very two years. What, then, is **bi-monthly**? The answer could be either twice a month or once every two months, so it should be avoided. Instead be specific and use twice-monthly, six times yearly, once every two months, etc.

Bible, bible

When referring to the Old and New Testaments, use a capital B, but use a lower case b in the context of, for example, 'His book on stamp collecting is regarded as the bible of philately.'

billion

It is well known that the **US billion** is a thousand million, and that the **British billion** is a million million. Unfortunately this considerable distinction escapes the media and financial institutions so that we now have, in Britain, a situation where much of the time a billion means a thousand million. To avoid ambiguity, say or write 1400 million, not 1.4 or 0.0014 billion.

blond, blonde

This may come as a surprise to many, but **blond** is used in the masculine context, and **blonde** in the feminine.

born, borne, bourne

'He was born on September 1, having been borne by his mother for the full nine months.' **Bourne** is an old English word for a stream that survives in place names such as Littlebourne, Bishopsbourne, etc.

both, each

Both embraces two things while **each** refers to one of two or more things: 'Both buckets had holes in them'; 'each of the three buckets was riddled with holes'.

bravery, bravado, bravura, courage, heroism

Bravery is the readiness to face danger or pain; **bravado** is the ostentatious pretence of bravery; **bravura** is a display of daring brilliance, often in an artistic performance. **Courage** is the quality required to meet confrontation or danger with firm resolve – a quality we'd all like to possess at times of stress or challenge. **Heroism** implies an act of selflessness that transcends normal human behaviour.

breach, breech

To **breach** is to break or violate, as in a breach (break or gap) in the wall; a breach (violation) of the peace. **Breech** (remember that breeches are the garment that covers the posterior) is the rear part of anything, as in breech birth.

Britain

Britain and Great Britain are synonymous, and mean the union of England, Scotland and Wales. The United Kingdom (full title: The United Kingdom of Great Britain and Northern Ireland, abbreviated to the UK) comprises England, Scotland, Wales and Northern Ireland. The British Isles include the UK, the dependencies of the Isle of Man and the Channel Islands.

---

broach, brooch

To **broach** is to open up: 'He eventually broached the delicate subject of marriage.' A **brooch** is jewellery, usually fixed to the clothing with a pin.

burgeon, burgeoning

Often used incorrectly, to mean growing or swelling. What it really means is something that's *starting* to grow, or sprouting.

burglary, robbery, stealing, theft

Stealing is to take or appropriate something belonging to someone else, without their permission. **Burglary** is entering premises with intent to steal or commit a felony. **Robbery** is stealing that involves violence or the threat of it. **Theft** is synonymous with stealing.

callous, callus

Callous is used to denote insensitivity in people: 'He was callous towards his animals.' A **callus** is a patch of hard skin.

can, may, might

Can and **may** each have two meanings. The first relates to possibility: 'I can go to the party (now that I've finished my chores)'; 'I may go to the party (if I feel well enough).' The second relates to permission, and in this context any difference between **can** and **may** is virtually extinct: 'Yes, you can go to the party'; 'Yes, you may go to the party.' Much the same applies to **could** and **might**: 'Could/might I go to the party?'; but **can't** has completely replaced **mayn't**.

capital, capitol

The **capitol** is the legislative building, while the **capital** is the city in which the legislature is situated. The Capitol in Washington DC always has a capital C.

casual, causal

A confusing pair of near opposites. **Casual** denotes accidental, unplanned, a chance happening, relaxed. **Causal** is the relationship between an effect and its cause: 'The causal element in their break-up was his casual attitude to money, and the lack of it.'

catholic, Catholic

With a small c, **catholic** means wide-ranging, comprehensive, near-universal: 'He had catholic tastes in music.' With a capital C, it is the shortened form for the Roman Catholic religion.

cavalry, Calvary

Cavalry are mounted soldiers, on horses, camels or wheels; **Calvary** is the mount near Jerusalem where Christ was crucified.

celibate, chaste

To be **chaste** is to be pure, modest, and sexually faithful. To be **celibate** is to abstain from marriage (and sexual intercourse) altogether, as with the members of many religious orders.

centre, middle

The **centre** of something is geometrically precise and measurable; the **middle** of something is a more general, approximate term.

Christian name, first name, given name

Be careful of using the term **Christian name** loosely; strictly speaking, the term should be used only when referring to the first or given names of Christians. The other terms are safer.

chronic, acute

Acute means sharp and quick, whereas **chronic** means almost the opposite, long lasting and recurring: 'The acute pains he suffered were symptoms of a chronic illness.'

claim, allege, assert, maintain

Just four of a group of words that are often used synonymously and wrongly. To **claim** is to demand or assert a right: 'He came to England to claim the crown.' It is, however, often used wrongly as a synonym for **declare**, **assert**, **protest** and **allege**. To **allege** is to assert without proof, and as it nowadays implies guilt should be used with caution: 'the alleged bribe'; 'the alleged crime'. **Assert** is stronger than **said** and means to declare positively. The primary meanings of

281

maintain are **hold**, **preserve** and **sustain**, so it is a supportive word: 'In the face of the allegations she maintained her innocence.'

climactic, climatic, climacteric

'The climatic conditions were almost unbearable' disposes of that one. **Climactic** relates to a climax, a high point, while a **climacteric** is a critical period in life, most usually the male or female menopause.

colony, protectorate, dependency

A **colony** is a territory annexed by another power; once numbering over a hundred, only a few of these now survive. These include former British Crown Colonies, now termed **dependencies**, which have their own legislatures – Belize, Cayman Islands, the Falklands and Hong Kong (until 1997) are examples. A **protectorate** is a territory protected and defended by a stronger state.

commonly, customarily, frequently, generally, habitually, ordinarily, usually

Commonly, **generally**, **ordinarily** and **usually** are virtually synonymous, meaning 'normally as expected'. **Customarily** differs by only a fine degree, meaning 'according to established practice'. **Frequently** means often, while **habitually** implies frequency as the result of habit.

compare to, compare with

These are a troubling pair but it is usually accepted that **compared to** is used to express dissimilarities to make a point: 'She often compared her boyfriend's intelligence to two thick planks.' **Compared with** is used to note the differences between two similar things: 'You

can't really compare Caruso's voice with
Pavarotti's.'

compose, comprise, constitute

Comprise is the odd man out and means 'consists
of': 'The building comprises seven rooms and
the usual offices.' It is a formal word that's falling
out of use. The meanings of **compose** and
constitute are similar – to form, or to make up:
'The pudding is composed of some weird
ingredients'; 'She hardly dared list the ingredients
that constituted the pudding.'

complement, compliment, supplement

A **complement** is that which makes something
complete: 'The hospital finally had its full
complement of nurses.' A **compliment** is an
expression of praise, and a **supplement** is an
addition to something already complete. They are
also used as verbs: 'She complemented the dish
with a swirl of cream and a cherry'; 'He
complimented her on the meal'; 'The doctor
supplemented her diet with a course of vitamins
and minerals.'

concede, accede

Accede implies willing agreement, while **concede**
implies grudging agreement or giving way: 'He
conceded the argument to his opponent'; 'He
acceded enthusiastically to the idea of a return
match.'

conscience, conscious, conscientious

A **conscience** is a person's sense of what is right
and wrong. **Conscious** implies self-awareness,
being aware of one's mental and physical state.
To be **conscientious** is to act according to a code
of principles.

consecutive, successive

Consecutive means following without an interval or break, while **successive** means following in order but without emphasis on the intervals. If jockey Lester Piggott had won nine **consecutive** Derbys he would have won the nine races over nine years; in fact he has won nine **successive** Derbys over 35 years.

consensus

A **consensus** is an agreement of opinion, so the cliché 'consensus of opinion' is to be avoided.

conservative, Conservative

With the small c it means opposed to change, moderate, cautious and conventional; with a capital C it means a member or supporter of a Conservative political party.

consultant, specialist

In medical parlance, patients are referred to a **specialist**, while a **consultant** is a specialist who is consulted by doctors.

continual, continuous

Continual means repeated at short intervals; **continuous** means uninterrupted.

converse, inverse, obverse, reverse

Of this quartet, all meaning opposite in some sense, **inverse** and **obverse** can be ignored unless you have a need for them – for example in coin collecting or mathematics. **Converse** and **conversely** (which is used loosely as 'on the other hand') denote a reversal of meaning: 'Every journalist knows that dog bites man – and its converse, man bites dog.' Note also that to **converse** means to have a conversation. **Reverse** is rarely misunderstood: 'He states that a fibre diet makes you fat; actually, the reverse is true.'

Contradictory words

When you **dust** an object, do you clean it of dust, or sprinkle fine powder on it? Why does a **seeded** bun have seeds baked on it, while **seeded** raisins have the seeds taken out? Does a child know the difference between **getting up** from the table, and **getting down**? These two-way words and terms are understandably the source of much confusion. Try looking up **ravel** and **unravel** in the dictionary: they can both mean the same. And **parboil**, a model of imprecision, means both to boil thoroughly, and to boil partially.

convince, persuade

Convince implies proving something to somebody by argument, by an exposition of the facts, while **persuade** suggests winning over someone to a point of view by appealing to reason or the emotions.

copy

See **replica, copy, facsimile**

correspond to, correspond with

If you **correspond with** someone, you exchange letters with them. **Correspond to** means to be in harmony with, or to tally with: 'Your version of the affair corresponds to that of Matilda's.' Don't get confused with **correspondent** (one who writes letters) and **co-respondent** (someone cited as 'the other party' in divorce proceedings).

couple, pair

A **couple** is two things that are united or joined together, as in a couple of drinks or a married couple. A **pair** is two things of a kind that are mutually dependent, as in a **pair** of scissors (joined) and a pair of gloves (not joined).

courage

See **bravery, bravado, bravura, courage, heroism**

curb, kerb

Curb means to check or restrain; **kerb** is the edge of the pavement, the drop between paved footpath and gutter. In the US they say the **curb** is the edge of the pavement.

currant, current

A **currant** is a small, dark, dried grape. **Current** has two meanings: a flow (of electricity, water, air); and existing in the present time: 'It is difficult to keep up with current events.'

cyclone, hurricane, tornado, typhoon

A **hurricane** is a violent gale with winds exceeding 75 miles an hour; a **cyclone** is a hurricane, the winds of which blow spirally towards a region of low barometric pressure. **Tornados** and **typhoons** are hurricane winds that rotate, creating funnel or cylindrical shapes.

cynical, sceptical

A **cynic** is someone who believes there is little good in anyone or anything; a **sceptic** is a doubter who has a problem believing anything without ample proof.

dais, lectern, podium, rostrum

A **rostrum** is a raised platform, and a **dais** is a rostrum on which several people can sit or stand.

A **podium** is a platform for a single speaker. A **lectern** is the stand on which the speaker props his notes.

The death watch

Watch out for the family of death words as they can spring unpleasant surprises.
Deadly can mean fatal, poisonous, relentless or even deadly boring; while **deathly** means 'like death': 'Her face was deathly pale.'
Deathless means immortal; its use today is almost always satirical, as in 'deathless prose'. **Deceased** is perfectly correct even though it is mostly used as a euphemism for **dead**; interestingly, animals are dead, never deceased.

debar, disbar

Debar means to exclude or to shut out; **disbar** means to expel, usually from a law court.

deceitful, deceptive

To be **deceitful** is to deliberately mislead or cheat. **Deceptive** describes the effect of a misleading circumstance: 'The bright sunshine proved deceptive, for it was really quite cold.'

decent, descent, dissent

Decent means good, respectable, morally upright; **descent** is a movement downwards; **dissent** is disagreement. Note also the spelling of the opposites, **ascent** and **assent**.

decimate

Used widely to indicate great destruction and even total annihilation, its true meaning is to destroy

287

one in ten – originally Roman legionnaires. Use carefully.

defuse, diffuse

Defuse means to remove a device or some circumstance likely to cause an explosion or an explosive situation. **Diffuse** means to spread: 'Unrest was diffused among the crowd, and he knew he had to defuse what was becoming an ugly situation.'

dependant, dependent

The difference here is that **dependant** is a noun and **dependent** is an adjective; a **dependant** is someone **dependent** upon some form of physical, moral or financial support: 'It was well known that the captain had half a dozen dependants in various ports'; 'The young man was unfortunately dependent on drugs.'

dependency

See **colony, dependency, protectorate**

deprecate, depreciate

To **deprecate** is to express disapproval while **depreciate** means to lower in value: 'The value of his holdings had depreciated by half.'

desire, want, need

Of this trio, **need** expresses the strongest requirement and urgency. **Want** implies a less urgent craving, while **desire** involves a degree of wishful thinking: 'He desired an easier life, wanted a house to live in, but meanwhile needed the price of a square meal.'

desiccated

It means dried, not chopped up.

device, devise

A **device** is something designed and made for a specific purpose; to **devise** something is to invent or create something: 'The man who devised the petrol engine gave us a device for propelling a car.'

diagnosis, prognosis

A **diagnosis** is an identification of or an opinion about a problem or disease, while a **prognosis** is a prediction about the outcome.

differ from, differ with

To **differ from** implies a contrast: 'Male views usually differ from those of females.' To **differ with** someone is to disagree.

Who's coming to dinner, supper, lunch or tea?

Depending upon your background, your work pattern and where you live in Britain, these terms can be very confusing. An invitation to **dinner** from strangers could be social dynamite! There are many people who eat **luncheon** around 1pm and their main meal, **dinner** (sometimes called **supper**), at 7–8pm. Others have **dinner** at midday and a main meal called **tea** at about 6pm, with a light **supper** before bedtime. Yet other families may have a **lunch** snack before noon, **dinner** at midday, **tea** at around 4pm and **supper** during the evening. **High tea** is a meal replete with meat or fish served late in the afternoon. And this by no means covers all the confusing gastronomic habits of Britain.

---

different from, different to

The latter is frowned upon, as is **different than**. Better to use 'dissimilar to' if you must.

dinghy, dingy

A **dinghy** is a small boat; **dingy** means grimy, soiled, shabby, and occasionally, gloomy.

disc, disk

The two spellings have been slugging it out for a couple of centuries, although today we tend to use **disc** to describe flat circular surfaces, and **disk** in connection with computers, as with floppy disk. But the usage is still far from uniform.

discreet, discrete

Discreet means careful, circumspect, prudent. **Discrete** means separate, unattached, distinct.

disinterested, uninterested

These are not synonyms. To be **disinterested** is to be impartial, to be uninvolved. To be **uninterested** is to lack interest in something, to be bored: 'Although he was asked to attend the meeting as a disinterested party, he was completely uninterested in the proceedings.'

disorient, disorientate

They both mean the same – to be confused or to lose your bearings – so why not use the shorter word?

doubtful, dubious

Doubtful is preferred, unless you wish to suggest something underhand: 'He was doubtful about the arrangement, especially with so many dubious characters involved.'

dual, duel

Dual means consisting of two, or double: a **dual** carriageway, **dual** brakes. A **duel** is a contest or combat between two adversaries.

due to

See **because, since, on account of, due to, owing to**

dwarf, midget, pygmy

A **dwarf** is a human, animal or plant of stunted growth. A **midget** is an extremely small person, while a **pygmy** is generally one of several tribes (including the Pygmy tribe), the members of which are undersized by normal human standards.

each

See **both, each**

eager

See **anxious, eager**

eatable, edible

Both are synonymous, perhaps with the distinction that **eatable** implies something more tasty than **edible**: 'The mushroom, once thought to be poisonous, is edible although bitter.'

effect

See **affect, effect**

effective, effectual, efficacious, efficient

This quartet causes much confusion. **Effective** means an action that produces the intended effect; while **effectual** (subtle, this one) means capable of producing the desired effect. **Efficacious** means having the power to produce the intended effect, while **efficient** means competent: 'He was an efficient judge, effective on the bench, with a style that was effectual in clearing up the backlog of cases; above all, he believed in handing out the sort of sentences that were efficacious.'

egoism, egotism

Egoism is a person's undue preoccupation with his or her self, obsessive self-interest. An **egotistical** person is also unduly self-interested but reveals it to all with excessive boasting and a predominance of 'I' in conversations.

either, any

Either means one or other of two: 'Either take it or leave it'; 'There were two books on the desk and I didn't take either of them.' Any refers to more than two: 'There were four books on the desk and I didn't take any of them.' **Either** and **neither** are both singular: 'Either you or I am lying.' Although correct it looks and sounds awkward, so reconstruct: 'Either you are lying or I am.' Also remember the **either/or** and **neither/ nor** rule.

Emergent words

New words are always creeping into the language. Many are useful or necessary, but some are not. Do we really need **proactive**? **Inputting**? **Debrief**? This last word makes little sense. If you devalue something you take away value, but how can you debrief someone, which is to take away information that person has gained, without a complete brainwash? It can't be done. As a grammarian wit observed, debrief makes as much sense as decircumcise.

---

elementary, alimentary, elemental

Elementary means returning to first principles, rudimentary, introductory; **elemental** describes something that relates to the primitive forces of nature. **Alimentary** refers to food and eating; hence the alimentary canal.

emigrant, immigrant

If John Smith leaves Britain to live in Australia, he's **emigrating** from Britain and **immigrating** to Australia, where he becomes an **immigrant** or, as forgetful Australians have it, a **migrant**.

eminent, imminent

An **eminent** person is somebody of note, distinguished: 'He was the most eminent doctor of his time.' **Imminent** means impending, threatening, about to happen: 'Everyone felt that war was imminent.' There is also a rare word, **immanent**, which means inherent.

empathy, sympathy

Sympathy is generally well understood, and means a sharing of emotions and a feeling of fellowship with another; also sometimes commiseration. **Empathy** is an extension of this to mean a very close identification with the thoughts and feelings of another: 'In his portrait, the artist reveals an unusual empathy with the sitter.'

enervate, energise

Enervate is often used wrongly; it means to drain and weaken: 'The succession of hot, humid days left them irritable and enervated.' **Energise** means the opposite.

enquire, inquire

Although not a hard and fast rule, **enquire** is used in a questioning sense, while **inquire** and **inquiry** refer to an investigation: 'The reporter enquired how the departmental inquiry was going.'

ensure

See **assure, ensure, insure**

envious, enviable, envy, jealousy

Although one of the seven deadly sins, **envy** can imply a casual longing for something as much as deep hatred and malice towards someone possessing something that one wants. **Enviable** is to be worthy of envy: 'He has got himself an enviable position in a bank.' To be **envious** is to feel or show envy. A near synonym is **covet** which is to lust after the possession of someone or something. **Jealousy** is the expression of personal unease about a situation, often involving rivalry, the transfer of affection or love to another, or a suspected infidelity, and tends to surface as irrational behaviour, resentment and spite.

especially, specially

Especially means in particular, exceptionally, while **specially** means of a special kind, individual, particular: 'That dog is my special friend, especially at feeding times.'

evacuate, vacate

Evacuate means to make empty (the bowels) or to remove from: 'The evacuation from the threatened town went smoothly.' **Vacate** means to give up occupancy.

evade, elude, avoid

Avoid means to shun, to keep away from. **Evade** and **elude** are similar and mean to avoid by cleverness or deception. Knowing the difference between avoidance and evasion is important when paying your tax; one is illegal and one is not.

evaluate
See **appraise, apprise, assess, evaluate**

everyone, every one, everybody
'There were ten apples and every one was rotten'; 'There were ten people in the room and everyone was drunk.' Note that they are both singular. **Everybody** and **everyone** are interchangeable; use according to taste.

evidence, proof, testimony
Testimony is the statement of a witness; **evidence** is information presented to support an argument; **proof** is evidence so factual or convincing as to remove any doubt.

evident
See **apparent, evident**

exasperate
See **aggravate, exasperate**

except, unless
Use **except** to imply an omission and **unless** to make a condition: 'I will work every day except Saturday unless you disagree.'

except
See **accept, except**

expect
See **anticipate, expect, hope**

expeditious, expedient
Expeditious means speedy and efficient, while **expedient** implies an action that is convenient for

the purpose: 'It was considered expedient to wind up the firm as expeditiously as possible.'

expertise, skill

Expertise is a posh word for **skill**, although it appears to have acquired a broader meaning, encompassing special skill and knowledge tempered by experience.

facility, faculty

Of the various meanings the one that causes most confusion centres on ability. By **facility** we usually mean the ability to do something with apparent ease: 'She had the charming facility to put people at their ease.' By **faculty** or **faculties** we mean our natural or inherent powers (intelligence, sight, hearing, smell, taste, intuition, etc): 'The task ahead was going to challenge all his faculties to the hilt.'

facsimile

See **replica, copy, facsimile**

faint, feint

Faint means weak, feeble, indistinct; and also to lose consciousness. A **feint** is a feigned or pretended attack intended to mislead.

farther, further

Word police insist that **farther** be used in the context of distance, and **further** when speaking or writing figuratively: 'He guessed that Bristol was much farther from London than Bath, but refused to think further about it.' Nowadays the two forms are interchangeable.

feel

See **believe, feel, think**

few, little, less

It is not unusual for a diet-conscious product to assert that it is **less** fattening, **less** expensive and has **less** calories. Two correct out of three; what is meant is '**fewer** calories'. Use **less** with singular nouns, **fewer** with plural nouns. The same goes for **little**: 'Although I have little spare time, I do have a few minutes to spare now.'

fiancé, fiancée

The first is masculine; the second, with the double ee, is feminine.

fill in, fill out

There's logic here; when you **fill in** something, you insert: 'I filled in the gaps; I filled in the form.' When you **fill out** something you add or complete: 'He filled out John's speech with some spicy anecdotes.'

flagrant, blatant

Flagrant is shocking and outrageous; **blatant** is loud and obvious.

flammable

See **inflammable**

flout, flaunt

Flout means to show contempt or deliberately defy; **flaunt** means to show off boastfully.

forego, forgo

Forego means to go before, to precede; **forgo** means to do without, or to give up something.

formally, formerly

Pronounced the same, spelt differently, and often confused. **Formally** means in a formal, ceremonious or established manner. **Formerly** means in past or earlier times.

fortuitous, fortunate

Something that happens by accident or chance is **fortuitous**; if the result is a happy one, it is also **fortunate**: 'Our meeting in the supermarket was fortuitous, and fortunately she remembered the money she owed me.'

frequently

See **commonly, frequently, generally, usually**

frightened, scared, alarmed, afraid

Afraid has a certain permanence about it: 'He was afraid of crossing roads.' To be **frightened**, **scared** or **alarmed** is more a passing experience. You are also frightened or scared *by* ghosts, not *of* ghosts.

gaol, jail

Both are correct but the former is increasingly regarded as being out of date.

genuine

See **authentic**; see also **replica, copy, facsimile**

genteel, gentle, Gentile

Two of these are well understood: **gentle** means tender and kindly, the opposite to rough, coarse and violent; and a **Gentile** is a non-Jewish person. **Genteel** is trickier; it originally meant well-bred and refined but is now mostly used in a mildly sarcastic way to send up ordinary people who ape middle-class lifestyles.

god, God

The Greeks had **gods**; Christians have **God**, the supreme being, always with a capital G.

gourmand, gourmet, epicure, glutton

Deepest in the trough is the **glutton**, who will eat anything and any amount of it. Then comes the **gourmand**, who, while appreciating what he's eating, loves to eat. Finally, the **gourmet** and the **epicure**, both of whom appreciate the finer points of eating and drinking except that to the **epicure** the joy of food is almost a religion.

guarantee, warranty

Although somewhat interchangeable, a **guarantee** is an agreement to repair or replace, while a **warranty** is a promise that what is being sold is the vendor's, and is serviceable and fit for the use claimed.

guess, suppose, think

To **guess** is to put forward an opinion; to **suppose** is to assume something is true; to **think** is to arrive at a point of view by meditating or remembering.

gynaecologist, obstetrician

A **gynaecologist** specialises in diseases of the urinary and genital organs of women; an **obstetrician** deals with all aspects of childbirth.

had had, had have

There are times when we all get boxed into a corner with the dual **had**: 'If I had had the time, I'd have . . .' Perfectly grammatical but not a pretty sight. Try to avoid it, and avoid totally **had have** and **had of**.

hence, thence, whence

Think of **here**, **there** and **where**: they went **hence** (from here); they advanced **thence** (from there, or that place); **whence** came the new arrival? (from where?).

hereditary, heredity

Hereditary means transmitting or passing by inheritance; **heredity** is the ability of living things to pass qualities from one generation to another. 'He was given a hereditary title; whether his intellect is a product of heredity or environment is anybody's guess.'

Hindi, Hindu

A **Hindu** is a member of the Indian religion of Hinduism; **Hindi** is the language.

hire, rent, lease, let

Modern marketing has introduced a large degree of interchangeability here: you can now **hire**, **rent** or **lease** a car; you can **hire** or **rent** a hall; you can **rent** or **lease** a building, although strictly speaking, **rent** is the money you pay. To **let** a flat means that temporary possession of the property is granted on payment of an agreed **rent**. He who lets is the **lessor**; he who pays the rent is the **lessee**.

hitherto, previously

Hitherto means up to this time, until now; **previously** means until then, prior to: 'Hitherto we have ignored the demands'; 'Previously, the demands were not unreasonable.'

hoard, horde

A **hoard** is a store or an accumulation; **to hoard** is to collect and store. A **horde** is an unruly and often unpredictable crowd of people.

homicide, manslaughter, murder

Homicide is the killing of one person by another. **Murder** is the unlawful killing of another with 'malice aforethought'. **Manslaughter** is the unlawful killing of another but without premeditation, usually under provocation, in the heat of passion, or through negligence.

hope

See **anticipate, expect, hope**

Hopefully

If you are seeking direction on the use of the word **hopefully** you may read this **hopefully**, or **full of hope**, for that is its traditional meaning. But recently a second meaning has intruded into the language: 'Hopefully, the team will play better next time.' Here, the meaning is **'let's hope'** or **'it is hoped'** and it has occasioned many visits from the word police. However its respectability in this sense can be readily defended; it originated from the German **hoffentlich**, meaning **'I hope so'** and travelled with German migrants to the US last century, there to be translated as – **hopefully**. More recently it crossed the Atlantic to Britain where it resides, a misunderstood and mocked orphan, in dire need of friends.

---

hotel, inn, public house, pub, bar

The services of **hotels** should include meals and accommodation; they need not necessarily be licensed to serve alcoholic liquor. **Public houses** or **pubs** are licensed, as are **inns** and **taverns**; they may or may not serve food or offer accommodation, and all the terms are more or less interchangeable. All have **bars**, from which are dispensed intoxicating drinks, but a **bar** can also be an establishment such as a **wine bar** or **gay bar**.

idea, opinion

An **idea** is a concept, a creation; an **opinion** is a view, judgement, assumption, belief.

Idioms

The words and terms in *Word Check* are almost without exception from the orthodox English vocabulary; what are known as idiomatic expressions – **pay through the nose, don't rub it in, take it to heart**, etc – are altogether omitted. In any case most people, perhaps instinctively, have little trouble with their use in their own language. But what does a foreigner, learning English, make of this group of idiomatic add-ons to the word **look**?

look slippery – be quick
look up – refer to
look out – be wary
look down on – scorn
look up to – respect
look daggers – angry stare
look yourself – act normal
look sharp – be alert
look alive – be awake
look see – make an inspection
look over – examine carefully
look for – search
look to – pay attention
look after – care for

---

if, whether

If an alternative is implied, use **whether**: 'Did you notice whether or not he returned the book?'; not 'Did you notice if he returned the book?'

illegible, unreadable

Illegible is usually taken to mean writing that cannot be deciphered because of fading or damage. **Unreadable** is most often used to describe writing that is bad, tedious or boring.

illiterate, ignorant

An **illiterate** person is not necessarily **ignorant** but for some reason has never learned to read or write.

illusion, allusion, delusion

An **illusion** is a deception of the mind or eye; an **allusion** is a passing reference to something, or mention of something; a **delusion** is a false belief.

immigrant

See **emigrant, immigrant**

imminent

See **eminent, imminent**

immoral

See **amoral, immoral**

imply, infer

To **imply** means to express indirectly, to hint or suggest; to **infer** is to deduce: 'I inferred that they had a bad attitude to working, and implied that I wasn't prepared to put up with their behaviour.'

impracticable, impractical

See **practicable, practical**

in, in to, into

In expresses a place, and is static: 'She is in the bathroom.' **Into** expresses motion and direction: 'She went into the bathroom.' And recognise the sense of purpose in: 'She walked towards the bathroom and went in to powder her nose.'

inapt, inept

Inapt means unsuitable or inappropriate; **inept** means clumsy, ill-conceived.

incredible, incredulous

Incredible means unbelievable or beyond belief, but is often used wrongly to mean surprising or wonderful. **Incredulous describes the inability to believe.**

infectious, contagious

Contagious diseases are transmitted by physical contact; **infectious** diseases are spread by germs in the air or in fluids.

infinite, infinitesimal

Two easily confused opposites. Something **infinite** is so great it has no limit; **infinitesimal** is so small as to be negligible: 'It is a mystery why the scientists took such infinite pains to measure such an infinitesimal difference.'

inflammable, flammable

Inflammable means intensely **flammable** but there is always the danger that, thinking the 'in' prefix means 'not' in this case, some people may assume that **inflammable** means **not flammable**. That's why we're seeing more and more **flammable** and **highly flammable** labels on products likely to catch fire.

ingenious, ingenuous

An **ingenious** person is clever and inventive; an **ingenuous** person is someone who is open, frank and candid.

initiate

See **begin, commence, initiate, start**

injury

See **accident, injury**

inquire

See **enquire, inquire**

insolvency, bankruptcy

Insolvency happens when a person can't pay his debts when they are due. If he cannot realise his assets he may be declared **bankrupt**, the official, public state of insolvency, when assets are distributed to creditors. When a company goes bust it goes into **liquidation**, either compulsorily or voluntarily.

insurance

See **assurance, insurance**

insure

See **assure, ensure, insure**

invariably, always

Invariably means fixed, unchanged and never varying; **always** means uninterruptedly, at all times. The difference is thus subtle and rarely observed.

irony, sarcasm, satire

You're waiting for a bus, the rain is belting down and you are splashed by passing cars. The next person in the queue says, 'Lovely day, isn't it?' That's **irony**: saying something the opposite of

what you mean with the intention of mocking.
Sarcasm is a bitter, derisory form of irony: 'Well,
thanks for telling everyone about our secret!'
Satire is the witty demolition of stupidity,
wickedness and folly.

It, its, it's

You cannot go through the day without
using **it** a few hundred times. Nor, it seems,
can you go through the day without seeing
its or **it's** used wrongly. The only time **its**
has an apostrophe is when it is used as a
contraction for **it is**: 'It's raining'. The
possessive form of **it** is **its**, always without
an apostrophe: 'The bird fell off its perch.'
When in doubt, read it: 'The bird fell off
it's perch' would sound like, 'The bird fell
off it is perch', which is plainly wrong. So
don't do it.

---

jail
See **gaol, jail**

jealousy
See **envious, enviable, envy, jealous**

Jew
You don't refer to a Christian as a Christian
person or a Hindu as a Hindu person, so why
say 'a Jewish person' or a 'person of the Jewish
persuasion' when you mean a **Jew**?

judicial, judicious
Judicial refers exclusively to justice and the law
courts; **judicious** means showing good judgment,
and also prudent and expedient.

306

kerb

See **curb, kerb**

kind of, sort of, type of

These are all interchangeable except in the informal sense of 'He sort of has a funny effect on me', and 'I felt kind of relieved it was all over.' The important grammatical point, however, is that **kind, sort** and **type** are all singular. 'This kind of TV programme' becomes in the plural 'These kinds of TV programme' and not 'These kinds of TV programmes'.

kipper, herring, bloater

Each of these is the sea fish **herring**. When split, salted and smoked it is called a **kipper**; a **bloater** is a herring cured whole without being split open.

laid, lain, lay, lie

Remember the difference between **lay** and **lie** by reciting: 'Lay down the law and lie on the floor.' In other words, to **lay** is to put or set down something, while to **lie** is to recline. The same goes for **laid** and **lain**: **laid** is something put down, while **lain** is something or somebody reclining: 'After he laid the table, he went to lie down.' 'The corpse was lying on the floor; it had lain there for days.' **Lay/laying/laid; lie/lying/lain**. What may give you grief, though, is **lay** when used as **lie** in the past tense: 'She simply lay there and cried.'

lama, llama

A **lama** is a Tibetan or Mongolian monk; a **llama** is a South American animal.

lawful, legal, legitimate

Lawful means permitted by law; **legal** means relating to law. **Legitimate** has a wider range of meanings – proper, natural, conforming to custom – but often refers to children born in wedlock or legally descended.

Lawyer, barrister, solicitor, silk

A **lawyer** is a member of the legal profession and is usually a barrister or a solicitor. A **barrister** pleads in the courts; a **solicitor** is a legal advisor to his clients and to barristers. An **attorney** is a practitioner in Common Law, while a **notary public** verifies contracts and deeds and administers oaths. A **silk** is a barrister who dons a silk gown on becoming a Queen's Counsel.

---

less

See **few, little, less**

libel, slander

A **libel** is something written, published or broadcast that damages the character and reputation of someone. **Slander** is spoken defamation.

licence, license

A **licence** (noun) is the piece of paper, evidence of permission granted; **license** (verb) is the act of authorising: 'He was granted a licence to sell liquor and became a licensed victualler.'

lightening, lightning

'As the sky was lightening at dawn, flashes of lightning illuminated the horizon.'

likely, liable, apt

Likely is a useful word to express degrees of probability: 'It is likely to be a fine day today.' **Liable** indicates a strong probability but, curiously, is almost always used in a negative sense: 'It is liable to rain today', derived no doubt from the word's primary meaning of being exposed to an obligation: 'We could be liable for damages.' **Apt** implies suitability, appropriateness or having a tendency to something: 'At his age he's apt to tire easily.'

literal, literary, literate, literally, littoral
If someone says, 'He literally hammered the guy into the ground', you should expect to see the flattened remains of a person merging with the earth. **Literal** means actual; unfortunately rather too many of us use it in the opposite sense; what we really mean is 'figuratively'. **Literate** means having the ability to read and write, and **literary** means pertaining to literature. **Littoral** is the odd man out; it is a shoreline.

loan, lend, lent
Loan is a financial transaction: you can raise a **loan** from a bank. However, you can **lend** someone a book: 'The bank loaned him £5,000'; 'She lent me the books last week.'

loose, lose
Use **loose** to describe anything free, hanging, unfastened: 'She loved loose clothing'; 'The vampire was on the loose again.' **Lose** describes loss: 'Give him money and he's sure to lose it.'

lunch
See **dinner, supper, lunch or tea**

maintain
See **claim, allege, assert, maintain**

majority, more, most

More means greater – in quantity, number, extent and importance; so does most, except that it implies an estimate. Majority also means more, but only of things that can be counted; minority is its opposite. The clichés, 'vast majority' and 'tiny minority' are therefore wrong.

malevolent, malicious, malignant

Of this similar trio, malevolent is the closest to evil intent; malicious implies a premeditated desire to hurt and injure; malignant means capable of harm to a life-threatening degree.

manslaughter

See homicide, manslaughter, murder

mantel, mantle

Mantel is the shortened form of mantelpiece, while a mantle is a cloak or covering.

masterful, masterly

Masterful means imperious, domineering, self-willed. Masterly implies extreme skill: 'With a flurry of masterly strokes he finished the painting.'

may

See can, may, might

may be, maybe

May and be are two words: 'It may be correct'; 'I may be ill tomorrow.' Maybe means perhaps or possibly: 'Maybe I'll be ill tomorrow.'

meantime, meanwhile

A lot of interchangeability here, as both can be used as adverbs and nouns: 'In the meantime, I waited in vain'; 'Meanwhile we waited as patiently as we could.'

media, medium

The **media** is the agglomeration of newspapers, magazines, television and radio stations, cable and telephone networks whose business is communications. **Media** is the plural of **medium**; *The Times* is a print medium; the BBC is a broadcast medium.

meretricious, meritorious

The first means superficial and flashy but empty and valueless; the second means excellent and praiseworthy.

Halfway test

Some of the statements below contain words that are used incorrectly. Can you identify them without reference to **Word Check?** Answers over the page.

1. Smoking adversely effected his breathing
2. He depreciated the comedian's efforts to amuse the crowd
3. She did the majority of her washing at the laundry
4. It was fortuitous that we bumped into each other
5. The explosive gas diffused through the city
6. The place was decimated; nobody was left alive
7. The captain was borne aloft by the delighted crowd
8. After an enjoyable shower he felt enlivened and enervated

---

middle
See **centre, middle**

midget
See **dwarf, midget, pygmy**

might
See **can, may, might**

millennium
The second **millennium** is just around the corner so watch the spelling. It's one thousand years.

minimum, minimal, minimize, minuscule
Minimum and **minimal** mean the smallest, the least possible: 'The minimum amount served from this pump is two litres'; 'He was taxed at the minimal rate'. To **minimize** is to reduce to the smallest possible amount, degree, extent or size. **Minuscule** (watch the 'u') means anything extremely small.

Misuse malapropisms

Here are some finely turned malapropisms from writers who should know better:

- The Saxons had coarse mating on the floor.
- In the Middle Ages, ploughs were drawn by bollocks.
- At ancient feasts the head of a bore was put on a platter.
- They found tools, dishes and bowels at the burial site.
- The restaurant will be remembered in the anals of gastronomy.
- The island people were much feared Satin worshippers.

moral, morale

Moral concerns right and wrong in human character and conduct; **morale** is a mental state of confidence and optimism: 'The moral standards of the officers had a bad effect on the morale of the troops.'

Answers to Halfway test

Statements 4, 5 and 7 are correct. The incorrect statements should read:
1. Smoking adversely **affected** his breathing. 2. He **deprecated** the comedian's efforts. 3. She did **most** of her washing at the laundry. 6. To **decimate** is to reduce by one in ten, so a better way of expressing the scene would be: 'The place was totally destroyed; nobody was left alive.' 8. After an enjoyable shower he felt enlivened and **energized**.

Moslem, Muslim

The latter is now the accepted form for a member of the Islamic religion.

murder

See **homicide**, **manslaughter**, **murder**

must

The overuse of the word **must**, as in, 'A visit to the British Museum is an absolute must', can be discouraged by remembering that in Anglo-Indian a **must** is the frenzied state of an elephant on heat.

mutual, common

There is a difference. **Common** means something shared by two or more or all; **mutual** implies something shared, experienced or felt between two: 'The boys' reluctance to share the blame was mutual'; 'In the end the various parties found common ground.'

nadir, zenith

The **nadir** is the lowest point of anything; the **zenith** is the highest point.

naturalist, naturist

A **naturalist** studies natural history; a **naturist** enjoys natural surroundings – in the nude.

nauseated, nauseous

If a terrible sight made you feel **nauseated**, you woud describe it as a **nauseous** sight.

necessities, necessaries, essentials

Few people preserve the differences here because they are extremely subtle. In usage, they have all come to mean about the same, which is why we are prone to add prefixes like 'bare necessities' and 'absolute essentials'.

negligent, negligible

To be **negligent** is to be careless and indifferent, to neglect something, often to a dangerous degree. **Negligible** means unimportant, trivial, insignificant.

neither, none, nor

Neither means not either of two, and thus, like **either**, is singular: 'Neither of his two novels is read much nowadays.' And while **either** is followed by **or**, **neither** is followed by **nor**: 'Neither Jane nor Thomas is to go out today.'

None simply means not one; whether it is singular or plural is open to argument and subject to circumstance: 'Not one of my colleagues is supporting me' could be written, 'None of my colleagues are supporting me'.

net, nett
The former is correct.

nevertheless, none the less
Nevertheless means however, yet, notwithstanding. **None the less** (in America written as one word) means 'not any the less': 'I was quite ill; nevertheless I felt I should go'; 'Although I was none the less eager to go, my illness prevented me.'

New York, New York

New York is both a city and a state, hence New York (city), New York (state). To avoid ambiguity, the city is called New York City (NYC). Manhattan is not New York City but one of its five boroughs; the others are Bronx, Brooklyn, Queens and Staten Island.

---

nice
Of the two meanings, only that of 'discriminating and precise' retains its original definition; the second meaning – variously agreeable, pleasant, attractive, kind – has through overuse attracted an entire layer of vague meanings. Replace by more specific adjectives to convey what you really mean.

noisome, noisy

Noisy needs no explanation, but noisome has nothing to do with noise: it means objectionable and offensive.

no one, no-one

No one is at home means that nobody, no person, not anyone is at home. It is written as two words for obvious reasons (noone!) although some prefer to hyphenate.

notable, noted, notorious

If you are **notable** you are a person distinguished by some aspect of worthiness or character. If you are **noted** it is usually because of some outstanding skill or achievement: 'He was a noted bassoon player.' If you are **notorious** you are a celebrity for all the wrong reasons.

noxious, obnoxious

See **obnoxious, noxious**

nutritious, nutritional

Certain foods may be **nutritious**, meaning nourishing, but not **nutritional**, which refers to the process of nourishing the body: 'The nutritional needs of the patients require at least two nutritious meals a day.'

objective, subjective

To be **objective** means to be uninfluenced by any prior beliefs, personal feelings or prejudices. To be **subjective** is to be the opposite, to be over-influenced by personal considerations or relationships.

obligate, oblige

Of the two, **obligate** implies a moral or legal duty, while **oblige** means to render a favour or to accommodate: 'The man had obliged him on several occasions, and now he felt obligated to repay the loan.'

obnoxious, noxious

Obnoxious is usually applied to personal behaviour and means aggressively unpleasant. **Noxious** is something potentially injurious.

obsolete, obsolescent

If something is **obsolete** it is out of use or out of date; if it is **obsolescent** it is in the process of becoming obsolete.

obstetrician

See **gynaecologist, obstetrician**

obviate, obliterate

Obviate means to remove, to make unnecessary: 'The new car park will obviate the need for people to park in the street.' **Obliterate** means to remove or efface by destruction.

odious, odorous

Odious means unpleasant and detestable; **odorous** applies only to smells, and may be pleasant. To describe a bad smell, use **malodorous**.

official, officious

Official implies the holding of a position of authority; **officious** means self-important and unnecessarily intrusive: 'The official in charge was officious in the extreme.'

off of

'He told us to get off of the grass' is wrong. Lose the **of**: 'He told us to get off the grass.'

one, one's, oneself

The use of **one** ('One isn't obliged to use the indefinite pronoun but it can be useful at times') can often lead to inelegancy and pompousness as any sentence containing it must use **one's** and **oneself**: 'No matter how much one tries to protect one's life, in a war it is only too easy to hurt oneself.' Many good writers go through life without ever using this form, preferring the more idiomatic: 'No matter how much you try to protect your life, you can still get hurt in a war.'

ongoing, continuing

Ongoing is an 'in-word' (ongoing dialogue/ situation/programme) for which there are better choices: **continuing**, **developing**, etc.

on to, onto

Until recently, **on to** as a single word was unrecognised. Both forms are interchangeable, except in the sense of: 'He refuelled, then drove the car on to his destination.'

opponent

See **adversary, opponent**

opportunity, chance, possibility

Chance, as any gambler knows, is a force by which things happen without cause; **opportunity** is the recognition of a favourable opening; **possibility** is the likelihood of something happening or existing.

Optical options

Ophthalmologists and **oculists** are medical doctors who specialise in diseases of the eye. An **optometrist** tests eyes and vision and prescribes, while an **optician** fills out prescriptions and makes and sells spectacles. Artificial eyes are made by **ocularists**.

or, nor
See **neither, none, nor**

oral, aural, verbal
Oral refers to the mouth, thus spoken; **aural** refers to the ear, thus heard. **Verbal** refers to words, spoken or written, and can be ambiguous if not used correctly. An **oral** examination is one that is spoken. A **verbal** agreement may or may not be in writing; if the former, specify 'written agreement'.

ordinary
See **average, ordinary**

orient, orientate
As with **disorient** and **disorientate**, they are interchangeable.

orthopaedic, paediatric
An **orthopaedist** was once the medical specialist who treated deformities in children, and this is why there is confusion between the two terms. Nowadays an **orthopaedist** treats the bone, joint and muscle problems of children and adults; a **paediatrician** treats children only.

overly

The use of this word is common enough ('She was not overly fond of cabbage') but continues to be frowned upon. Purists might suggest: 'She was not over-enthusiastic about cabbage.'

paediatric

See **orthopaedic, paediatric**

pair

See **couple, pair**

palate, palette, pallet

The **palate** is the roof of the mouth; a **palette** is an artist's board on which colours are mixed; a **pallet** is many things but most visibly the robust timber tray on which are stacked bulky goods for easy lifting and transportation.

parameter, perimeter

A **perimeter** is a boundary or limit. A **parameter**, a very much misused jargon word, is a mathematical term for a constant, with variable values, used to determine a problem – nothing to do with boundaries at all.

part from, part with

To **part from** someone means to leave; to **part with** something is to give it away or give it up.

partial, partially, partly

Partial can mean either prejudiced, or incomplete, so only use it when the meaning is clear: a 'partial account' of some event could mean either. The same applies to **partially**, so if in doubt, use **partly**.

Passable pairs

Quite a few words in the language have evolved with two spellings, both of which are acceptable. Here are some examples:

gipsy, gypsy	leaped, leapt
hoofs, hooves	learned, learnt
movable, moveable	leaned, leant
hiccup, hiccough	racism, racialism
instal, install	spelled, spelt

passed, past

'We saw the car pass at tremendous speed'; 'We told the police that the car passed at a great speed'; 'But that was ages ago; it was in the past.'

per, a

'We worked ten hours per day' is considered inferior to the plain 'We worked ten hours a day.' Restrict the use of **per** to commercial or legal contexts, as in 'per annum'.

perceptible, perceptive, percipient

Perceptible means observable or able to be recognised or measured. **Perceptive** means 'quick to see and understand'; **percipient** is a near synonym, except that in this case the perceiving has a hint of the unexplainable about it.

peremptory, perfunctory

Peremptory means final, decisive, precluding questions and objections. **Perfunctory** means careless and half-hearted: 'After drilling in such a perfunctory manner, the squad was peremptorily ordered to the cookhouse.'

permanent, perennial

Perennial does not, as many people seem to believe, mean 'year after year'; its correct meaning is **permanent**, unfailing, unceasing, long-lived.

perpetrate, perpetuate

Perpetrate means to commit something, to carry something out; **perpetuate** means to preserve by making eternal: 'He perpetrated such a wonderful hoax that the event was perpetuated by an annual dinner.'

perquisite, prerequisite

Easily confused. A **perquisite** (perk) is a benefit or privilege, often regarded as a right; a **prerequisite** is a precondition: 'One of the men's prerequisites for a settlement was not to take away the car parking perquisite.'

personal, personnel

Personal is an adjective ('I've been going through my personal expenses') while **personnel** is a noun meaning the staff of a company or organisation.

perspicacity, perspicuity

The first means 'clearness of understanding'; the second, 'clearness of statement'. As Eric Partridge put it: 'Perspicacity is needed to grasp the distinction, and perspicuity to explain it.'

persuade

See **convince, persuade**

peruse, read

Peruse is often believed to mean reading something casually, at a glance. It means the opposite, which is to read and examine carefully and critically.

petition, partition

A **petition** is a request, a plea, a formal written supplication to some authority; a **partition** is a dividing wall.

Petrol and other hydrocarbons

Petroleum is what comes out of the oil well, and **petrol** (**gasoline** or **gas** in the US) is refined from it. **Paraffin** (**kerosine** in the US, Australia and other countries) is also distilled from petroleum. What comes out of the pumps marked **derv** (Diesel Engined Road Vehicle) is **diesel** oil, one of the heavier fractions broken down from the crude petroleum.

---

plaid

See **tartan, plaid**

podium

See **dais, lectern, podium, rostrum**

possible, plausible, feasible

Possible means that something can exist, happen, or be done; **feasible** means that something is capable of being done. If an argument or statement appears to be reasonable or true it is **plausible**: 'The plan was plausible, for although the river was subject to flooding it was still feasible to construct the bridge.'

practicable, practical

Practicable means feasible, capable of being done and put into practice. **Practical** has a wider range of meanings, including useful, usable, sensible, realistic, efficient: 'It was practicable to climb the wall with a rope, but a more practical plan was to get a ladder.' Their opposites, **impracticable**

and **impractical**, mean 'unfeasible, impossible, unattainable' and 'useless, ineffective' respectively.

practically, virtually

These often confused words have quite different meanings. **Practically** means in practice, effectively, while **virtually** means almost, very nearly: 'Living on anything they could find, the people were practically starving, and clean water was virtually non-existent.'

practice, practise

'The doctor had **practised** medicine for nearly forty years, thirty of them from his **practice** in Harley Street.'

precede, proceed, supersede

To **precede** is to go before or come before; to **proceed** is to continue or to go forward: 'As they proceeded to the altar, the Archbishop **preceded** the Queen.' **Supersede** means to displace or replace someone or something: 'Many people regretted that the Authorised Version had been superseded by the Revised English Bible.'

predicate, predict

Predicate seems to be catching on as a synonym for **predict**, which it is not. **Predict** means to foretell, while the original meaning of **predicate** is to imply, affirm or assert: 'He predicated that the election result would turn on the issue of inflation but declined to predict the result.' In the US, **predicate** almost always means **based**: 'His views on economic policy are predicated on the need to lower inflation.'

pre-empt, prevent

To **pre-empt** is to do something or obtain something beforehand, to appropriate something in advance of other claims. To **prevent** is to hinder or stop.

premier, première

Premier means first or foremost and is often used as a title for a country's leading statesman. **Première** is used exclusively for first performances of plays and films: 'After its **première** in London next week the play will **première** in New York in August.'

prescribe, proscribe

The words are opposites: **prescribe** means to recommend a course of action or lay down rules, while **proscribe** means to banish or forbid: 'Smoking is proscribed on the Underground.'

presume

See **assume, presume**

preventative, preventive

Both mean 'to prevent something from happening or recurring', but a fine difference is emerging. **Preventative** is used as a noun: 'Against the common cold, vitamin C is an effective preventative; that's the view of preventive medicine.'

previously

See **hitherto, previously**

principal, principle

A very tricky duo. The meanings of **principle** are fairly straightforward: a fundamental truth, a belief or doctrine, an agreed rule of action or conduct. **Principal** can be an adjective (meaning of chief importance) or a noun (meaning the leader, the head; or a sum of money on which interest accrues): 'The school principal said his principal aim was to insist on students observing a code of strict moral principles.'

Of proctors and prostates

A not uncommon malapropism goes something like this: 'He's seeing the doctor because of his prostrate trouble.' **Prostrate** means to lie face down, while the **prostate** is a male reproductive gland that tends to peter out with age. And a **proctor**, perhaps because it rhymes with doctor, is sometimes thought to specialise in diseases of the anus. In fact a **proctologist** does that; a **proctor** is a university official, one of two elected annually.

---

prognosis
See **diagnosis, prognosis**

program, programme
Programme (program in the US) is still preferred in Britain, although **program** has made considerable inroads in the computer industry.

prone, prostrate, recumbent, supine
The good news is that they all refer to lying down. The bad news is that they all have different meanings. To lie **prone** is to lie face downwards; **prostrate** assumes the same position but suggests exhaustion and helplessness. **Recumbent** is lying in any comfortable position, while **supine** is lying listlessly on the back, looking upwards.

proposal, proposition
While both mean 'something suggested', **proposal** is more of an offer, as in a **proposal** of marriage; a **proposition** is a stronger suggestion, even an assertion, that might invite discussion

before agreement. That said, they are both fairly interchangeable.

Psycho matters

This is an area of potentially embarrassing confusion. **Psychosis** is the generic term for disorders of the mind marked by a loss of touch with reality; **psychotics** suffer from **psychoses**, and **psychiatry** is the branch of medical science which deals with mental disorders and their diagnosis, treatment and prevention. **Psychotics** may be **psychopaths**, persons with anti-social personality disorders; **schizophrenics**, whose minds and feelings have parted, causing a withdrawal from reality; or **neurotics**, persons with unbalanced minds suffering from obsessive behaviour, unreasonable fears and hysteria. **Psychology** is the study of the mind and its behaviour; **psychoanalysis** is a treatment method based on the patient's memory of his or her past life; **psychotherapy** is a treatment based on action on the mind itself and not on the use of drugs or operations.

---

purposely, purposefully

Purposely means on purpose, intentionally. **Purposefully** means the same but with added determination, and with some definite purpose or objective in mind.

quantitative, qualitative

Quantitative refers to quantity and proportions, of amounts, size and volume; **qualitative** refers to quality, of characteristics, properties, attributes and singularities.

quantity, number

Use **number** only when the total can be counted:
'To make the juice you use a large number of
oranges and a large quantity of water.'

quantum leap

This term is used rather loosely; strictly speaking
it is a change or an advance of unprecedented
magnitude with no apparent connection with
anything that preceded it.

quite, rather

Because the meaning of **quite** is completely,
entirely, absolutely ('He flung himself down,
quite exhausted') it seems odd that we persist in
using it to mean **somewhat, sort of** and **rather**:
'The horse was going quite well until the fifth
jump.' **Rather** is preferred.

quorum, quota

A **quorum** is the agreed number of people
required to be present before a meeting can be
held; a **quota** is a proportion, a limit, an agreed
number or amount.

rain, reign, rein

Rain we all know about; **to reign** is to rule and a
reign is a period during which a particular
monarch rules; to **rein** is to check or control, and
a **rein** is the strap which controls and guides a
horse: 'The constant rain of criticism did nothing
to stop Henry VIII giving full rein to his appetites
throughout his entire reign.'

raise, raze, rise

To **raise** is to elevate; to **raze** is to do the reverse:
to destroy completely, to level with the earth.
Raise is also creeping in to mean 'rear children',
but most people would prefer to **raise** sheep and

bring up a family. You also **raise** your head but
rise in the morning and **rise** from your chair.
British English still prefers a **pay rise** to the
American **raise**.

rapt, wrapped

Rapt means engrossed and absorbed; **wrapped**
means enveloped, enfolded, blanketed.

react, respond

A **reaction** is a **response** to some stimulus, so
react is an extremely vague term. To be more
precise, use words like **respond** and **reply**. 'His
immediate response was to reply in no uncertain
terms.'

really

See **actually, virtually, really**

rebut, refute, repudiate, deny

There are several shades of meaning among this
lot. To **rebut** is to contradict by argument; to **deny**
is to assert that an allegation or statement is false;
to **repudiate** is to disown, reject or refuse to
admit a charge or claim; and to **refute** – the
strongest and most convincing denial of all – is
to prove that an accusation is false.

receipt, recipe

A **receipt** is a written acknowledgement that
something has been received; a **recipe** is a
formula of ingredients and instructions to make
something, usually in cookery. However, in the
past, receipt meant the same as recipe.

recoup, recover

Recoup means to regain or replace a loss, usually
financial; **recover** is used in a broader way:
'When he recovered from the fainting spell he
also recovered his composure.'

reduce, lessen

Virtually interchangeable, except that **lessen** tends to be used where numbers are involved in the quantity: 'By reducing his petrol consumption, he lessened the number of weekly trips to the garage.'

regretful, regretfully, regrettable, regrettably

The first two mean to feel sorry or show regret, while the second pair is used when sorrow or regret is caused: 'Regretfully, I am forced to cancel our plans'; 'The problems caused by the cancellation are regrettable, but I had no other option.'

regulate, relegate

Regulate means to adjust, control or restrict; **relegate**, as any football fan knows, means to consign to an inferior position.

reiterate, repeat

Repeat is to do, make or say something again. If there is a difference it is that **reiterate** tends to be used to express the repetition of a word, statement, account or request often in order to stress it.

relatively, comparatively

Use only when there is something to be relative to, or something to compare with: 'Although it appeared to be a most ambitious project, it would occupy relatively/comparatively little of his time.'

replica, copy, facsimile

It is generally accepted that a **replica** is a duplicate made by the original artist, or made under his supervision. A **facsimile** is a copy exact in every respect and detail. A **copy** is the most general term and can be a duplicate (a Xerox) or state-of-the-art colour reproduction, or anything in between.

replicate, repeat

Although increasingly used as a synonym for **repeat**, **replicate** means rather more than that. Technically, a **replication** is a repeat of a study or of research, using the same data and methods, to confirm whether the result will be the same.

repudiate

See **rebut, refute, repudiate, deny**

respectably, respectfully, respectively

Respectably means in a way that is honest, decent and deserving respect. **Respectfully** means with respect. **Respectively** means in the order given: 'John, Amy and Sarah are aged twelve, nine and five respectively.'

restful, restive, restless

Restive and **restless** are the opposite to **restful**, which means peaceful, calm, inviting rest. A **restless** person is one who cannot be still or quiet, while a **restive** person (although more often a horse) is one who frets under restraint.

restaurant, restaurateur

The latter owns or manages the former; note the spelling.

revenge, avenge

Revenge is personal retaliation: 'I eventually got my revenge by having him arrested for harassment.' To **avenge** a wrong, the punishment is meted out by a third party as a form of rough justice: 'They avenged my father's murder.'

reverse
See **converse, inverse, obverse, reverse**

review, revue
'The revue had been enthusiastically received but the cast was shattered by the savage review in *Variety*.'

rheumatism, arthritis
Rheumatism is a term covering a variety of painful diseases of the joints and muscles; **arthritis** is local inflammation of a particular joint.

robbery
See **burglary, robbery, stealing, theft**

Roman Catholic
See **catholic, Catholic**

rostrum
See **dais, lectern, podium, rostrum**

saccharin, saccharine
The first is the sugar substitute; the second means excessively sweet.

sacred, sacrosanct
Sacred means dedicated to religious use: holy, and not to be profaned. **Sacrosanct** is more intensive, and means 'incapable of being violated, pure and incorruptible'.

sadism, masochism
Sadism is the desire to inflict physical pain on others and derive pleasure [usually sexual] from it; **masochism** is the desire to be physically abused or humiliated by another [usually for sexual pleasure].

salary, wages, remuneration

A **salary** is usually fixed as an annual rate, and divided into months or weeks; **wages** are rates paid by the day or week. **Remuneration** is payment for a service, not necessarily on a regular basis.

same, similar

'Harry sold six cars last week, and a similar number this week.' What is meant here is 'the same number this week'; **similar** means resembling something or someone.

sanatorium, sanitarium

The first offers curative services, as with health farms and rest homes; the second is a little-used term for a hospital.

sarcasm, satire

See **irony, sarcasm, satire**

sceptical

See **cynical, sceptical**

Scotland, Scotsman, Scot and Scotch

Natives and institutions of Scotland are Scottish or Scots: Scotswoman, Scottish smoked trout, Scottish writers. There are a few exceptions including Scotch broth and, of course, Scotch whisky (not whiskey, that's made in Ireland).

---

see, witness

To **see** is to observe something with your eyes; to **witness** something is to observe with the eyes

333

and other senses: 'I saw the car go past but did not witness the accident.'

sensitive, sensual, sensuous

Sensitive means acutely susceptible to influences, highly responsive to stimulus, easily offended. A near synonym is **sensibility**, but this has come to mean heightened feelings for what is socially correct. **Sensual** pleasure derives from physical indulgences like eating, drinking and sex; **sensuous** refers to arousal through all the senses: listening to music, smelling a flower, watching a sunset, feeling silk, etc.

sewage, sewerage

Perhaps you may need to know this one day: **sewerage** is the sewer system, and **sewage** is what passes through it.

shall, will

Full directions for the correct use of **shall** and **will** would frighten most people, so it's not surprising that the distinctions have largely disappeared, helped on their way by the increasing adoption of the contractions **I'll**, **she'll**, **he'll**, **they'll**, which can mean either. Churchill further hastened the rot with his 'We shall fight on the beaches . . .' speech, in which he consistently used **shall** instead of **will** in the first person to express determination. Writers and speakers wishing to preserve traditional usage are advised to consult any good grammar book. Meanwhile, the use of **shall** is now almost confined to 'officialese': 'Passengers shall not talk to the driver while the vehicle is in motion.'

should, would

The fate of **shall** has also befallen **should** because of an overdose of complex rules. 'I should like to see some of your work' looks and sounds elegant but in modern usage it has largely been replaced by **would** or **I'd**.

silicon, silicone

Silicon is the chemical element which is all about us in the form of sand; **silicone** is a synthetic silicon compound used to make lubricants, water repellants and a range of other products.

simile, metaphor

A **simile** uses a direct comparison, usually preceded by as, as if, or like: 'He was as thick as two planks'; 'The party went like a house on fire.' A **metaphor** makes an analogy: 'You're a doll'; 'She's a pain in the neck.' A **mixed metaphor** combines two incompatible metaphors: 'We've got a real headache on our hands'; 'This decision is a very hard blow to swallow.'

It's a problem situation

A **situation** is, simply, a position or location, or a state of affairs. Yet the word is being increasingly used superfluously ('crisis situation' to mean crisis; 'emergency situation' to mean emergency) and ambiguously (a mother–daughter situation – meaning what?). Be wary.

---

slander

See **libel, slander**

sleight, slight

Sleight means dexterity, as in the 'sleight of hand' of a magician; **slight** means small, slim, insignificant.

so-called

This is regarded as a put-down or sneer term, like **self-styled, would-be** and **self-proclaimed**. It indicates that what follows is to be held up to question or ridicule: 'The so-called animal lovers said they had collected a petition of ten thousand names.'

solecism, solipsism

In linguistic terms, a **solecism** is a violation of conventional usage, more or less confined to faulty syntax and incorrect pronunciation. **Solipsism** is the theory that only the self is real and knowable.

sort of

See **kind of, sort of**

source, cause

The difference is illustrated by: 'The source of his headache was that blow to his head.' In fact, the blow was the **cause**; the **source** may have been a punch by a boxer, a thrown brick or running into a wall.

specially

See **especially, specially**

specialty, speciality

The first is preferred in the US, but both are interchangeable.

stationary, stationery

Stationary means fixed, not moving, standing still; stationers sell writing material, which is called **stationery**.

straightened, straitened

You **straighten** something by making or bending it straight; **straitened** means restricted: 'The couple lived in straitened circumstances.'

strategy, tactics, stratagem

Strategy is the planning of an operation, while **tactics** involve putting the strategy into effect. A **stratagem** is a scheme designed to deceive.

Stroke, coronary, heart failure

A **stroke** is a cerebral haemorrhage, a burst blood vessel in the brain that often results in paralysis. A **coronary**, or more correctly a **coronary thrombosis**, is caused by a clot in the coronary artery, stopping the supply of blood to the heart. **Heart failure** or **heart attack** covers a variety of disorders in which the heart is suddenly unable to cope with pumping blood to the body. Most heart failures are treatable.

---

subconscious, unconscious

Subconscious has two meanings: that of being only partly aware, and, more commonly, the thoughts that occupy the hidden level of the mind and influence our actions. To be **unconscious** is to be unaware: 'She was unconscious of the danger she was in.' It can also mean total loss of consciousness: 'After the accident he was unconscious for two days.'

subjective

See **objective, subjective**

substitute, replace

A subtle but interesting difference: **substitute** means to 'put in the place of', while **replace** means to 'put back again in place': 'She carefully replaced the candlesticks but substituted a cheap imitation for the priceless bowl.'

successive

See **consecutive, successive**

supersede

See **precede, proceed, supersede**

suppose

See **guess, suppose, think**

surely, certainly, definitely

Certainly and **definitely** are interchangeable and so, for the most part, is **surely**. However **surely** can also imply safely and securely: 'He made his way slowly but surely up the cliff face', and is also used to emphasise a question: 'Surely you're not going to climb up there?'

swingeing, swinging

Swingeing (pronounced swinjing) means severe in degree: 'People tend to forget that the Swinging Sixties also saw swingeing tax increases.'

sympathy

See **empathy, sympathy**

synthesis

See **analysis, synthesis**

tactics

See **strategy, tactics, stratagem**

Tales from the clypt

As long as there are words that look and sound alike, the merry list of malapropisms will run forever:

- Mrs Connor's doctor was arrested for possession of heroine.
- One of the restaurant's specialties was barely soup.
- He was so angry we thought he'd blow a casket.
- We wrecked our brains trying to think of the answer.
- Most Chinese speak the mandolin dialect.
- I never did like that cold slaw.

tartan, plaid

Tartan is the distinctive patterned cloth used for certain Scottish garments, including the kilt and the **plaid** – the shawl worn over the shoulder.

tasteful, tasty

Tasteful is something that embodies or employs aesthetic discrimination or good taste: 'The reception rooms were tastefully furnished.' **Tasty** means flavourful to the palate, although colloquially it has also come to mean sexually attractive.

testament, testimony

A **testament** is a will, the document by which a person disposes of his estate after death. **Testimony** is evidence, proof or confirmation, often given under oath. See also: **evidence**, **proof**, **testimony**

theft

See **burglary**, **robbery**, **theft**

That, which, who

That and which are relative pronouns that are becoming more and more interchangeable despite the rules about their use. However, a couple of these rules should be observed. **That** is used to refer to persons, animals and things; **which** to animals and things; **who** and **whom** to persons. Use **that** to restrict or define the meaning or intention of the preceding word or phrase: 'The hotel that Helen stayed at has burnt down.' **That** defines or identifies the hotel for us. Use **which** when the identifying information is already supplied in the sentence: 'The Imperial Hotel at Bath, which Helen stayed at last year, has burnt down.' Whether to use **who** or **that** for persons can be a problem, but generally, **that** is used to refer to any person, and **who** to a particular person: 'The mechanic that fixed this car ought to be shot'; 'My mate Jim, who was supposed to fix the car, ought to be shot.' Most people now solve this problem by using **who** indiscriminately.

their, there, they're

They look different but sound the same and often confuse. **Their** is a possessive pronoun: 'It is their car.' **There** means in or at that place: 'She left the car there; now it's gone.' **They're** is a contraction of 'they are'.

think

See **guess, suppose, think**

though

See **although, though**

till, until

Till is a short form of until, meaning 'up to the time when': 'I'll stay until the bar closes.' Both are interchangeable, but **until** is preferred.

titillate, titivate

The first means to tickle or excite; the second means to smarten up.

TNT, dynamite, gelignite

Dynamite, a compound of liquid nitroglycerin and absorbent material, was the invention of Alfred Nobel in 1866; he followed this with blasting gelatin or **gelignite** in 1875. **TNT** or tri-nitro-toluene is the most recent of the trio and safest from friction and shock.

---

ton, tonne

An English **ton** is 2,240 lbs; a short or American **ton** is 2,000 lbs; a metric **tonne** is 1,000 kilograms or about 2,200 lbs.

tortuous, torturous

Tortuous means twisting, winding, devious; **torturous** means inflicting torture and pain: 'Following the dark, tortuous passages became a torturous nightmare.'

toward, towards

Both, meaning 'in the direction of' or 'in respect of', are interchangeable. Use according to taste, appearance and sound: 'They steered toward/ towards the horizon'; 'The storm broke towards dawn.'

truth

See **veracity, truth**

try and, try to

Try to is correct, and in most cases, sounds better to the ear. Although **try and** is so common as to be considered colloquial, **try to** avoid it.

turbid, turgid

Turbid means clouded, muddy, opaque; **turgid** means swollen, bloated, inflated. A river in flood can be both turgid and turbid.

unaware, unawares

Two different words, two meanings. If you are **unaware** (adjective) you are not aware or you are ignorant of something; if you are caught **unawares** (adverb), something has happened without warning and you are surprised.

unconscious

See **subconscious, unconscious**

under

See **beneath, under**

uninterested

See **disinterested, uninterested**

unique

Unique means without like or equal, the only one of its kind. Yet we persist in using pointless modifiers like 'so unique', 'absolutely unique', 'most unique' and so forth. If you think something may be **unique**, don't say 'nearly unique' but, 'It is so rare, so exceptional, that I think it may be unique.'

unless

See **except, unless**

unprecedented

The free use of this word, which means first, original, unparalleled, unheard-of, can land you into trouble. Announce something or some event as **unprecedented** and the chances are that they are not; further, someone is likely to pop up and smugly point out your error. Make sure of your facts before using it.

unreadable

See **illegible, unreadable**

until

See **till, until**

upon, on

With a couple of exceptions, **upon** and **on** are interchangeable: 'She sat upon/on the chair.' However, you would hardly begin a fairy story with, 'Once on a time . . .'; nor does the ear respond favourably to, 'The suburbs stretched mile on mile . . .'

urban, urbane

Urban refers to the city, as in urban living, urban architecture; **urbane** means poised and sophisticated: 'Ten years of urban life had transformed the country boy into a witty, urbane gentleman.'

use, utilise, usage

Use is synonymous with the other two words in most cases and should be preferred. **Utilise** has the narrow meaning of making useful, or turning to profitable account: 'The company utilised the old factory to manufacture office furniture.'
Usage – especially in the context of the English

language – is the recognised practice of something; it is also applied where quantities are involved: 'Water usage in Kent rose 30% last month.'

valuable, invaluable, valued

Valuable means having great value, or being worth a lot of money. **Invaluable** means priceless, precious beyond valuation: 'Her friendship at this difficult time was invaluable to him.' Apart from its use as 'I'm having my watch valued', meaning to estimate the worth of something, **valued** means esteemed and highly regarded: 'Of all the things he valued most, her friendship was paramount.'

veracity, truth

Truth is something that is true, that is fact. **Veracity** is the capacity for being truthful, accurate and honest: 'We can depend upon his admirable veracity for the truth to come out.'

verbal

See **oral, aural, verbal**

viable, workable

The true meaning of **viable** is 'the capability to maintain independent existence in life'. It has, however, become an overworked and inaccurately used buzz-word, to the extent that a doctor once claimed: 'Suicide is a viable alternative to painful terminal illness.' Try to limit its use to mean capable of surviving and thriving independently: 'The Channel Tunnel is expected to be operationally viable by the year 2010.' **Workable** means something or some plan that is practicable and can be made to work. (See **practicable, practical**; also **possible, plausible, feasible**)

Vicars and other men of God

The differences between **parsons**, **rectors** and **vicars** are largely historic. **Parsons** and **rectors** were the most fortunate because their parochial posts (called a living) included church property and income (called the benefice) and revenue from the parish (called the tithe). The poor **vicar** got none of this, nor did the **curate**, who was an assistant to the parish priest. Their respective residences are called the **parsonage**, **rectory** and **vicarage**. A **curacy** is a position, not a residence.

vicious, viscous

Vicious implies a propensity for vice, hatred, spite and desire to hurt; **viscous** means thick and sticky, and is usually applied to liquids.

virtually

See **practically, virtually**

wages

See **salary, wages, remuneration**

waive, wave

These two are often confused. **Waive** means to relinquish, not to insist on something: 'He waived his right to speak.'

want

See **desire, want, need**

whatever, whatsoever

Whatever means 'no matter what' ('Whatever the problems, I promise to finish the job') and also 'what' ('Whatever is the matter?'). **Whatsoever** is vaguely synonymous in the context of 'at all': 'Have you no manners whatsoever?' But the usage that has grown into a monster has resulted from the hijacking of **whatever** to mean 'and so on and so forth and who cares anyway?': 'On Saturdays I usually do some shopping, wash my hair, empty the cat litter, generally slob around and, you know, whatever . . .'

whether
See if, **whether**

To whomever it may concern: who and whom

Without getting into personal, relative and predicate pronouns and objects of finite verbs, it is not easy to explain the rules governing the use of **who** and **whom**. As a consequence, popular usage all but abandons **whom** on the grounds of (a) the likelihood of using it incorrectly, and (b) it sounds pompous. Furthermore, exclusive users of **who** are probably right 8o% of the time. But if you wish to take a stab at **whom**, the rough-and-ready **who/whom** – **he/him** – **she/her** formula will help: simply substitute **he** or **she** for **who**, and **him** or **her** for **whom**. Thus 'He is a man who/ whom I know is honest.' He is honest? Him is honest? The answer is he, and therefore the correct choice is **who**. You can remember this with the celebrated Hemingway mnemonic. Which sounds right: 'For Whom The Bell Tolls? It tolls for him'; or 'For Who The Bell Tolls? It tolls for he'?

which

See **that, which, who**

will

See **shall, will**

witness

See **see, witness**

workable

See **viable, workable**

would

See **should, would**

wrapped

See **rapt, wrapped**

Xerox

Many of us say, 'Can you Xerox this for me, please?', even though the copier might be a Canon or some other make. Like Hoover, Durex and Cellophane, Xerox is a trade name, not a generic name, and should be capitalised.

your, yours, you're

Your means belonging to you: 'I love your house'; 'Is that your opinion?' **Yours** denotes the particular one belonging to you: 'Is that jacket yours?'; 'That son of yours is a real tearaway.' It is never spelt with an apostrophe. **You're** is often confused with **your** but it is a contraction of **you are**; thus the contraction of 'You are quite mad!' is 'You're quite mad!'

Yours sincerely, Yours truly

Yours does not have an apostrophe; if it did it would mean 'your is'. **Yours Truly** and **Yours Faithfully** are customarily reserved for impersonal letters; **Yours Sincerely** when the addressee is named.

zenith
See **nadir, zenith**

Style

Introduction
Into the jungle, with machete and cleft stick

Let us be brave. We are about to hack our way into a jungle. The dense, tangled world of obscure and difficult language. Officialese. Jargon. Circumlocution. Verbiage. Pomposity. Cliché. All the ugly growths that prevent us understanding a piece of writing.

Perhaps the obstacle is a letter from the town council, which for all we know might have a drastic effect on our future.

Perhaps a newspaper story which makes us stop and re-read, seeking its meaning.

Or perhaps an advertisement for a job we might fancy . . . if only we knew what the wording meant.

This guide, though, is not meant to help the baffled reader to fight his way through the thickets of spiky legalisms, prickly abstractions and choking verbosity.

It is an effort to help you, the **writer** of the letter, memo, report, manifesto, survey or press release, to make sure your writing is cleared of such obstacles to understanding.

Don't be a sloppy copycat

In business and bureaucracies, it is easy to fall in with the writing habits of everyone else around you: sloppy, vague and clumsy.

A letter, memo or report from someone who is known to write clearly and with precision will obviously be more welcome, and read more keenly, than a dreary wodge of waffle and obscurity.

Your own writing will be most effective when it is clear and direct. People who write in a straightforward way always shine out against the dim grey mass of Sloppies.

As a writer, you have to be tighter

The usual advice on clear expression is: 'Write as you

speak.' That advice is sound enough – but in everyday conversation we do not generally need the clarity and precision we should aim for in the written word, which cannot be helped along with the odd smile, shrug, frown or particular tone of voice.

Perhaps the advice should be amended slightly, to: 'Write as you speak – but make it tighter.'

People can lose sight of the purpose of putting something in writing. The purpose is usually not to compose a fancy array of words, but to say what you mean. Clarity can be its own form of elegance.

Before you begin to write, THINK –

- What do I want to say?
- Am I making just one main point, or several?
- If several, what's the order of importance?

You may find it worthwhile to jot down your points before starting your letter, notice, press release or story. If you use a word processor, of course, it may be just as easy to get all your thoughts down first, then sort them into an acceptable order, on the screen. (*See* Wonders of the Word Processor, p. 439.)

It is easy to confuse even the simplest message by using language that is not clear, or to lose the reader's attention by being too complicated – or simply going on too long.

Sometimes, of course, it may be undesirable to be too clear and concise, if your words are likely to commit you or your employers to something better avoided. Even then, you should be clear exactly what you are trying not to say, and why. That kind of imprecision requires skill, not mere sloppiness.

The shorter the better, but don't be a machine-gun

Your English will be clearer and crisper if, in the main, you keep your sentences short. But this can be overdone. Short sentences, yes. But not all the time. Otherwise your reader may feel he or she is being sprayed with a machine-gun.

A 'crescendo' effect of short and longer sentences – for example, short/short/shortish/long – makes easier, more interesting reading:

> The vicar looked strained. The usual smile was missing. Mrs Parrot had no idea what might be the matter. But she was determined to get to the bottom of it, before going home that night.

Take a tip from a master-novelist

But they didn't devote the whole evening to music. After a while, they played at forfeits; for it is good to be children sometimes, and never better than at Christmas, when its mighty Founder was a child himself. Stop! There was first a game at blind-man's buff. Of course there was. And I no more believe Topper was really blind than I believe he had eyes in his boots.

Charles Dickens, *A Christmas Carol*

The English language can be a bewildering jungle, if you let it. But there are plenty of markers to guide us. If we keep our nerve steady, our eyes wide open and our cutting-blade sharp, together we can hack a way through . . . and emerge into the sunny glade of clear, concise English.

And, once safely back to the relative civilisation of the office, with the machete and cleft stick stowed in the stationery cupboard, how satisfying to stand at the copier with your crisp, fresh document . . . watching as a less well-schooled colleague's handiwork, sodden with cliché, drenched in jargon, swamped with officialese, comes oozing out of that machine.

From Here to Obscurity: The Baffling Art of Officialese

If language can be a jungle, officialese is the minefield laid among the thorny thickets and clinging creepers of that jungle. Faced with a mass of pure officialese, the bravest of us is likely to radio for a rescue helicopter.

Despite the successes of the Plain English Campaign, officials in government, local councils and other bureaucratic organisations still too often try to lure us into their own well-loved, baffling word mazes.

A railway announcer may proclaim: *Due to an earlier person on the line, trains will be subject to intervals.*

Intervals between services are certainly a sound way of avoiding collisions: otherwise the announcement is typical, thoughtless officialese.

The language of officialdom can obliterate all meaning. Feel the undergrowth closing in, as you try to fight your way out of this tiger trap dug by the Department of Health and Social Services . . .

Case of the crippled sentence

> A person shall be treated as suffering from physical disablement such that he is either unable to walk or virtually unable to do so if he is not unable or virtually unable to walk with a prosthesis or an artificial aid which he habitually wears or uses or if he would not be unable or virtually unable to walk if he habitually wore or used a prosthesis or an artificial aid which is suitable in his case.

> taken from *Gobbledygook*,
> published by the Plain English Campaign

This would-be 'sentence' first of all reflects a legalistic terror of punctuation: the full stop or comma which, misplaced, might lead the Department all the way to a House of Lords appeal.

Let us take our machete to the undergrowth, bring in the wire-cutters, and try to discover what, if anything, this passage struggles to convey. A step at a time, for fear of booby-traps.

A person shall be treated as suffering from physical disablement . . . treated? This is not intended as medical advice, but since the background is medical, the reader may, however briefly, be confused. Lift out *treated*. Replace it with *considered*. And that chance of confusion disappears.

Suffering from physical disablement Why not simply *physically disabled?* And while we are at it, we don't need *as* after *considered*. Pluck it out, hurl it into the jungle shrubbery.

So far, in our cleaned-up version, we have 'A person shall be considered physically disabled' – and we don't seem to have lost any of the intended meaning.

Such that he is either unable to walk or virtually unable to do so Wrench away the clumsy *such that he is* and replace it with *which makes him*. Next, we cut out *either* – because we don't need it.

We now have 'which makes him unable to walk, or virtually unable to do so.' More tightly expressed as 'which makes him unable, or virtually unable, to walk'.

Peering into the gloom, we next tackle *if he is not unable or virtually unable to walk with a prosthesis or an artificial aid which he habitually wears or uses . . .* Stop! The rest is just the gibbering of jungle monkeys. This seems to mean that the poor chap can get around, but only with the help of a prosthesis or other artificial aid. The word *even*, before *if he is not* would have helped. But we simply do not need this tangled heap of words at all.

The entire 'sentence', if it means anything, must surely mean this:

A person is regarded as physically disabled if he always needs an artificial aid to walk.

This was a prime example of the need to think 'What do I want to say?' And then to say it, the simple way.

A serious case of effluxion

From a London borough council, this smokescreen:

> And take further notice that under the provisions of Section 47(2) of the said Housing Act 1974 in relation to any land consisting of or including Housing Accommodation in a Housing Action Area, a landlord must not less than four weeks before the expiry by effluxion of time of any tenancy which expires without the service of any Notice to Quit, notify the council in writing that the tenancy is about to expire in accordance with the said schedule 4 . . .

A model of mixed officialese and legalese: you can almost see the glint of watch-and-chain on the Town Clerk's egg-stained black waistcoat. How do we turn it into something like English, without losing any legal force the passage might be required to have?

For a start, there seems no need for *And take further notice*. If the reader is not going to take notice, there seems little point in the writer finishing his masterwork. Next: *under the provisions of Section 47(2) of the said Housing Act 1974* – the words *the provisions of* are redundant. Let's lose them. The same goes for *said*.

And next: *in relation to any land consisting of or including*. The lawyers can keep their *consisting of or including*, just in case they are struggling to cover, say, a backyard where someone lives in a caravan. But *in relation to* can shorten to *concerning*.

We have now brought *concerning* clumsily close to

356

consisting, so let us replace *consisting of* with *that consists of*. The word *Accommodation* after *Housing* is not needed. And once *Housing* is left standing by itself, the capital H becomes even more obviously unnecessary.

Plodding on: *a landlord must not less than four weeks before the expiry by effluxion of time . . .* Quickly to the dictionary, to seek out this excitingly unfamiliar word, *effluxion*. We find:

> Efflux, n. Flowing out (of liquid, air, gas: also fig.)
> That which flows out. Hence effluxion, n).

From its meaning the word suits the prose style, if nothing else. But we can do without *effluxion*. We can also do without *expiry*.

Now, what is the rest of the council's message?

It seems to be that in a Housing Action Area, if a landlord knows that a tenancy is running out, and no notice to quit is needed, he must warn the council in writing, at least four weeks before that tenancy is due to end.

Let us tack that piece of information on to our earlier repair:

> Under Section 47(2) of the Housing Act 1974, concerning any land that consists of or includes housing in a Housing Action Area, if a landlord knows that a tenancy is due to end without need of a notice to quit, he must tell the council in writing at least four weeks before the tenancy runs out.

Still scarcely slick or smooth. But perhaps a shade less forbidding than the original mess.

How axiomatic is your bus shelter?

From the West Yorkshire Passenger Transport Executive:

I refer to your recent letter in which you submit a request for the provision of a bus passenger shelter in Ligett Lane at the inward stopping place for Service 31 adjacent to Gledhow Primary School. The stated requirement for a shelter at this location has been noted, but as you may be aware shelter erection at all locations within West Yorkshire has been constrained in recent times as a result of instructions issued by the West Yorkshire Metropolitan County Council in the light of the Government's cuts in public expenditure and, although it seems likely that the Capital Budget for shelter provision will be enhanced in the forthcoming Financial Year, it is axiomatic that residual requests in respect of prospective shelter sites identified as having priority, notably those named in earlier programmes of shelter erection will take precedence in any future shelter programme.

Let us briefly mop our brows and try to fathom what the poor, befuddled author was battling to say, before we set about helping him say it in English.

At a guess, the passage could be summed up as:

I refer to your request for a bus shelter in Ligett Lane . . . Unfortunately, because of Government spending cuts, West Yorkshire Metropolitan County Council has in turn ordered a curb on bus-shelter building. Although there may be more money for such work in our next financial year, shelters already on the waiting list will obviously be built first.

Where did the author go wrong? Let us lay this Frankenstein's Monster on the slab, and dissect:

I refer to your recent letter in which you submit a request for the provision of a bus passenger shelter in Ligett Lane . . . If the writer identifies the subject clearly enough, there is no need to remind his correspondent of all the details. The correspondent wants a Yes, No or even Maybe – with an explanation, if the answer is No or Maybe.

The stated requirement for a shelter at this location has been noted. Of course it has. Otherwise, the official would hardly be writing at all.

but as you may be aware . . . Word-wasting. It doesn't matter if the correspondent is *aware* or not. Your job is to make sure he knows the facts now.

shelter erection at all locations within West Yorkshire has been constrained in recent times . . . No purpose is served by *at all locations*. There is no reason to use *within* rather than *in*, no matter how widely this particular verbal fungus has spread.

constrained should be replaced by the easier-to-take *restricted*.

in recent times is another redundancy. So is *as a result of instructions issued by*.

Granted that *West Yorkshire Metropolitan County Council* is rendered with a rare and forceful clarity, not a syllable wasted. But then we slide back into the Monster's pit . . . *in the light of the Government's cuts in public expenditure* . . . The only meaning of *in the light of*, here, is *because of*. Your reader, rightly or not, will still blame the Government for the lack of a bus shelter, whether you use the clear or the foggy expression. So why go for the fog? (See *Fog Index*, p. 430)

and, although it seems likely that the Capital Budget for shelter provision will be enhanced in the forthcoming Financial Year . . . The reader is less interested in what the bus-shelter fund is called, than what it will do for him, and when. Ditch *the Capital Budget*. And since a shelter is a shelter, *provision* is yet another unneeded word.

enhanced, in this context, means *increased*. There seems no reason to evade the more common word.

it is axiomatic that An axiom is a self-evident truth. *Axiomatic* is presumably meant to convey *self-evidently*

359

true. If something is that obvious, the writer is wasting his Transport Executive's paper and his reader's time in saying it.

residual requests in respect of prospective shelter sites identified as having priority, notably those named in earlier programmes of shelter erection Hurling a swift grenade into the middle of this, we are left with *Shelter requests not met by earlier building programmes*.

will take precedence in any future shelter programme. Not much, for once, to argue with there – apart, perhaps, from the repetition of *shelter programme*.

The deskbound, wordbound Frankenstein who created our Monster may be sad, even annoyed, at the way we have slimmed down his offspring. But at least he can now discover what he really meant to say.

Q and A to save the day

None of the sorry examples quoted need have happened, if only the writers had held this conversation with themselves:

Q What's it all about?

A It's about when somebody is classed as disabled/ special duty of a landlord in a Housing Action Area/ someone wanting a bus shelter built.

Q What do we want to say?

A We want to say that someone who can't walk unaided is officially disabled/ Housing Action Area landlord has to warn the council when there's about to be a tenancy available/ we can't afford the requested bus shelter just now.

Q Very well. Why don't we just SAY it!

Jargon: smart talk that soon gets tiresome

Jargon – words and phrases which may have started life among a particular circle of people, trade or profession, but spread among others who wish to appear up-to-date.

The Concise Oxford Dictionary explains jargon as 'unintelligible words, gibberish; barbarous or debased language; mode of speech full of unfamiliar terms; twittering of birds.'

Not all jargon is that dreadful, and there is no harm in using a little, every so often. But a lot of it is just a distortion of language – and that can only interfere with meaning.

Some of the worst modern jargon is spoken, rather than written. It is hard to imagine even the most modish jargonaut writing down disc-jockey nonsense such as: 'The time at this hour is twenty-five ahead of the witching hour of twelve noon.'

Technical terms, used among experts as a shorthand language, are not jargon of the kind we are discussing – however opaque they may seem to outsiders. But there are less excusable vogue expressions that have encrusted the language, and we should all take the chisel to them.

Help wanted in the job-ads swamp

Company advertisements offering jobs have created their own hideous swamp of non-language.

cultivational – a fortunately rare sighting, in an English National Opera advertisement for a 'development officer – events', to be responsible for *co-ordinating and administering cultivational and fundraising events.* It is just possible that *cultivational* really means something. Our only guess is that it is something to do with sucking up to people to get them to put some money into a project. Your guess, obviously, is just as good.

driven – as in *quality-driven service organisation*. As with *orientated* (see below), this is merely meant to indicate the firm's sense of priority – in this case, to produce high-quality goods or services.

environment, meaning, usually, the place where the worker will do the job. The firm which boasted a *quality-driven organisation* also promised . . . *a demanding and results orientated environment*. Another company required a background of *progressive sales or marketing environment*. In this case, *environment* presumably meant *business*. In which case, *sales or marketing* would have sufficed. *Progressive* can only mean forward-looking – and few firms are to be found in need of backward-looking candidates.

Should have experience in a fast-moving, multi-assembly environment. Assuming that *multi-assembly* has its own recognisable meaning in the business concerned, why not simply require *experience in fast multi-assembly?*

Environmental hazard on the line

London Underground Ltd, advertising for a Director of Human Resources (see below), demanded *broadly based blue-chip HR experience in unionised environment*. Apart from the *blue chip* nonsense, presumably meaning senior level in a successful company, London Underground clearly wanted someone experienced at dealing with trade unions. In which case, why not say so?

Human Resources (people). Replacement for *personnel*, which, though also bureauspeak, at least does not have the ghastly pretentiousness and pseudo-caringness of *Human Resources*.

motivated is one of the most hard-worked jargon words in job advertisements . . . *the ability to motivate, lead and be an effective team player*; *management and motivation of the sales force*; *should be self-motivated*. In the first two examples, we can substitute *inspire* and *inspiration*. In the third, it is harder to guess what the applicant will be required to prove. *Enterprising*, perhaps. Or *should show initiative*. Or, if those sound too revolutionary for the company's taste, *able to work unsupervised*.

pivotal role. Fancier version of *key role*. Neither means much, to explain a job. If the importance of the post needs to be stressed, what's wrong with *important*?

positive discrimination (favour/preference)

orientated, as in *results-orientated environment* (see *environment*, above). The word is presumably meant to convey what the firm considers important. In this example, its use is *nonsense-orientated*. A company that is not keen on getting results will not be placing job advertisements for much longer. So the whole phrase can be cut out.

Another advertisement required someone *success-orientated*. There is a perfectly good word to replace that: *ambitious*.

postholder (employee)

proactive, mostly found in social services advertisements, describing the approach to a particular job. It means initiating change where needed, as opposed to merely responding to events – *reactive*. Difficult to think of a crisp equivalent, but at least we can try to keep the word out of our everyday language.

363

remit, meaning *responsibility*. It may be shorter, but is not otherwise commonly used, and is pompous.

remuneration package simply means *salary and perks*. If *perks* is too racy, try *other benefits*. Lots of companies do!

skills At first sight, a reasonable word to expect in job advertisements. There are, though, some odd uses, as in *interpersonal skills*, which presumably means *good at dealing with people*.

specific, as in *The main duties of the post will include: developing country-specific and/or product-specific marketing activity plans*. That, heaven help us, came from an advertisement by the personnel department of the University of Cambridge Local Examinations syndicate. They could have said: *Developing plans for selling to particular countries and/or selling particular batches of information.*

structured, as in *it is likely that you will have worked successfully in a sizeable, structured organisation*. You would hardly go recruiting in an *un*-structured organisation.

Of all jargon, among the most impenetrable can be found in council social services departments. An advertisement about a home for teenagers: *The aim of the home is to enable older young people who still have substantial emotional and personal deficits to make planned progress towards personal autonomy* . . .

Even from social worker to social worker, this is garbled nonsense. Surely no professional catastrophe will happen if we simply say: *to enable teenagers with troubled personalities to learn to cope for themselves.*

experience of managing a multicultural urban environment and the ability to integrate equalities considerations into areas of work activity.

This passage, from an advertisement for a Deputy Director of Social Services, is a real polysyllabic mess. *Multicultural urban environment*, despite modern delicacies, simply means *racially-mixed part of town*. And *integrate* may mean here *build in*. Or it may have been misused to mean *include*.

Every trade is entitled to its own jargon . . . up to a point. So let us allow that *equalities* is immediately understood among social services people as meaning equal treatment regardless of race, sex and, probably, physical handicaps – though *equality* in the singular serves the purpose as well, or better.

That passage, converted into plain English, could read:

Experience of dealing with a racially-mixed town area and ability to ensure that equality is part of departmental life.

The same advertisement required *ability to organise intervention in the community to establish the needs of potential service users*. Meaning, presumably, *ability to go out and find what people need us to do*.

Social workers do not have the battlefield to themselves, when it comes to jargon. An advertisement for a health worker in Brazil said:

You will assist the team in formulating and implementing a health policy, evaluating and developing appropriate responses to specific health problems in indigenous areas . . .

365

Meaning: *You will help to plan and carry out a policy to deal with health problems among local people.*

A breathless advertisement by the English National Board for Nursing, Midwifery and Health Visiting, seeking a director of midwifery education, brought the equivalent of motorway carnage to the English language:

> essential qualities include innovative abilities, proven inter-personal and communication skills, an energetic pursuance of goals and a positive approach.

What a spectacular pile-up! What on earth *were* they looking for?

Computerspeak horrors

From the world of computers, source of some of the worst non-language, comes:

> Driven and focused by seeing the world from the customer's perspective, we continue to build an organisation where quality is embedded in every aspect of endeavour . . .

From the same advertisement:

> Our continued growth in the network computing industry mandates that we now identify and attract the most talented and creative Sales and Marketing Professionals . . .

Mandates? This announcement sounds as if it was written by someone for whom English was not the first language, and whose dictionary had a bad coffee-stain on the relevant entry.

Perhaps those who draft such monstrosities should

study this one, tucked among the large, expensive advertisements in the same newspaper's pages:

> KITCHEN DESIGNER (Trainee considered) for thriving Chelsea Studio. Drawing experience essential. Salary negotiable dependent on experience. If you are aged 20–30, educated to at least A-level standard, have a bright personality, thrive on hard work and are happy to work Saturdays, tell me about yourself by leaving a message on my Ansaphone, not forgetting to leave your phone no., or write with brief CV to . . .

Bright. Un-pompous. Direct. And above all, *clear*.

Jargonaut's lexicon

The nastiest entries are graded with j symbols – more js, worse jargon.

accessible, as in *make Shakespeare accessible to the millions* (understandable/attractive) [j]

activist, as in *political party activist* (worker/campaigner)

address, as in *address the problem* (tackle, face, deal with) [j]

airlifted (flown). *Airlift* was originally military jargon for a bulk movement of materials or people by plane. It is hardly warranted in describing, say, a helicopter flight taking a road casualty to hospital. [j]

ahead of, as in *shares rose ahead of the company report* (rose before the company report was published/over expectations from the company report) [j]

albeit (even if/although)

all that jazz (and so on/etcetera) [j]

at risk, as in *these children are on the at-risk register* (danger)

blueprint, as in *this is a blueprint for disaster* (this will end in/means/could mean disaster)

bullish (confident) [j]

cash-strapped/strapped for cash (hard up/short of money) [j]

chair/chairperson (chairman/chairwoman) [jj]

chauvinism – originally obsessive patriotism, after Napoleon-worshipper Nicolas Chauvin. Nowadays usually refers to *male chauvinism*, a vogue expression meaning a man's unwarranted belief in his automatic superiority over women (male arrogance) [j]

come on stream, as in *the new model Rolls Royce will come on stream in April*. Suitable enough as oil-producer's jargon, but now often misapplied to some unlikely fields, from bus production to new radio stations and hospitals (begin production/start working/get under way/open for business) [j]

come to terms with (accept/understand)

concept (idea/notion/plan/proposal) [j]

core curriculum (basic curriculum) [j]

cutback – needless expansion of cut [j]

de-manning (cutting jobs) [jjj]

de-stocking (letting stocks dwindle/shrink/run down) [jjj]

down that road, as in *if we go down that road, what will happen?* (if we do that) [j]

downplay, as in *he tried to downplay the gravity of the case* (play down/minimise/belittle) [jj]

end of the day, as in *at the end of the day, what have we got?* (in the end – or just cut it out!) [j]

final analysis, as with *in the final analysis, it makes no difference* (treat as for *end of the day*) [j]

funded (paid for, backed, supported) [j]

geared to (suited to) [j]

go for the burn (go all out/make the last big effort) [jjj]

go through channels (get authority/follow correct routine) [j]

hands-on, as in *he adopted a hands-on approach to his job as manager*. This seems to mean no more than *he did the job he was paid to do, rather than sit back in his office with the cocktail cabinet permanently open*. A less respectful meaning, possibly in the minds of staff working for this hands-on hero, might be *He's always on our backs and under our feet*. There seems no real need for this expression. [jj]

heading up – use *heading* or *leading*. The *up* is mere cottonwool. [j]

innovative – applied to a person, this presumably means someone with bright ideas – a little longer, certainly, but more immediately understood. Applied to a product, project or work of art or literature, there seems little wrong with *novel*, *inventive* or even *new*, according to context. [jj]

An acute case of the inputs

A core post is available for a Senior Research Associate to take a leading role in the programme. The first projects involve relating nursing inputs to patient outcomes in acute hospitals.

University of Newcastle upon Tyne advertisement

---

input – horrid germ picked up from the computer world, where it is used as a verb meaning *enter*, as in *he inputted the whole file into the computer*. Now likely to turn up elsewhere, as in *planned input of personal supervision*. At best the word means *contribution*. At worst, as in this example, it means nothing. [jjjj]

insightful (perceptive/shrewd) [j]

interface. As a noun, just means *contact*. As a hideous verb, *interface with* means *negotiate with*, *discuss with* or *meet*. Any of these is preferable. [jjjj]

jury is still out, as in *as to whether this move has saved Sterling, the jury is still out* (is not yet known/decided/certain/clear) [j]

logistics, as in the *logistics of the situation* (practicalities) [j]

meet with/meet up with (meet) [j]

methodology (absurd way to convey method) [j]

name of the game, as in *the name of the game is making money* (object) [jj]

new high (new/record high level/height) [j]

new low (new/record low level/depth) [j]

non-stopping, as in *eastbound services will be non-stopping at the following stations . . .* (will not stop) [jjj]

operational, as in *eastbound services are now fully operational* (now working/running) [j]

outgoing (friendly) [j]

overview (broad view) [j]

no way, as in *no way will I do that* – irritating, dated way to say *I will not* [j]

on the back of, as in *shares rose sharply on the back of a good profit forecast* (after/because of) [jj] *ongoing*, as in *we have an ongoing supply problem* (continuing) [j]

pre-condition – a condition is something that has to happen before something else will happen. It is not possible to impose a condition on the past. So *pre-condition*, however popular among politicians (*there must be no pre-conditions for the peace talks*) is nonsense (condition) [jjj]

proven – so rarely used in real language that there seems no excuse for preferring it to *proved*. Certainly it should never have appeared in, of all contexts, a BBC advertisement for a sub-editor with *proven journalistic skills*. Let us hope they found one whose *proven skills* enable him or her to spot irritating jargon at a thousand paces. [j]

put in place (ready/get ready/prepare) [j]

put on the back burner (put off/put back) [jj]

set to, as in *The Emperor was reported to be set to abdicate* (expected to, intending to, about to)

spend, as in *a total advertising spend*. An abbreviation no doubt meant to convey the need for terribly-important executives to save syllable time (expenditure, spending) [jj]

state of the art (newest/latest) [jj]

take on board (accept/understand/comprehend) [j]

terminal (fatal) [j]

track record – except for an athlete, perhaps, *track* record means nothing more than *record*. The next time you draft such an advertisement, be a pioneer: shun *proven track record*. *Experience* will normally do. [j]

user-friendly (easy to use) [j]

viable alternative (alternative/choice/option) [jj]

within, as in *a minimum of 5 years marketing experience within a quality-driven service organisation* (in) (see also *driven*, above) [j]

So long, scenario

Scenario has lately been distorted from its real meaning, which is an outline of a play or film.
- *worst-case scenario* (at worst)
- *completely different scenario* (different sequence of events)
- *scenario for World War Three* (How World War Three might happen)

Depending on context, you can use *prediction*, *programme* or *plan*.

Reach for the de-iser

One increasingly popular and lazy habit is the addition of *ise* to create a verb. Sometimes this does not get in the way of meaning, but at other times it does.

Some *ise* words are part of our orthodox language – for example, *idolise*, *mechanise*, *mobilise*. But in recent years the *ise* has been tacked on, less comfortably, to other words.

normalise, though not much used by real people, is probably too much part of the language of politicians to be got rid of. The humbler of us can make do with *return/get back to normal*.

hospitalise is still rarely heard in Britain, and long may that be so. For conveying direct meaning to the reader, it can never replace *taken to hospital*.

unionise is probably in the same class as *normalise*.

criminalise (transform non-criminal behaviour into criminal), like *politicise* (draw a person or topic into politics), fortunately seems to remain the verbal property of political agitators and social workers who presumably understand each other.

marginalise, meaning *belittle* or *push to one side*.

None of these invented noun-plus-ise 'words' helps clarity.

When in is out
in-flight/in-house/in-car

As with *in-flight movie*, where, assuming we are talking to air passengers, only *movie* or *film* is needed.

As with *brochures produced in-house* – meaning *by the company's own staff* or *on the company's premises*. Using the jargon, we may save a few words. Without it, the meaning will be more immediately obvious to people who do not use it themselves.

As with *in-car entertainment*, grandiose way of saying a radio and tape cassette/CD player. Even retaining entertainment, we can at least get rid of that intrusive *in-*.

In-car has not yet invaded the language as thoroughly as *in-flight* or *in-house*. But these expressions, too, were once as unfamiliar as they are ugly. It would be a bold gambler who bet against *in-car* becoming part of our common speech.

Circumlocution – The Long, Long Trail A-winding

> Bournemouth was on Monday night thrown into a state of most unusual gloom and sorrow by the sad news that the Rev. A.M. Bennett – who for the last 34 years has had charge of St Peter's Church and parish, and who has exercised so wonderful an influence in the district – had breathed his last, and that the voice which only about a week previously had been listened to by a huge congregation at St Peter's was now hushed in the stillness of death . . .

> *Lymington Chronicle*, January 22, 1880

When a writer or speaker fills you with the urge to shout 'Get on with it!', he or she is probably committing the sin of circumlocution. Even in the most purple of today's newspapers, the example above would be a collector's item.

Politicians, of course, are notable circumlocutionists: they often have a keen interest in not being pinned down. Not so long ago, a British political leader went on television to explain his attitude to the introduction of a single currency for all countries in the European Community.

Before you continue reading, it might be as well to find a comfortable seat . . .

> 'No, I would not be signing up: I would have been making, and would be making now, a very strong case for real economic convergence, not the very limited version which the Conservatives are offering, so we understand, of convergence mainly of inflation rates, important though that is, but of convergence across a range of indicators – base rates, deficits and, of course, unemployment – together

with a number of indexes of what the real performance of economies are . . .'

(Perhaps a brief tea-break would be in order here.)

'. . . the reason I do that and the reason why that
is an argument that must be won before there is any
significant achievement of union is not only a British
reason, although it is very important to us, it is a
European Community reason: if we were to move
towards an accomplished form of union over a very
rapid timetable without this convergence taking
place it would result in a two-speed Europe, even
to a greater extent than now – fast and slow, rich
and poor – and the fragmentation of the Community, which is the very opposite of what those
people who most articulate the view in favour of
integration and union really want; when I put that
argument to my colleagues in, for instance, the Fed-
eration of Socialist Parties, many of whom form the
governments in the EC, there is a real understanding and agreement with that point of view . . .'

So what precisely might the gentleman have been
hoping to convey? Probably this:

'I do not want a single European currency until
various other factors affecting the question have
been dealt with. The factors are these . . .'

America's then President, George Bush, was of course
famous for his bemusing circumlocution, as in this
speech defending his accomplishments:

'I see no media mention of it, but we entered in –
you asked what time it is and I'm telling you how
to build a watch here – but we had Boris Yeltsin
in here the other day, and I think of my times
campaigning in Iowa, years ago, and how there was

375

a – I single out Iowa, it's kind of an international state in a sense and has a great interest in all these things – and we had Yeltsin standing here in the Rose Garden, and we entered into a deal to eliminate the biggest and most threatening ballistic missiles . . . and it was almost, "Ho-hum, what have you done for me recently?" '

Circumlocution does not always come in such generous helpings. It is more likely to pop up phrase by phrase. A police officer may prefer *an explosive device*, or even *an infernal machine*, to a *bomb*. *Except* is also frequently contorted into *with the exception of*.

The words *nature* and *character* do heavy circumlocutory duty: *inquiries of a delicate nature/ character* – when *delicate inquiries* is enough. Or *items of a suspect nature will be removed and destroyed* – for *suspect items*.

Well embedded in poor English usage are *with reference to . . . with regard to . . . with respect to . . .* when the writer need only say *about*.

Circumlocutionist's lexicon

As to whether (whether)
as yet (yet)
at the time of writing (now/at present)
at this moment in time (now/at present)
avail ourselves of the privilege of (accept)

Consequent upon (because of)
consonant with (agreeing/suiting/matching)
could hardly be less propitious (is bad/unfortunate/
unpromising)

During such time as (while)
during the course of the day (during the day)

Few in number (few)
for the very good reason that (because)

Give up on (give up)
go in to bat for (defend/represent/help)

I beg to differ (disagree)
in accordance with your instructions (acting on/
following)
in accordance with the regulations (under)
in addition to which (besides)
in all probability (probably)
in anticipation of (expecting)
inasmuch as (because)
in association with (with)
in close proximity to (near)
in consequence of (because of)
in contention (competing)
in contradistinction to (compared to/with)
in connection with (about)
in excess of (over/more than)
in favour of (for, or, with a cheque, to)
in less than no time (soon/quickly)
in more than one instance (more than once)
in many instances (often)

in no time at all (quickly)
in respect of (about/concerning)
in the absence of (without)
in the context of (for/considering)
in the near future (soon)
in the recent past (recently)
in the vicinity (near/nearby)
in view of (because of)

Large in stature (large/big)

Nothing if not (very)

Not, not! Who's there?

The double negative is usually confusing. But it is occasionally useful.

The bomb attack was not unexpected.

If you lived in a terrorist-ridden area, where to be bombed sooner or later was no great surprise, *not unexpected* would convey a suspended kind of expectation better than *was expected* or *was no surprise*.

Generally, though, the double negative is pompous and needlessly confusing:

The Prime Minister is not unmindful of the damage already suffered . . .
The company proposes a not-ungenerous compensation payment . . .

Of a high order (high/great/considerable)
of the opinion that (think/believe)
on a temporary basis (temporary/temporarily)
on the ground that (because)
on the part of (by)

Prior to (before)

Subsequent to (after)

To the best of my knowledge and belief (as far as I know/I believe)
to the extent that (if)

With a view to (to)
with reference to (about)
with regard to (about)
with respect to (about/concerning)

Tautology

Free gift! Added extra! Added bonus!

Exciting claims. Wasted words. All examples of tautology – the use of more than one word to convey the same thought.

A gift, if not free, is not a gift – except in the slang usage 'That car was an absolute gift at £3,000'.

Something *extra* is clearly something *added*. And a *bonus* is normally an *addition*. Even if the word is used to describe something apart from money, an *added bonus* is an *added addition*. Nonsense, obviously. Yet we hear and read *added bonus* every day, from people who have not thought what they are saying, or do not care.

Tautologist's lexicon

absolute certainty (certainty)
added bonus (bonus)
added extra (extra)
quite/very/markedly distinct (distinct)
each and every (each/every)
end result (result)
following an earlier incident – public transport announcements about delays (following an accident)
forward planning (planning)
future plans (plans)
future prospects (prospects)
free gift (gift)
past history (past/history)
really excellent (excellent)
revert back (revert/return/go back)

Quite so

Perfect. Excellent. Unique.

These are words that cannot be qualified. A vase is either perfect or it is not. It cannot be *better* than perfect. So *quite perfect, absolutely perfect* are tautologies. The same goes for *excellent*.

Unique means *the only one of its kind*. You can't get much more unique than that. Not even *quite unique* or *absolutely/utterly unique*.

Witter Words: Dump Your Witter in the Bin

The language is sprinkled with Witter Words –
expressions that clog a sentence and add nothing to the
information or meaning. In this, Witter Words differ
from circumlocution, which certainly adds
information, but adds it in the wrong order, holding
back the main point.

In our elaborate Victorian death notice for the Rev.
A.M. Bennett(see p. 374)the reader has to plod through
53 words before arriving at 'breathed his last'. But those
53 words tell us the place and time of death, how long
he had been vicar, the name of the church, the extent
of his influence and the reaction in the parish to news
of his death.

Witter Words, on the other hand, tell us nothing.
Some are more often heard in speech, especially among
the prattlers of radio and television. But many appear
in writing.

Witter warning list

As it were
As such – as in *the rules, as such, do not preclude* . . .
Often mistakenly used where the writer would do
better to say *the rules, by themselves* or *the rules, alone*
. . . carrying the implication that however limited the
strict rules, there is some other obligation to consider.

By and large
By definition

Funnily/strangely/oddly/curiously enough

Having said that

I am here to tell you

I am the first to admit
If you like – as in *he was, if you like, a rebel*
I have to say, here and now
In a manner of speaking
In point of fact
It goes without saying

Let me just say, right here and now
Let's just be clear about this

Needless to say

Quite simply – as in *quite simply, they are starving*

Shall I say – as in *it is, shall I say, a novel approach*
So to speak

The fact of the matter – as in *the fact of the matter is, the Government were wrong.* Generally used by a politician for *the claim I hope to get away with . . .*

Unless and until – as in *unless and until they pay, there will be no more food for them.* The *unless* is not needed. *Until* makes the necessary condition.

When all is said and done – as in *when all is said and done, we came out on top.* Not entirely meaningless, but perhaps better replaced with *still/however/nevertheless.* With all due respect/the greatest respect
Within the foreseeable future

Here is a sentence which includes three Witter phrases:

> *Needless to say*, we are, *if you like*, facing difficulties which, *when all is said and done*, we did not create ourselves.

The sheer lack of meaning in those phrases becomes

more obvious when we find we can move them around the sentence, to no effect:

> We are, *if you like*, facing difficulties which, *needless to say, when all is said and done*, we did not create ourselves.

Or:

> *When all is said and done*, we are, *if you like*, facing difficulties which, *needless to say*, we did not create ourselves.

All those extra Witter Words, just to say:

> We are facing difficulties which we did not create ourselves.

Saying it ever so nicely

They are called euphemisms: words and phrases with which people avoid making a statement that is direct, clear and honest.

A euphemism is often used out of kindness, when the direct expression might give needless offence. For example a deaf person may be described as *hard of hearing*, a part-blind person as *partially sighted*.

This is taken to an absurd extreme with ultra-euphemisms such as *visually* or *aurally challenged*.

Poor people are *in a lower income bracket* or *under-privileged*. Their slum homes are *inner city areas of deprivation*. When the city decides to clear away its slums, the process is called *urban renewal*, rather than slum clearance.

If part of a city has people from a variety of racial backgrounds, the result is an *ethnic mix* of citizens, any of whom may be proud of his or her *ethnicity*.

Euphemisms abound, and have done for centuries,

when sex is discussed. Adultery was once *criminal conversation*. When lovers met, it was highly likely that *intimacy occurred*. The human body in particular has attracted the euphemists. *Winkle, willy, John Thomas, Percy, todger* and *tool* are only a few of the euphemisms for the male organ; for the female, *pussy, fanny* or simply *down below*. A facetious person might call his backside *my nether regions*. And someone seeking a sex-change operation will find it is called *gender reassignment*.

If the surgeon is *the worse for wear* or *a bit merry*, or has *taken a drop to drink*, a slip of the scalpel may turn the patient into a dead person – *the dear departed*. The body is handed over to a *funeral director*, who will still be unable to shake off the traditional expression, undertaker. Any unwanted belongings will be carted away by a *refuse collector* or *cleansing operative* – whose Old Man would have been a plain dustman.

At the inquest on the departed, someone may allow a false impression to be given, by holding back information – being *economical with the truth*. If the patient's body is lost, somewhere between funeral parlour and graveyard, embarrassing publicity may be dealt with by the undertakers' *corporate public relations director*, or *publicity manager*. The *customer liaison assistant* whose mistake led to the re-routing of the corpse is likely to be subjected by his *Director of Human Resources*, formerly personnel manager, to *outplacement* – the sack.

This news may well drive the customer liaison assistant on an urgent *call of nature* to the *Gents, loo, WC* or *Little Boys' Room*, where once stood the lavatory. A female assistant, of course, would choose the *powder room*, or *Ladies*. (An American is likely to talk of *visiting the bathroom*, even when referring to the family dog's use of a lamp-post.)

A Bit of a Muddle

Muddled writing occurs when the author is not really thinking about what he or she is putting on paper.

Disaster at lunchtime

> The lunch hour is not what it appears to be for the majority of workers.
>
> An hour is more likely to be fewer than 30 minutes for two in every five workers, while a mere 5 per cent take a more leisurely attitude and admit to exceeding the traditional time limit.
>
> *The Independent*

An apparent attempt at being jokey turns the first part of paragraph two into a muddle of statistics likely to dissuade the reader from finishing the sentence.

Mixing ordinary figures with percentages is another irritation: the reader has to stop and work out how the two sets compare. Perhaps the passage can be rescued, though:

> For 40 in 100 workers, that 'hour' is likely to be under 30 minutes. Only five in 100 take a more leisurely attitude and admit to exceeding the traditional time limit.

A nasty mess in the vestibule

> The high for the day was achieved for a marble Georgian chimney-piece circa 1770 with superbly carved tablets of Diana and her hounds.
>
> It went on estimate for £23,650 to Bartlett, the Bermondsey dealer in architectural fittings who paid £330 for three piles of marble at Castle Howard last

year which he has since sold to America for about £150,000, reconstructed as a 15ft vestibule by Sir John Vanbrugh.

Daily Telegraph auction report from the Duke of Westminster's Eaton Hall estate in Cheshire.

A thorough mess, isn't it? Ignoring the jargonaut's *high* in the first sentence (see *Jargonaut's Lexicon*, p. 23), we are violently wrenched from the latest doings of Bermondsey Bartlett to an entirely different event, year and place.

What exactly was it that Bartlett from Bermondsey sold to America? The marble? Castle Howard? Last year itself? And what exactly was *reconstructed as a 15ft vestibule by Sir John Vanbrugh*? Marble? Castle Howard?

And wasn't Sir John Vanbrugh, by then, rather old to be reconstructing anything, being already 62 when he officially died in 1726?

By cheating a little and looking at a reference book, we see that Sir John was an architect as well as a playwright. Castle Howard, in Yorkshire, was the first building he designed. So could it be that the *three piles of marble* had originally been a 15ft vestibule which he designed? Let us assume so. Let us also assume that *sold to America* does not mean *sold to the United States government*.

It now becomes possible, with heavy lifting-gear and wearing our hard hats, to reconstruct this pile of literary rubble – not, perhaps, as a grand 15ft vestibule, but at least as a piece of clear English.

It went at the estimated price, £23,650, to Bartlett, the Bermondsey dealer in architectural fittings. Last year, at Castle Howard, the same dealer paid £330 for three piles of marble, originally a 15ft vestibule by the castle's architect, Sir John Vanbrugh. Bartlett has since sold the marble in America for

£150,000. It has been used to reconstruct the vestibule.

And not a scrap of valuable verbal marble vandalised.

After the smart card, the smart book

> This passbook is required by the Society when making a withdrawal.
>
> Building Society notice

What a clever little book, able to make its own withdrawals. Perhaps the Society has a special aversion to the words *you* and *must*. Otherwise the wording could have been simpler, clearer and more direct –

> You must show this passbook to withdraw money.

To visit, or not to visit

> Trust staff, the report discloses, have been advised that they should only visit the area after midday in the event of an emergency.

That snippet could mean:

> Trust staff have been advised that if there is an emergency, they should not visit the area in the morning.

It could also mean:

> Trust staff have been advised that the only time to visit the area is after midday – and even then, only if there is an emergency.

That word *only* is part of the problem. Pedants have
388

always fretted about the correct placing of the word. In this example, they would be right to fret. Does the writer mean *only visit that area*? Or *visit that area only after midday*? Or *visit after midday only if there is an emergency*?

The other part of the problem is the piece of verbiage, *in the event of*, meaning, in clearer English, *if there is* or *unless there is* an emergency.

What the sentence so clumsily failed to convey was this:

> Trust staff have been advised not to visit the area after midday, unless there is an emergency.

Doorstep body horror

This absurdity, taken from a newspaper, is a masterpiece of muddle:

> A Texan undertaker left the body of a man on the doorstep of his son because he could not afford a cremation.

Apart from the pen-of-my-aunt construction – whose son owned the doorstep? The dead man's son? The undertaker's son? – who could not afford a cremation? The dead man? His son? The undertaker?

At first sight, this dreadful sentence is easy to rewrite without confusion or loss of fact. But try doing it also without repetition, which the writer may have been desperate to avoid:

> A Texan undertaker dumped a dead man on the man's son's doorstep because the son could not afford a cremation.

Clumsy, as well as repetitive.

> A dead man was dumped on his son's doorstep by

a Texan undertaker because the son could not afford a cremation.

Still repetitive.

A dead man whose son could not afford a cremation was dumped on the son's doorstep . . .

Yet again, repetitive.

Just one more heave:

A Texan undertaker who found that a dead man's family could not afford a cremation dumped the body on the son's doorstep.

It is taking no great liberty to introduce the word *family*, and in this context *the* son is normal usage.

Like as not

Lazy (or ignorant) use of *like* can change the writer's intended meaning:

Like the Heath administration more than 20 years ago, the miners have weakened a Tory government's authority.

Now, it is possible – even likely – that a government would weaken itself by sheer cackhandedness. But that is obviously not what the writer wanted to say. It is the *miners* who are alleged to have weakened governmental authority on both occasions. Replace *like* by *as with*, and the problem is solved.

   Like is also widely misused to introduce examples:

It included stars like Frank Sinatra, Bob Hope and Michael Jackson.

Were these mere lookalikes? Or do we really mean stars *such as*? It is lucky, since this misuse is so common, that it rarely causes misunderstanding.

Might or may

Misuse of *may* instead of *might* is common and can confuse. *May* is correct when an outcome of fact is still unknown. *Might* is right when an *if* is lurking in the background – when we discuss something that was likely or possible on some past occasion.

RIGHT: If it had not been for the police, I might have died. (But I didn't.)
WRONG: If it had not been for the police, I may have died.

RIGHT: I accept that I may have been mistaken. (I am still not sure.)
WRONG: I accept that I might have been mistaken.

RIGHT: It might have been a mistake to turn right, so I didn't. (At the time, I wasn't sure.)
WRONG: It might have been a mistake to turn right, because I hit another car.

RIGHT: It may have been a mistake, but I turned right. (I still don't know it if was a mistake or not.)
WRONG: It may have been a mistake to turn right, so I didn't.

Overloading can Sink a Sentence

Consider this passage from the *Daily Telegraph*:

> Seven of the 33 buildings in St James's Square, in the heart of one of the most expensive parts of the West End, display For Sale or To Let signs.

Nothing wrong there. But then:

> The sight of some of the capital's most exclusive business addresses languishing empty – when not long ago they were snapped up as corporate head-quarters – brings home the impact of the recession as financial controllers cut costs by letting out spare space vacated by staff who have been made redundant or exiled to less costly locations.

Now, readers of 'quality' newspapers may be perfectly able to wind their way through that sentence. But why should they have to?

Let us count the items of information that the author has loaded in:

1: some of the capital's most exclusive business addresses
2: are empty
3: when not long ago they were snapped up
4: as corporate headquarters
5: impact of the recession
6: financial controllers cutting costs
7: by letting out spare space
8: . . . which was left empty when staff either were made redundant
9: or were moved
10: to somewhere cheaper

Clearly, the structure ought to be dismantled and

reassembled in more manageable form. The major pieces of information are: (a) The situation is caused by an economic recession; (b) The recession meant that offices were emptied because staff were sacked or moved to cheaper accommodation; (c) Companies also saved money by renting out offices they used to occupy themselves.

What could the author have done instead? If we indulge his taste for *languishing* buildings, he could have written:

> The sight of some of the capital's most exclusive business addresses languishing empty brings home the impact of the recession. Offices have been left empty as staff were made redundant, or moved to cheaper accommodation. Financial controllers have cut costs by letting out the space their companies no longer need.

Sentence under the cosh

The same newspaper carried a less formidable, but nevertheless overloaded, opening paragraph:

> A man living alone was attacked by seven armed robbers who forced him at gunpoint to open the front door of his secluded country cottage before leaving him so badly beaten that he is now afraid to return home.

To cure this, we need help from the second paragraph:

> Mr __, a former England Boys rugby player who weighs 22 stones, was returning to his home in __, Kent, on Thursday from his nearby garden furniture company when the gang struck . . .

393

The main news points seem to be: (a) A man was badly beaten by robbers in his secluded cottage; (b) He was beaten so badly that he is now afraid to return home – presumably from hospital. The additional facts, that there were seven robbers, that they were armed, that they forced him at gunpoint to open the front door, can wait a moment.

The opening paragraph could have read:

> A man living alone in a secluded cottage was beaten so badly by armed robbers that he is afraid to go home. Seven armed men struck as he approached the house, and forced him at gunpoint to open his front door.

In danger of decomposing

From another newspaper, the *Independent*, comes this:

> Cage studied for a time with Schoenberg, in Los Angeles, and electing to follow the Viennese composer's path as opposed to the Stravinskyan alternative available in the 1930s, but finding he had none of the harmonic sense which Schoenberg deemed fundamental to musical structure, he set himself up as primarily a percussion composer interested in the pure unfolding of time and, subsequently, in the pure operation of chance.

Even though this obituary was addressed to people who know their musicians, the sentence still seems to pack in more information than the reader should have to cope with, in one gulp.

Let's break it up, inserting the occasional comma for extra clarity:

> Cage studied for a time with Schoenberg, in Los Angeles, and elected to follow the Viennese

composer's path, as opposed to the Stravinskyan alternative available in the 1930s. Finding he had none of the harmonic sense which Schoenberg deemed fundamental to musical structure, he set himself up as primarily a percussion composer, interested in the pure unfolding of time and, subsequently, in the pure operation of chance.

These slight amendments may still not make the passage comprehensible to those of us who don't know much about that corner of the musical world. But at least they offer a better chance of getting to the end.

Danger: Here be Clichés

Many favourite phrases which once added colour to the language have been worked far too hard, over the years. We all drift into using them: some people can hardly manage a sentence without a cliché or two.

You don't have to give up all clichés for ever: sometimes the hackneyed phrase is the neatest way of expressing yourself. But before plunging on with your cliché, ask yourself: Are you sure? Or might a quick rewrite avoid the need for it?

If you make up your mind to watch out for creeping clichés and ration them, you will be surprised how easy it becomes to do without – and how much fresher your writing becomes as a result.

Here are a few to watch for:

Abdicating our responsibilities
accidentally on purpose
according to plan
act of contrition
acid test
add insult to injury
all at sea
all in the same boat
all over bar the shouting
all things considered
almost too good to be true
arms of Morpheus
angel of mercy
angry silence
as luck/fate would have it
as sure as eggs is eggs
at the end of the day
at this point in time
at your peril
auspicious occasion
avid reader

Bad omens
bag and baggage
ball and chain (marital)
barometer of the economy
bat an eyelid
batten down the hatches
battle lines being drawn
beavering away
between a rock and a hard place
between the Devil and the deep blue sea
beware the Greek bearing gifts
(the) bird has flown
bit of a bombshell
blanket coverage
bleed them white
blind drunk
blind leading the blind
blinkered view
blissful harmony
blissful ignorance
(my) blood boiled
blood out of a stone
bloody but unbowed
blot on the landscape
blow the whistle
(it) bodes ill
bored to death
(the) bubble burst
borrowed time
brought to book
bruising battle/encounter
bumper-to-bumper traffic jams
burden of proof
but I digress

Call of the wild
call the shots/tune
callow youth
calm before the storm

came in from the cold
camp as a row of tents
captive audience
card up his sleeve
cards stacked against
cardinal sin
carrot-and-stick treatment
carte blanche
cast of thousands
cast the first stone
(given a) clean bill of health
catalogue of misfortune/misery
cat among the pigeons
Catch-22 situation
catholic taste
caustic comment
cautious optimism
centre of his universe
chain of events
(as different as) chalk and cheese
chapter and verse
cherished belief
chew the cud
chew the fat
chip off the old block
chop and change
chorus of approval/disapproval
chosen few
come to the crunch
complete and utter candour
compulsive viewing
conspicuous by his absence
consummation devoutly to be wished
cool as a cucumber
cool, calm and collected
copious notes
crack of dawn
crisis of confidence
cup of sorrow runneth over

current climate
cut any ice

Damn with faint praise
Dark Continent
dark horse
dark secret
deadly accurate
deafening silence
deaf to entreaties
deep gloom
depths of depravity
despite misgivings
devour every word
dicing with death
dirty raincoat brigade
doom and gloom merchants
drives me up the wall
(wearing the) Dunce's cap

Eagerly devour
enjoy the fleshpots
eternal regret
(to my) eternal shame
eternally in your/my/their debt
evening of our lives
every man jack of them
every stage of the game

Face the music
fair sex
feed the Inner Man
few and far between
(the) final insult
fine-tooth comb
finger in every pie
finger of suspicion
fit as a fiddle
follow like sheep

fond belief
fraught with danger/peril
frenzy of activity
fresh fields and pastures new
fudge the issue

Generous to a fault
gentle giant
gentler sex
glowing tribute
golden opportunity
go to the ends of the earth
green with envy
ground to a halt
guardian angel

Hand-to-mouth existence
happy accident
happy medium
happily/comfortably ensconced
having said that
heaping ridicule
heart and soul
hell hath no fury
(come) hell or high water
high and dry
hit the panic button
hive of activity
Hobson's choice
hoist with his own petard
horns of a dilemma
horses for courses
howling gale/tempest

Ill-gotten gains
ill-starred venture
(the) impossible dream
inch-by-inch search
inordinate amount of

(one/not one) iota
it seemed an eternity
it will all end in tears
I must fly

Just not on

Keep your head above water
keep your own counsel
knocked into a cocked hat

Lack-lustre performance
large as life
lavish ceremony/banquet/hospitality/praise
leave no stone unturned
leave no avenue unexplored
level playing-field
lick his wounds
little local difficulty
little the wiser
living in the Dark Ages
long arm of the law
long hot summer
lost cause
lost in admiration
lost in contemplation
love you and leave you

Made of sterner stuff
make a killing
man of straw
method in his madness
Midas touch
(the) mind boggles
mixed blessing (worse still, not an unmixed blessing –
see *Circumlocution*, p. 30)
(a) model of its kind
more honoured in the breach than in the observance
more in sorrow than in anger

more sinned against than sinning
mortgaged up to the hilt
move the goalposts
much-needed reforms

Necessity is the mother of invention
no peace for the wicked
not a scrap of evidence
not to put too fine a point upon it

Offer he couldn't refuse
older and wiser
olive branch
one fell swoop
operative word
own worst enemy

Package of measures
painstaking investigation
palpable nonsense
part and parcel
path of virtue
pinpoint accuracy
plain as a pikestaff
plain as the nose on your face
poison/ed chalice
pomp and circumstance
press on regardless
prime candidate
pure as the driven snow
(when/if) push comes to shove

Resounding silence
rings a bell
roll out the red carpet
rose between two thorns
(one) rotten apple in a barrel
ruffled feathers

Sale of the century
search high and low
seething cauldron
set in stone
shake the dust from their feet
shot across the bows
simmering hatred
skin of our teeth
snatch defeat from the jaws of victory
snatch victory from the jaws of defeat
solid as a rock
sorely needed
splendid isolation
spoken for
standing ovation
stick to our guns
steady as a rock
stir up a hornets' nest
straight and narrow
strain every nerve
strange as it may seem
strange to relate
strapping great fellow
straw that broke the camel's back
strike a chord
stuff and nonsense
suffer in silence
suffer fools gladly
sugar the pill

Tarred with the same brush
technological wizardry
tender mercies
there, but for the grace of God
this day and age
thunderous applause
time flies
time heals all ills/wounds
time waits for no man

(in a) time warp
tip of the iceberg
tireless campaigner/crusader
tissue of lies
to all intents and purposes
to my dying day
to my utter chagrin
too awful/terrible/horrible to contemplate
too many cooks
torrential rain
towering inferno
tower of strength

Utter bilge
ultra-sophisticated
(take an) unconscionable time
unequal task
up to his neck in debt/in it

Wages of sin
wash my hands of it
(all) water under the bridge
wealth of evidence/experience/knowledge/material
wedded bliss
welter of evidence
wheels within wheels
whisked to hospital
(idea/man/political party) whose time has come
winter of discontent
with a vengeance
without a shadow of doubt
without fear of contradiction
wringing of hands

What's your cliché rating?

How many from that list are you aware of having
written lately?

More than ten? If there were such a thing as a cliché-holic, it would be you. If your job involves much writing, someone in the office is probably making a secret collection of your greatest excesses. Study the list again. Then promise yourself a thorough cliché clear-out.

Between five and ten? You're not a hopeless case – yet. But do run the cliché detector over your next piece of writing before you let anyone else see it.

Up to five? Not so bad – but don't slacken. If five clichés can get past you, so can six, seven . . . and before you know it, you'll be standing in Cliché Corner *wearing the Dunce's Cap* (see list).

Not one? Almost (as the cliché would have it) too good to be true. But if you're sure you are not even slightly cheating, congratulations on helping to keep the English language fresh and alive.

Complete the cliché

How many of these well-worn expressions can you complete with the missing word?
(Answers below)

1. a gift from the . . . .
2. . . . . scepticism
3. . . . . averted
4. like peas in a . . .
5. . . . . . savage
6. light at the end of the . . . . . .
7. overweening . . . . ./. . . . .
8. blown off . . . . . .
9. address the . . . . .

Awfully Abstract: Soggy Words for Soggy People

An abstract noun represents nothing of substance.
Using one can knock the stuffing out of what you are
trying to say. There is nothing wrong with the words
themselves. They all originally meant something.
Aspect, for example, is correctly used to mean *way of
looking* at a subject: *When viewed from the aspect of
England's interests, it was unsatisfactory.*

But when the word is used to mean *part* or
consideration, your sentence suddenly becomes soggy:
We had to consider the money aspect.

Sogginess is the general effect of the Awful Abstract.
Here are some of the abstract nouns and adjective/
adverb phrases to be found crawling all over the
language nowadays . . .

(in) abeyance (suspended)

abrogation (breach/rejection/spurning)

amenity, as in *the school has gymnasium and swimming
    amenities* (gymnasium and swimming pool)

aspect, as in *the major aspect of the plan* (the important
    part of the plan)

attitude, as in *he adopted a menacing attitude* (he looked
    menacing)

availability, as in *supplies will be subject to limited
    availability* (supplies will be limited/scarce)

basis, as in *he worked on a part-time basis* (he worked
    part-time). The word can sensibly be used when it
    means basis: a foundation, beginning or main
    ingredient. (*He marshalled his troops on the basis of a
    spy's information/ the basis of their romance was a shared
    love of music/ the basis of her pudding was bread.*)

capability/capacity, as in *they have a chemical warfare capability/capacity* (they have chemical weapons)

cessation, as in *a cessation of hostilities was hoped for* (it was hoped hostilities would cease/stop/end)

character, as in *the parcel was of a suspect character* (the parcel was suspect)

degree, as in *she showed a considerable degree of restraint* (she showed considerable restraint)

description, as in *they had no plan of any description* (they had no plan)

desirability, as in *he questioned the desirability of the proposals* (he asked whether the proposals were desirable)

degree, as in *he displayed a high degree of courage* (great courage)

element, as in *there was a rebel element* (there were rebels)

expectation, as in *expectation of jam tomorrow was expressed by the government* (the government expected jam tomorrow)

factor, as in *remember the unemployment factor* (remember unemployment)

feature – see *aspect*

function, as in *following a complete review of the Greater Manchester Police Press and Public Relations Function* (review of Greater Manchester Press and Public Relations)

level, as in *the general level of conduct was unsatisfactory* (in general/generally, conduct was unsatisfactory)

manner, as in *he drove in a reckless manner* (drove recklessly)

nature, as in *arrangements of a temporary nature* (temporary arrangements) *operation*, as in *these lifts are not in operation* (not working)

participation, as in *there was enthusiastic participation on the part of the members* (the members took part enthusiastically)

persuasion, as in *he was of the Methodist persuasion* (he was a Methodist)

situation, as in *please let me know the present state of the situation* (please let me know how things are)

Sharpen Up Your Memos

Writing to an old friend, or your grandmother, you can ramble as much as you like – just as you might, on a cheap-rate phone call.

Business correspondence, of course, is a different matter. You need to be succinct and to get to the main point or points straight away.

Let's imagine you have to tell your boss that a pet project of his has not gone entirely as planned. The bad news is bound to irritate him anyway. And his irritation will not be soothed by having to hunt through a wordy preamble before he stumbles across it.

How not to tell it

You instructed me to organise a 'Knees-up' in a Brewery, to celebrate the 100th anniversary of Hardboiled Eggs plc.

I was asked to approach certain local brewery companies with a view to establishing whether one or other of them would be able to accommodate our function on one or other of our preferred dates, bearing in mind that it has to be held as close as possible to Founder's Day, Friday, February the 13th.

My first inquiry was to Messrs WhatBrew, of Staggering Way, the closest to our own offices. In principle, they were keenly interested, but on checking their bookings for similar events were regretfully forced to conclude that none of our required dates was available, though they certainly hoped to be able to be of service on some future occasion.

I next contacted Messrs Tallyho Breweries, of Stumbling Lane – rather further afield but with an excellent reputation for organising these affairs.

Unfortunately, it appears that they no longer do them, owing to difficulties in obtaining damage and injury insurance for events involving stockbrokers and Rugby players (it was thought commercially unwise to be seen to discriminate against these particular groups).

This left, in practice, only the much smaller firm of Messrs Tipsy & Droppitt, of Hiccups Corner, mentioned in conference by one of the sales force. After several fruitless efforts to contact this brewery, I learned that in fact, as recently as the middle of last summer, they went into liquidation, as a result of the Chief Accountant leaving his wife and five children in order to abscond to Latin America with a considerable sum of his company's VAT money and the MD's third wife (the MD being a hopeless alcoholic).

It unfortunately appears that unless we are prepared to go a good deal further afield for our Knees-up, there is likely to be considerable difficulty in adhering to your original plan.

You may wish to call another conference, or perhaps we could discuss privately any alternative suggestions.

No doubt the boss would be intrigued by the bits of gossip you have picked up during your research. But not when it gets in the way of the main point: What progress with the Knees-up Plan?

By the time the boss got to the fairly muted confession, he or she would have been foaming like a pint of hot WhatBrew's Special XXX, and the writer clearing his desk within the hour.

Much better, then, to come clean from the start.

The quick (and nearly painless) way

> Our plan for a Founder's Day Knees-up in a brewery has run into a difficulty.
>
> Of the three breweries a reasonable distance from our offices, one cannot offer any of our suggested dates, on or near Friday, February 13th; another no longer does such functions and the third has gone out of business.

If you feel a little cringeing might be in order over your failure to deliver, you could add:

> I am sorry I have not been able to carry out your instructions. Perhaps we could discuss other possibilities.

The same get-it-over-with approach also applies if you find you have to put a proposal which you know the boss will not like – or even when you have *good* news!

Making it look good

A long letter or memo – assuming all those words really are necessary – can be made less forbidding if you break it up with simple tricks of layout.

It is common enough to give a main subject heading –

PROPOSED FOUNDER'S DAY
BREWERY KNEES-UP

But you can also break up the slab of text under it with subheadings, preferably at the side –

Why the plan has not worked

WhatBrew, of Staggering Way, could not offer any of our suggested dates . . .

Or inset, like this –

> **Why the plan has not worked**   WhatBrew, of Staggering Way, cannot offer any of our required dates

Another way to put a bit of air into your memo would be an extra bit of display, using asterisks or 'bullets' – full stops, the bigger the better (see *Wonders of the Word Processor*, p. 439).

> Of the three breweries I was told to contact –
> * One could not manage any of our required dates
> * Another no longer does these events
> * The third has gone out of business

Sometimes it may be useful to number your subsections, though this can look boring.

Sum up to start with

It is often a good idea to start your long missive – one that runs to more than a single page – with a short, sharp summary of the most important points. Make sure you don't leave out something vital: your busy boss might just rely on the summary to keep up with what is happening, and so miss that important point.

Although our Brewery Knees-up message is not long enough to need a summary, let us stick to it for our example.

> PROPOSED FOUNDER'S DAY
> BREWERY KNEES-UP
>
> * We are unable to use any of the three breweries discussed.
> * No other brewery is within reasonable distance of our offices.
> * Should we discuss what else to do?

Having summarised, take care, in expanding your points, to do it in the same order.

Dear Sir, Please find enclosed some nonsense

When writing to someone outside your office – a customer, for example – keep in mind that, hectic though the pace in your business may seem, the person you are writing to is likely to have no more time to waste than you have.

This was a letter from a building society, about a passbook which a customer had accidentally left at its office:

> I write to confirm that I have enclosed your passbook which was left at our Branch today.
>
> I trust that this is in order, and if I can be of any further assistance, please do not hesitate to contact me.

What a relief to recover the missing passbook! And what a polite letter! And how devoid of genuine thought!

In the first paragraph *I write to confirm that* is meaningless, if there has been no previous discussion of the matter.

I have enclosed is an odd way to say *I enclose* – or even, to defy tradition, *Here is*.

The initial capital for Branch might be office style, and doesn't get in the way of the meaning, but is unnecessary.

This passage easily comes down to:

> I enclose your passbook which was left at our branch today.

The second paragraph, in the circumstances, is pointless. What might *not* be *in order*? Is the customer likely to protest at the return of his passbook? And what *further assistance* can be rendered, concerning the book – unless perhaps the customer discovers unexplained withdrawals of his money?

That second paragraph wastes the time of both writer and reader. It can go.

In this word-processor age, it would be a good idea to make sure that even if the computer is to churn out automated letters, the text has some bearing on the subject.

Don't let the machines take over!

Your opening shot

There is no logical reason to start a letter, whether business or personal, with the word Dear. But the habit is so ingrained that if you began with a blunt *Mr Smith* you would be considered rude. It would have a *Now look here* . . . tone. So perhaps the Dear custom is not one to abandon.

And how do we proceed after that?

Replying to somebody's letter, a businessman or woman will generally refer to it at once. Very practical, too. But some people go about it in an incredibly clumsy, stilted style.

> We are in receipt of your letter . . .

> Your letter of 13th February is hereby acknowledged . . .

> We are obliged for your communication of . . .

> This letter is by way of reply to yours of . . .

All more satisfactorily expressed, as so many people fortunately do, with *Thank you for your letter*.

Making the above examples even more gruesome, occasionally, are the terrible twins, *inst.* (for *instant*,

414

meaning this month) and *ult.* (for *ultimo,* meaning last month).

Given the dwindling number of Latin scholars carrying on business today, there is no real demand for either of these.

And finally . . . the sign-off

None of the usual business-letter sign-offs makes much sense, from the simple *yours faithfully, yours truly* or *yours sincerely* to the archaic flourish of *I beg to remain, your Obedient Servant.*

Another form from the foggy past is: *We would be grateful if you would be kind enough to reply/supply the information/settle this account/ at your earliest convenience, and oblige . . .*

Even if the letter is some sort of threat, *and oblige . . .* has an enfeebling effect: the snivelling tone of an anxious tailor beseeching the Squire to pay at least a little something . . .

But why do we use even the simpler sign-offs? Answer: they're there because they're there. And even today, it would seem a little brusque, even impolite, not to put *something* between your letter and your signature.

So how do we decide which is the more suitable form? Once, the rough-and-ready rule was that if you got a letter ending *Yours faithfully,* you adopted the same style in your reply. And similarly with other sign-offs.

Of the three basic insincere sign-offs, *Yours sincerely* is obviously the warmest-sounding. *Yours truly* is probably the most meaningless. There seems no harm in continuing *Yours faithfully/sincerely.* But use *sincerely* only if you are addressing someone by his or her name, not as Dear Sir/s. *Best wishes* or *Kind regards* also still have their place, when you want to add a flicker of warmth.

You may of course want to be the pioneer who dispenses with all of them.

In which case, jolly good luck – but check with the boss first (unless you *are* the boss).

Letters From Home

Domestic matters that in the past were dealt with by letter are often disposed of nowadays by a quick phone call. But there are still occasions when a letter is better. And at those times, you will usually need to express yourself as clearly as possible . . .

To the council, about a pavement

> Dear Sirs: It's an absolutely bloody disgrace that anybody could leave things until they get in such a state! ! !
>
> I've very nearly broken a leg several times tripping over it and one poor old soul a couple of doors down is terrified to even step outside any more, in a manner of speaking, since her tumble last month (I'm talking about the pavements that you have let go to rack and ruin for the last 18 months, if a day.)
>
> Wake up, can't you, and get something done around here before there's a really serious tragedy. And I warn you, if it's me, I shall sue! ! !

That, of course, is how not to do it. The greatest weakness of the letter, as a complaint demanding action, is that it does not explain at once what the writer is fuming about.

However angry you may be about something, let off steam by kicking the dustbin over – but keep your letter cool and factual. Imagine that this is an office matter, and use the restraint you would feel obliged to exercise in making a business complaint.

TRY THIS INSTEAD

Dear Sirs:

<u>Dangerous Pavement</u>

The paving outside this house and several others
is broken and dangerous.

I have stumbled on it several times and at least
one other resident, an old lady, is afraid to risk
walking on the pavement for fear of an acccident.

Will you please get the paving repaired, urgently.

To a magistrates' court, about a parking fine

You'd have thought there was enough real crime
going on in our streets without the long arm of the
law wasting time picking off innocent motorists like
this.

I told the silly bitch I'd broken down but she still
went ahead and wrote the ticket out. What was I
supposed to do? Sling a ton of saloon car over one
shoulder and hike it off to a garage?

If you think I'm paying good money after that, you
are fooling yourselves.

I want this ticket cancelled, not be hauled into court
to explain why, because I can't afford the time off
work and this letter ought to be good enough explanation for anybody.

As with the broken-pavement letter, this complaint lets
the routine jibe about police work get in the way of
the real point: the writer feels it unfair that a parking
ticket was issued in the circumstances described.

The abusive tone does not help. There is nothing
novel about an indignant motorist: the average driver
is born indignant. At best, your justifiable spleen will
be shrugged off: at worst, it will annoy an official who
might otherwise have sympathised.

418

I enclose a parking ticket which I believe should not have been issued to me.

The ticket was put on my car, in my presence, at the corner of Smith Street and Brown Street, on Friday October 7 at 10.05 a.m. At the time, as I explained to the parking warden, my car had broken down.

I would have liked to contest the case in court, but cannot afford to take time off work to do so.

However, I hope you will agree that, in the circumstances, the ticket was unfairly issued and should be cancelled.

To a noisy neighbour

I'm fed up hammering on the bedroom wall till my knuckles hurt and this noise has got to stop or I'll be calling in the police.

Night after night after night my good lady and I lie awake forcibly listening to that stereo of yours and if it's not the stereo it's the TV and if it's not the TV it's the lot of you charging about knocking things over and making a general hullabaloo.

This is your final warning.

It's the police next time. Plus the council, who are very hot on noise nuisance, I gather.

At least this letter gets the subject of complaint into the first paragraph.

But if the nearest to a formal rebuke has previously been a lot of knuckle-bruising on the bedroom wall, the threats and general tone are premature.

If the neighbours are that noisy, they probably have

not even heard the drumming on the wall. They may be absolute pigs, but it is better to start with the assumption, however unlikely, that they have no idea what a nuisance they have been creating.

The threats, the police and the Noise Abatement Man can come later, if necessary.

TRY THIS INSTEAD

> My wife and I are regularly kept awake by loud sounds from your house in the early hours. Last night, for example, pop music was still playing loudly at three a.m.

> You may not realise how easily the sound from stereo, TV and even loud conversation can go through the party wall.

> We would be grateful if you would reduce the amount of late-night disturbance.

Life and people being what they are, you will no doubt need to turn to officialdom in the end. But your opening shot will read most reasonably in court.

To a holiday firm that let you down

> My wife and I have just returned from a quite expensive holiday booked through your firm and I have to state that it was utterly disappointing.

> Call yourself a tour operator? Don't make me laugh. The things you promised in that brochure of yours, it turned out to be nothing like, from the state of the pool to the food, etcetera.

> We are hereby demanding a refund of at least £1,000 on it.

Supposing you are lucky enough to have booked with

one of the dwindling number of tour firms staying in business, you will need to be much more explicit about what was wrong with the holiday you paid for.

It may also be a mistake to offer an *at least* settlement figure, because that immediately becomes, to the holiday firm, *at most* – at best.

The first paragraph is reasonably direct, though *I have to state* is a waste of space (see *Witter Words*, p. 382). But then the letter becomes vague as well as sneery. You have to set out your complaints, one by one, against the promises of the brochure.

> The hotel pool was unusable: there were still many traces of the recent rainstorm of bats' blood and giant frogs, during which the cover was apparently left off.

> Meal service, described in the brochure as 'super de luxe attention par excellence', was inexcusably slow. My wife's *turbot à la Japon* was eventually brought to us in the bar, shortly after we had ordered teatime cocktails.

> It also smelt unpleasant and we put it straight into the dustbin for fear of food poisoning. This obviously does not support the brochure's claim that food at our hotel was the 'creme de la creme of the Costas'.

> The hotel itself looks out on to a derelict filling station, tyre dump, sewage farm and train shed, according to where you stand. We could not see the sea, golden sands, waving palm trees or quaint whitewashed villas not only described but also pictured in the brochure.

> My wife was especially disturbed by one room-service waiter, who each morning barged into our room on some pretext or other, always managing to catch her, a mature lady, half-dressed or completely naked.

This unfortunate timing was explained when we discovered a peephole in the door. I tackled the waiter about it and he hit me in the mouth, knocking out two teeth.

I complained about all this to the reception clerk, who merely shrugged and said: 'A lady so old and fat should be so lucky, and you still got plenty teeth.'

Finally, our baggage was apparently stolen from a 'secure storage space' before it even left the hotel on our journey home.

Please let me know, within seven days, your proposals for compensation over this entirely unsatisfactory holiday.

To an interfering Granny

Bill and I are both fed up to the teeth with the way you keep trying to force us into sending our kids – *our* kids, not yours – to a private school when that is completely against our principles.

Opening a fund for the fees without asking us first was bad enough.

Constantly telling the kids how lovely it was going to be was even worse.

Now you have had the audacity to put their names down for, in one case, Eton, and in the other case, Roedean. Yuk!

This nonsense has got to stop. Until we have your solemn written promise to leave the education of our children to us, their parents, you will not see either of them again.

And don't bother contacting your precious son, either, because he agrees with me!

Well, that certainly told Granny, didn't it? You could scarcely be accused of lack of clarity, conciseness and directness. Or that valuable attribute, low cunning.

Every family, of course, has its own grievances, loathings, jealousies and obstinacies. Only the details vary. So it may just be possible to tiptoe into this particular affray and suggest how, although the battle has clearly been going on for years, the softer approach might – just *might* – achieve the desired end, which is to Stop Granny Interfering So Much.

TRY THIS WAY

> You already know how Bill and I feel about private schools, and although your generosity would otherwise have been appreciated, we do not think it is fair of you to go over our heads as you have been doing.
>
> Obviously, wherever you have put our children's names down, there is no chance of their going to those schools. So the result is just confusing to them, a waste of staff time and money for the school – and a waste of our own time and money making sure the school is not misled about our intentions.
>
> We know you worry about your grandchildren's future, and we share your worry. We just have different ways of trying to cope with it.
>
> We don't want the children to become victims of a battle between you and us. But we have to answer for their welfare in every way.
>
> Could you think about dropping the private-school idea? There is so much else you could do for them – such as music and riding lessons.

It might lack the fun of all-out warfare. But there is a chance that Granny might calm down.

Spare the Comma, Spoil the Sentence

Writers often worry about commas and other punctuation. What to use, when to use it.

This is not a guide to grammar (see Chapter 1). But it is an attempt to help you write clearly as well as concisely. And misused, misplaced punctuation can cause confusion.

You may have been taught never to put a comma before *and*. Discard the advice. Advancing through the language jungle, treat your comma as an ever-ready hip-flask, available for any emergency. If your sentence looks like flagging without one, administer a strong comma, at once.

Too many commas, spattered pedantically about your page, can just get in the way. But if you are too miserly with them, the reader may be left to puzzle out where the sentence is supposed to be going. Or, just as likely, he or she will give up and read something else.

Watch where you put them

An ill-placed comma can completely alter the sense of what you write.

> Women who are bad drivers present a danger to the public.

No doubt as true of women as of men. But see how peril on the road can spread, if the writer gets comma-happy:

> Women, who are bad drivers, present a danger to the public.

Confusion can also be caused when your sentence needs a single comma, but you use more:

424

RIGHT: The driver having been charged, the police phoned his wife.
WRONG: The driver, having been charged, the police phoned his wife.

That comma after *driver* leads the reader to believe that you are about to reveal what the driver did next, not what someone else – in this example, the police – did next. You have just given the reader an unnecessary jolt. Too much of that, and you are likely to lose your reader altogether.

A comma-free solution, of course, would be:

After the driver was charged the police phoned his wife.

There is an argument for a comma after charged, but you can do without it. Suit yourself, it's a free comma!

You don't always have to use them

Many sentences, even quite long ones, are instantly understandable without a comma in sight. Others are not.

One that is:

I do not suggest there is ever likely to be another politician whose standing in the eyes of the public comes anywhere near to equalling that of the late Sir Winston Churchill in the earliest stage of the Second World War.

One that is not:

There were of course going to be exceptions to the rule as with any field of human activity though this was no reason he pointed out why the courts should slacken in their response to the problems of crime in general.

This stumbler needs four commas to pick it up off the pavement.

> There were of course going to be exceptions to the rule, as with any field of human activity, though this was no reason, he pointed out, why the courts should slacken in their response to the problems of crime in general.

Beware of overdosing

You could shovel in even more commas:

> There were, of course, going to be exceptions to the rule, as with any field of human activity, though this was no reason, he pointed out, why the courts should slacken, in their response to the problems of crime, in general.

But that, as the jargon goes, might be three or four commas too far.

Every little comma has a meaning of its own

The comma may be a mere speck of ink on the paper, but, properly used, it can add nuance and intrigue, as well as clarity, to a statement.

> I walked into the room and found the gasman there.

So what? He's only looking for the meter. But now add a comma.

> I walked into the room, and found the gasman there.

Hello, hello, hello – what's going on here? Your comma has introduced a tiny hesitancy into the sentence. A suggestion that something is not quite right, or ordinary, about the gasman's presence.

If you really want to point the finger, try a loaded full stop instead.

> I walked into the room. And found the gasman there.

A comma is not a full stop

One firm DON'T is: DON'T use a comma instead of a full stop:

> He said he was just going to the pub, he never returned.

There are two separate statements. The comma leads your reader to expect another one, to complete the sentence:

> He said he was just going to the pub, he never returned and we have not seen him again to this day.

If you want your two statements in a single sentence, insert *but* before *he never*. Then you can keep your comma or take it out, as you please. Otherwise, take out the comma and put in a full stop.

> He said he was just going to the pub. He never returned.

Make a dash for it

The dash is another useful piece of equipment in your journey through the jungle.

A single dash serves to add emphasis to a phrase or word:

> He opened the envelope, which was not properly sealed and found – a cheque.

The single dash can also be used to attach a comment to a sentence:

> He opened the envelope, which was not properly sealed, and found a cheque – at last.

A pair of dashes is useful to fence off a thought that is an aside:

> He opened the envelope – it was not properly sealed – and found a cheque.

Try not to get too fond of dashes. They can turn your writing into a scatty, breathless mess:

> He went to the front door – the postman had just been – and found an envelope – not properly sealed – in which was a cheque.

Ration yourself to no more than one or two every fourth or fifth paragraph.

Case for the colon . . .

The colon (:) is often used instead of a full stop. The liveliest explanation of what a colon is for comes in *Fowler's Modern English Usage* (Oxford University Press): 'delivering the goods that have been invoiced in the preceding words'.

> It was not so much the mystery of the vanished gas meter: that, it turned out, was only the beginning.

Nobody would really quarrel with a full stop there, but the colon has us on our toes, waiting for the follow-up.

... and the semi-colon

It is possible to get through life without feeling the need of a single semi-colon. But the semi-colon is a useful instrument to have in your writer's toolkit.

You may have two statements which could be given as separate sentences, but which are so closely linked that a full stop seems too much of an interruption in the flow of thought. Using a full stop:

> He is doing well, so far. I just wish he had improved much earlier.

Using a semi-colon:

> He is doing well, so far; I just wish he had improved much earlier.

A semi-colon is useful also when you have a sentence containing several commas, and in which you need a stronger break, at some point. Without the semi-colon:

> She thought back to the hurtful things he had said to her, about her face, her figure, her hair, her clothes, jibes for which he would never be able to make amends.

There is a slightly bewildering effect, when the lady's plaintive catalogue ends on a mere comma.

Replace the last comma with a semi-colon:

> She thought back to the hurtful things he had said to her, about her face, her figure, her hair, her clothes; jibes for which he would never be able to make amends.

Measure the Blinding Fog

The Fog Index, to measure the readability of a piece of writing, was invented by an American anti-jargon pro-clarity crusader named Robert Gunning.

A Fog Index of 13 or over is a warning that the writer may have made the going unnecessarily heavy for the reader. However, this is *not* a template to work with when you write – and it is fallible. Treat the Fog Index as a semi-serious guide to the clarity of what you have written.

This is how it works:

Choose a section of the written work, at least 100 words long. Count the number of words. Divide the total by the number of sentences. That will give you the average sentence length. If a long sentence contains two or more complete thoughts, separated by a comma, colon or semi-colon, treat each thought as a sentence, for the purpose of judging clarity.

Now go through the same passage, counting the words of three or more syllables. Ignore proper names and words which become three-syllable only because *-ed*, *-s* or *-es* has been added to the basic word – for example, *invent-ed*, *transpose-s*. Also ignore words formed by combining short, simple words: *caretaker*, *maneater*.

Get out the calculator and find the *percentage* of multi-syllable words (*Divide* multi-syllable total by word total, *multiply* result by 100).

Add your average-sentence-length figure to your multi-syllable-percentage figure. *Multiply* the total by 0.4.

The result is the FOG INDEX for that piece of writing.

Let us try this Fog Index test on some examples of published work.

A leading article in the *Sun* newspaper:

A fortnight today Britain's future in Europe will be decided. /
Not by the voters of Britain, / but by the voters of France. /
Our Government has made it clear that if the French say 'Non' in their referendum, the Maastricht Treaty is dead. /
If they say 'Oui', we can all go happily forward / with no regard to how the British people may feel. /
This is unacceptable. /
Our people have never had the chance to vote on European unity. /
Maastricht was not an Election issue / so it is quite arguable that Britain should have a referendum. /
Mr Major believes that this kind of poll is 'undemocratic'. /
Surely it can't be wrong if the ordinary man and woman – as well as MPs – have their say. /

Total words: 122. Over two syllables: 11. Percentage: 9.
Total sentences: 12. Average sentence length: 10.

Add 10 and 9 = 19. Multiply by 0.4.

FOG INDEX: **7.6**   Sparklingly clear.

From the *Sunday Telegraph* editorial on the same topic:

The spectacle of the French being allowed their say, / while the British people are silenced, / grows daily more intolerable. / We seldom have anything to learn about democracy from the land of Robespierre and Bonaparte, / but we do now. / On September 20 French voters will have the chance to give their verdict on the Maastricht Treaty, / and our own Government has said it will be bound by their decision. /

The leaders of both main parties have conspired to supress debate about Europe, / which they know would expose deep divisions among their followers. / They prevented Europe from becoming an issue in our general election / by the simple expedient of agreeing with each other. / The voter wishing to register his or her opposition to Maastricht was given no serious party for which to vote. /

Our politicians have thereby spared themselves the disagreeable task of justifying their European policy to the public. /

Total words: 149. Over two syllables: 16. Percentage: 10. Total sentences: 13. Average length: 11.5.

Add 11.5 and 10 = 21.5. Multiply by 0.4.

FOG INDEX: **8.6**   Despite the more elaborate construction, hardly less clear than the tabloid *Sun*.

From an editorial in the *Independent* newspaper:

More worldly ministerial advisers than the bishop might have put the issue with great cynicism yesterday: / There is little to be gained by further flogging a dead horse. / If the TUC is not dead, it is possibly in terminal decline / after 13 years of maltreatment by Conservative administrations. / Moreover, the emergence of a handful of super-unions, well able to handle their own affairs and to offer their members the material benefits associated with service unionism, / makes it hard to see the purpose of a large and costly central union bureaucracy. /

Some of the more optimistic delegates gathered at Blackpool are taking consolation from the fact that the Secretary of State for Employment, Gillian

Shephard, is demonstrably bored with the plans for further union reforms inherited from her predecessor, Michael Howard, who delighted in reviving the union bogey. / She will push ahead with his proposals to introduce greater freedom for workers to join the union of their choice / and to render more difficult the system of 'check off' / (under which employers deduct union dues from workers' pay packets), / then turn her mind to questions of industrial training and job creation. /

Total words: 191. Over two syllables: 27. Percentage: 14. Total sentences: 11. Average length: 17.

Add 17 and 14 = 31. Multiply by 0.4.

FOG INDEX: **12.4** Dangerously close to the edge of the fog.

From *The Second World War: Triumph and Tragedy*, by Winston Churchill, regarded as a master of English prose:

The final destruction of the German Army has been related; it remains to describe the end of Hitler's other fighting forces. / During the previous autumn the German Air Force, / by a remarkable feat of organisation, / but at the cost of its long-range bomber output, / had greatly increased the number of its fighter aircraft. / Our strategic bombing had thrown it on to the defensive / and 70 per cent of its fighters had to be used for home defence. / Although greater in numbers their effectiveness was less, largely owing to fuel shortage caused by our attacks on oil installations, / which it became their principal duty to prevent. / German high-performance jet fighters perturbed us for a time, / but special raids on their centres of production and their airfields

433

averted the threat. / Throughout January and February our bombers continued to attack, / and we made a heavy raid in the latter month on Dresden, then a centre of communications of Germany's Eastern Front. / The enemy air was fading. / As our troops advanced the airfields of the Luftwaffe were more and more squeezed into a diminishing area, / and provided excellent targets. /

Total words: 186. Over two syllables: 13. Percentage: 6.98.
Total sentences: 17. Average length: 11.

Add 11 and 6.98 = 17.98. Multiply by 0.4.

FOG INDEX: 7.2   Churchill remains an example to us all.

From *The Way through the Woods*, by Colin Dexter:

As he had just considered the photographs, it was the man himself, pictured in two of them, who had monopolized his interest: / a small- to medium-sized man, in his late twenties perhaps, with longish fair hair; / a man wearing a white T-shirt and faded-blue denims, / with a sunburnt complexion and the suggestion of a day's growth of stubble around his jowls. / But the detail was not of sufficient definition or fidelity for him to be wholly sure, / as if the cameraman himself –/ or almost certainly the camerawoman –/ had scarcely the experience needed to cope with the problems of the bright sunlight that so obviously pervaded the garden in which the snaps had been taken./

Total words: 117. Over two syllables: 12. Percentage: 10.25.
Total sentences: 8. Average length: 14.6.

Add 14.6 and 10.25 = 24.85. Multiply by 0.4.

FOG INDEX: **9.9**   Well clear of the mist.

**Letter from Queen Victoria to Sir Robert Peel,
7 September 1841:**

> The Queen wishes that Sir Robert Peel would men-
> tion to Lord De la Warr / that he should be very
> particular in always naming to the Queen any
> appointment he wishes to make in his department, /
> and always to take her pleasure upon an appoint-
> ment before he settles on them; / this is a point
> upon which the Queen has always laid great stress. /
> This applies in great measure to the appointment of
> Physicians and Chaplains, / which used to be very
> badly managed formerly, / and who were appointed
> in a very careless manner; / but since the Queen's
> accession the Physicians and Chaplains have been
> appointed only for merit and abilities, by the Queen
> herself, / which the Queen is certain Sir Robert Peel
> will at once see is a far better way, / and one which
> must be of use in every way.

Total words: 143. Over two syllables: 13. Percentage: 9.
Total sentences: 10. Average length: 12.

Add 12 and 9 = 21. Multiply by 0.4.

FOG INDEX: **8.4**   Well done, Your Late Majesty!

**From *A Good Enough Parent: the guide to bringing
up your child* by Bruno Bettelheim (Thames and
Hudson):**

> Psychoanalytic doctrine is deeply committed to the
> conviction that how these inherited characteristics
> will be shaped depends on a person's life experi-

ences. / Thus it subscribes to a historical view, / according to which later events are to a considerable degree conditioned by what has happened before; / therefore, the earliest history of the individual is of greatest importance in respect to what he will be like in his later life, / not only because it is the basis for all that follows but also because early history largely determines how later life will be experienced. / While genetic and evolutionary history creates an individual's potentialities, / his early personal history more than anything that follows accounts for the forms these potentialities will take in the actuality of his life. /

Total words: 125. Over two syllables: 20. Percentage: 16.
Total sentences: 7. Average length: 17.8.

Add 17.8 and 16 = 33.8. Multiply by 0.4.

FOG INDEX: **13.5** Not the kind of writing to struggle with if you're looking for urgent help to fend off an enraged infant.

Yet the Bettelheim is lucid, compared with this example from our Officialese section (p. 352):

A person shall be treated as suffering from physical disablement such that he is either unable to walk or virtually unable to do so if he is not unable or virtually unable to walk with a prosthesis or an artificial aid which he habitually wears or uses or if he would not be unable or virtually unable to walk if he habitually wore or used a prosthesis or an artificial aid which is suitable in his case. /

Total words: 78. Over two syllables: 19. Percentage: 24.
Total sentences: 1 (The sheer overall obscurity prevents

our splitting this piece into sub-sentences.) Average sentence length: 78.

Add 78 and 24 = 102. Multiply by 0.4.

FOG INDEX: an impenetrable **40.8**   Someone was unable, or virtually unable, to write English – prosthesis or no prosthesis.

Testing the experts' expert – *Fowler's Modern English Usage*:

> The use of semi-colons to separate parallel expressions that would normally be separated by commas is not in itself illegitimate, / but it must not be done when the expressions so separated form a group that is itself separated by nothing more than a comma, if that, from another part of the sentence. / To do this is to make the less include the greater, / which is absurd . . . /
>
> . . . As long as the Prayer-Book version of the Psalms continues to be read, the colon is not likely to pass quite out of use as a stop, / chiefly as one preferred to the semi-colon by individuals, or in impressive contexts, or in gnomic contrasts (Man proposes: God disposes); / but the time when it was second member of the hierarchy, full stop, colon, semi-colon, comma, is past.

Total words: 133. Over two syllables: 12. Percentage: 9. Total sentences: 6. Average length: 22.

Add 9 and 22 = 31. Multiply by 0.4.

FOG INDEX: **12.4**   Just the right side of the fog bank, according to Robert Gunning's test.

As we said, the Fog Index is fallible. You would expect

the extract to get the all-clear: after all, it was written by that master of correct language, H.W. Fowler, author of *Modern English Usage*. The extract was in fact taken from a revised edition of the book produced by that apostle of plain English, Sir Ernest Gowers. And it does get the all-clear, just.

But there is another test by which that excerpt would get a much worse score for unreadability. It's the Commonsense Test.

Wonders of the Word Processor

If you do a lot of writing, you probably already own a computer word processor. For those still holding back from the 'new' technology, here are a few processed words on its advantages – and drawbacks.

A word processor will do more tricks than a mere glorified typewriter. But a glorified typewriter is what most writers want.

Its biggest single advantage is that it lets you play around with the words on screen until you have got them right. Whole blocks of text, or a single word, can be moved up and down the page, or deleted, without so much as the rustle of a sheet of A4.

The writer yearning for perfection might think hard before deciding to mess up a much-revised page with correcting fluid, or use scissors and paste and then type the whole thing again.

With a word processor, you leave the satisfactory bits alone and fiddle only with the unsatisfactory bits. Then, when all is ready, you print your document.

How does it work?

The cheaper types of word processor need to be fed with instructions from a removable disc, each time you switch on. Dearer models have a built-in 'hard disc' which also has to be fed, but only once.

There is a wide range of word-processing languages, some easier to use than others. Some of the most popular are Wordperfect and Wordstar. Some work by a 'menu' list of instructions for you to choose from; others wait for you to enter a simple code from the keyboard.

Your writings are recorded on either a removable disc or the hard disc. The hard version can hold a stupendous amount of work. Even the removable kind can contain an entire book.

More attractive display becomes possible: you should be able to use italics, bold face, underscore and a variety of small, large or condensed type.

The work comes out on a printer attached to the computer: the printer may not be able to handle all the fancy touches which the computer offers, but there should be enough to help you smarten up your printed page.

If possible, get a friend who is already using a computer to help you through the earliest phase of getting to know yours. The manual supplied may not be a model of clarity, and many a beginner has come near to blows with his machine before it agreed to understand his wishes.

Read the words on the screen with extra care until you get used to your new machine: it is surprisingly easy to miss a mistake which might have glared at you from a printed page. And because adjustments are so easy, you may be tempted to waste a lot of paper, making your document ever more beautiful.

The Name Book

What's in a name? Here is everything you ever
needed to know about surnames, Christian names,
nicknames and odd names: what they mean, where
they came from and how they evolved. *The Name
Book* includes an insider's section on people who
have entered the language as words, a name-
dropper's list of those who have changed them and
an invaluable pronunciation guide.

The Secrets of Speed Reading

How fast do you read? Reading faster not only enables you to absorb more material in any given time, but also improves comprehension and enhances enjoyment. With *The Secrets of Speed Reading*'s proven technique and sequence of instruction, exercises and self-tests, you can reach double, even triple, your present speeds for your own benefit and satisfaction – at home, at work, or even on holiday.